D0908147

UNDER THE TUMP

OLIVER BALCH

Under the Tump

*Sketches of Real Life
on the Welsh Borders*

FABER & FABER

First published in 2016
by Faber & Faber Ltd
Bloomsbury House
74–77 Great Russell Street
London WC1B 3DA

Typeset by Faber & Faber Ltd
Printed in the UK by CPI Group (UK) Ltd, Croydon, CR0 4YY

A CIP record for this book
is available from the British Library

ISBN 978–0–571–31195–8

FSC
www.fsc.org
MIX
Paper from
responsible sources
FSC® C101712

2 4 6 8 10 9 7 5 3 1

I fy meibion, Seth a Bo, gyda fy holl gariad

Contents

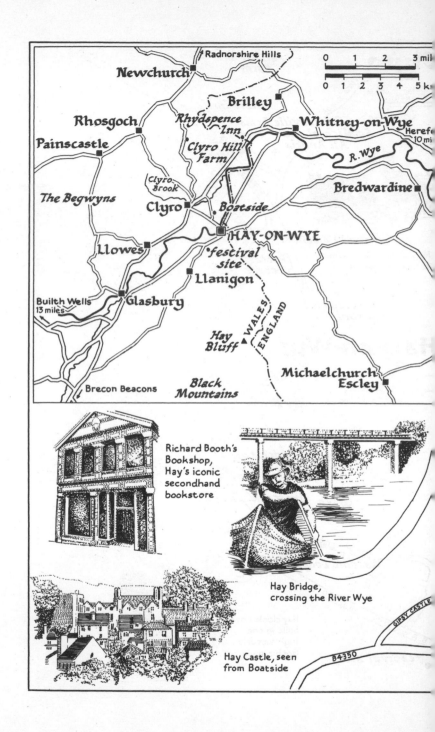

Newchurch

Radnorshire Hills

0 1 2 3 mil
0 1 2 3 4 5 k

Brilley

Rhosgoch

Rhydspence Inn

Whitney-on-Wye

Heref
10 mi

Painscastle

Clyro Hill Farm

R. Wye

Clyro Brook

Bredwardine

The Begwyns

Clyro

Boatside

HAY-ON-WYE

Llowes

festival site

Llanigon

WALES
ENGLAND

Builth Wells
13 miles

Glasbury

Hay Bluff

Michaelchurch Escley

Brecon Beacons

Black Mountains

Richard Booth's Bookshop, Hay's iconic secondhand bookstore

Hay Bridge, crossing the River Wye

Hay Castle, seen from Boatside

GIPSY CASTLE

B4350

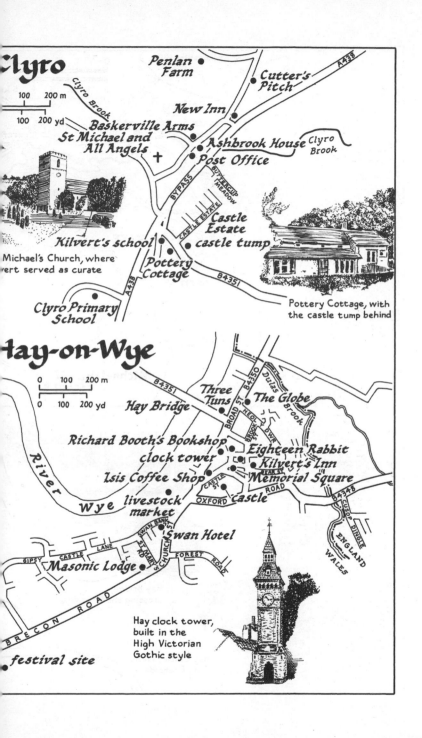

Clyro

100 200 m
100 200 yd

Clyro Brook

Penlan Farm

Cutter's Pitch

New Inn

Baskerville Arms

St Michael and All Angels

Ashbrook House

Clyro Brook

Post Office

BYPASS

BUTTERCUP MEADOW

CASTLE ESTATE

Castle Estate castle tump

Kilvert's school

Pottery Cottage

B4351

A438

Michael's Church, where
vert served as curate

Clyro Primary School

Pottery Cottage, with
the castle tump behind

Hay-on-Wye

0 100 200 m
0 100 200 yd

B4351

Hay Bridge

Three Tuns

BROAD ST

B4350

HEOL DWR

Dulas Brook

The Globe

Richard Booth's Bookshop

clock tower

Isis Coffee Shop

Eighteen Rabbit

Kilvert's Inn

BEAR ST

Memorial Square

CASTLE ST

OXFORD

CASTLE ROAD

castle

B4348

River Wye

livestock market

SWAN BANK

ST MARY'S

CHURCH ST

Swan Hotel

CUSOP DINGLE

ENGLAND

WALES

GIPSY

CASTLE LANE

FOREST ROAD

Masonic Lodge

BRECON ROAD

festival site

Hay clock tower,
built in the
High Victorian
Gothic style

The people of Clyro are still sufficiently Welsh to be suspicious of strangers, and an Englishman would probably not be thoroughly liked and trusted till he had lived for some years in the country. But there is not in Radnorshire the same hostility and bitterness of feeling that is shown towards the Saxon in many parts of Wales. In fact the people, as a whole, are singularly civil, courteous and obliging, and this pleasant characteristic is not merely superficial, for to those who are kind to them they are demonstrative and really affectionate.

Reverend Francis Kilvert
(Curate of Clyro, 1865–1872)

Reverend Francis Kilvert

Born near Chippenham, Wiltshire, on 3 December 1840, Robert Francis Kilvert was educated under his uncle's tutelage at Bath and later at Wadham College, Oxford.

The son of a vicar, he served a brief stint as curate in his father's parish in Langley Burrell, a few miles from his birthplace, before becoming curate of the village of Clyro in Radnorshire. In 1872, after seven years in the Welsh borders, he returned to Wiltshire. Four years later he was back in Radnorshire as vicar of St Harmon, before taking up the living of Bredwardine in Herefordshire the following year.

In August 1879 he married Elizabeth Ann Rowland, but only one month later, with the wedding decorations still hanging in the trees, Kilvert died of peritonitis. His body lies close to the banks of the River Wye, in the graveyard of Bredwardine's parish church.

In early 1870 Kilvert began keeping a diary, the many volumes of which would pass to his widow and, later on, to a niece. After some judicious censorship by his relatives, a collection of his journals came into the hands of William Plomer half a century after Kilvert's death. Plomer, a young editor at Jonathan Cape, published during 1938–40 an edited version in three volumes. A single-volume abridged edition, *Kilvert's Diary, 1870–1879*, appeared in 1944.

In 1948 the still-flourishing Kilvert Society was established with the aim of fostering future interest in the acclaimed Victorian diarist and the rural life he wrote about so fondly.

UNDER THE TUMP

Introduction

We sat to take our luncheon upon the turf of the Beacons beside a tinkling rivulet . . . A sweet fresh wind was moving upon the hills and brilliant gleams of green and purple cloud shadows were flying upon the great landscape. In the narrow green sunny lanes the nuts still hung from the hazel tree and a small farmer driving a herd of fat red oxen put us into the right way with the beautiful courtesy of Radnorshire.

Kilvert's Diary, 14 September 1874

'Don't wait there. Knock and come in,' the farmer's wife says, her tone both forthright and welcoming. 'You're in Radnorshire now.'

I step through the doorway of her hilltop farmhouse, my arms bubbling with goose pimples from the cold. It is our first day in her holiday cottage and I sense her appraising me.

I was thinking about going for a jog, I tell her, standing there in my running shorts and trainers. Could she recommend a possible route? Her bemusement intensifies, my question sending her eyebrows arching upwards. The effect is discomfiting.

'You know we're on the top of a hill?' she says. I do, I tell her. 'Like running downhill, do you?' I nod. 'And uphill?' No, uphill I'm less keen on, I have to admit, and we both laugh, which helps break the ice and bring her eyebrows back down.

A few minutes later, I am heading along the road at the end of the farmyard with a sketched map in my hand. After a gradual descent, I bear off down a narrow country lane that is barely wider than a car. A thick hedgerow lines its bends and blind corners, its back and sides clipped by tractor flails into a mile-long crewcut. The luge-track road has no verge and I silently pray that no vehicle comes the other way.

The height of the hedges restricts my view of the surrounding countryside. I have to wait for the farm gates to catch glimpses through the gaps, although, with my fitness levels not what they should be, I am mostly focused on just keeping going. Having grown up in the flatlands of East Anglia, hill-running is an unwelcome novelty. We don't do steep.

I am a mediocre runner and ten minutes in I am struggling. After the initial descent, the road began to climb. So far, it hasn't stopped. My legs are heavy, my chest tight, my heart pounding.

My body wants to stop. This same urge creeps up on most runs, although seldom so close to the start and rarely with such insistence. I really, really want to stop. The road peaks about 400 yards ahead. I'll rest when I get to the top, I tell myself. With leaden steps, I stagger on.

There, at the crest of the hill, I stop. Bent over, hands on my knees, I gasp for breath. A gusty wind generously tries to revive me. Not until I straighten up do I realise how strong it is. The hilltop is exposed on every side, the hedgerows stopping further down the slope. I glance down at the map, which reveals a sharp corner, next to which is etched the somewhat chilling pair 'Cold Blow'.

'You'll guess it easy enough,' the farmer's wife had said. Leaning on a nearby fence post, I think I've located it.

My lungs still straining, I look around me. In the foreground, fields of billiard-baize green stretch out on every side. The weather in the Marches is flighty. Gun-grey and inclement one moment; cloudless, azure skies the next.

The one constant is green, the colour of hope, of spring, of new life. Almost every type of green imaginable is on show. The greens of grass and leaf, fern and lichen, weed and shrub, moss and plant, all woven together in a chlorophyllous patchwork without stitch or edge.

Each field houses its own population of sheep, woolly white cue balls unruffled by the wind. To my left, in a sag just below the ridge line, the sheep are sharing their quarters with a herd of pedigree Hereford cattle, handsome brown-suited creatures with white tabards fastened to their chests.

Riding the thermals above is a fork-tailed red kite, its feathered limbs spread wide, on its aerial prowl for lunch. As I watch it swirl and turn, my eye is drawn to the backdrop behind it, where a spectacular crescent of corrugated escarpments frames the far horizon, a jagged zip-fastener binding earth to sky.

The mountains sweep upwards from the east, a surging wave of rock and scree erupting from the languid seabed flats of the Wye valley. Having scurried to the top, they cruise for a while, creating a knobbly plateau that continues for several miles. Then, as though the ancient river were calling them back, they tumble downwards to the rich grasslands below. Today the Black Mountains are dressed in cerulean blue.

After a short sprint across the lowlands, the Black Mountains give up the chase. On the muddied banks of Llangorse Lake, under the gaze of Afanc, the horse-headed Monster of Llyn Syfaddon, they hand over the reins. Seizing their chance, the Brecon Beacons take up the race and bound off to the south in a denture-shaped arc. Poking up through the mountains' rocky skin, the stubby tips of two tiny milk-teeth jut upwards. Corn Du and Pen y Fan, the highest points in southern Britain.

The wind is blowing directly in my face and beginning to make my eyes water. I turn to gaze out in the opposite direction, where the hills are closer yet more outstretched, as though anxious to get away and beat a rolling retreat into the heart of Wales proper. Each hill folds into the next, gently heading westward in a lapping tide towards the country's watery edge.

These are the Radnorshire hills, bare-backed and weather-smoothed. Down in the nearest valley trough below, an ancient line of Celtic outposts clings to the banks of the Bachawy brook. Rhosgoch, Llanbedr, Painscastle, Bryngwyn. Villages of sturdy homes built in ashlar stone, accustomed to damp and shy of the sun.

On the higher land, signs of human habitation are scant. The dark smudge of a farmstead occasionally blots the hillside. Otherwise, it's open fields and barren moorland tops, mile upon mile of heather and sedge and sheep. Endless sheep. Noses always downward, diligently strimming the earth one patch at a time.

I turn right and set off westward from the cloud-high crossroads. The wind is on my back and almost straight away I am plunging downwards along a steep slalom slope to the Bachawy below. At the bottom, another back road takes me north towards the village of Newchurch and the prospect of English soil underfoot.

I keep a steady pace for a few miles, the residual charge from the mountain views bringing a modicum of life back to my legs. Before I reach the border, I take a turning off to the right beside an abandoned phone box, which has me doubling back up a vertiginous pitch to the farm where I started. It is a cruel climb to end on. I check the map, now smeared with sweat. The 'X' marking the farmhouse still looks a fair way off. I will have to walk.

*

Some weeks later I buy a map of the immediate area. Unfolding it on the table of our hillside rental cabin, I trace my finger along the route I ran that first afternoon. I locate the farm and Cold Blow, Rhosgoch and the fearsome final slope.

Lured by the open space on the page, I imagine alternative routes further afield. The names of hills perched above narrow contour squiggles speak of a wild hinterland: Aberedw, Glascwm, Rhulen, Llandeilo, Gwaunceste.

The designation *Tumulus* appears next to each. The term is both italicised and capitalised, as though its subject is special yet somehow in doubt. Other similarly shadowy references dot these roadless voids. Words like *Castell* and *Standing Stones* and *Pillow Mounds*. Princelings' forts and Druids' rites fill my imagination. It would be months before I put on my trainers and braved any of these hill-strewn wastelands in person.

I continue drawing a line northwards until I reach the top of the map. It finishes after about fifteen miles, near a farm called Bwlch-y-cefn Bank. The isolated hill farm neighbours another farm called Bwlch-llywn Bank, which is just above another settlement called Bwlchau. I study them closely. Balch and Bwlch. I wonder if our paths might have crossed before.

Ten or fifteen miles beyond the edge of the map lies the Ithon valley. Fast and plucky, the River Ithon takes its name from the Welsh *eithon*, meaning 'talkative'. A major left-bank tributary of the River Wye, it rises in the uppermost reaches of Radnorshire, in the saddle between the Kerry Ridgeway and the wonderfully Tolkeinesque Hill of Glog. From these mythological beginnings, the Ithon twists and chatters its way south towards its broad-banked parent and the ebbing tides of reality.

Close to the mouth of the Ithon, a few miles from the riverside village of Llanbadarn Fynydd, is a large, square-jawed house called Pen Ithon Hall. It stands on its own at the end of a long driveway lined with sycamore sentries. My parents first took me there when I was six months old and I have been back on holiday every year since. As young children, my brother and sister and I would spend our days roaming outside in the sprawling grounds, making dens and building dams, kicking cowpats and flying kites. Now I look on as my own two boys, Seth and Bo, aged five and six respectively, do the same.

It is the landscape of rural Radnorshire that I had foremost in mind when my wife Emma and I decided to move. We had left London for Argentina shortly after we were married, setting off in search of something new, determined to spread our wings before they were clipped by jobs and mortgage payments and rush hour on the Northern Line. We told ourselves we'd go for just a year. We ended up staying seven. Throughout that time, Argentina constantly veered and wobbled, as is the country's wont. At a personal level, however, life remained good. We travelled, we made friends, we bought a house, we had our two boys. It's true that we mostly lived hand-to-mouth, but we kept our outgoings low and our responsibilities were few. In the round, there were far more years of feasting than famine. It helped that the sun shone and the music played, of course.

Then, very naturally, it felt as though our adventuring abroad had run its course for the time being. The boys were approaching school age and I realised I wanted them to experience something of what I had known as a child, with the white Christmases and changing seasons, the FA Cup Saturdays and Sunday walks to the pub.

This urge to return came with a conundrum. Where exactly to move back to? Our work is such that we can live anywhere as long as we have a phone line and internet access.

Going back to where we had grown up – Yorkshire in Emma's case, Essex in mine – would have been the most obvious choice. But neither of us had lived there since leaving school almost two decades ago, and we had few friends left in either area.

That wasn't always the case. At primary school I knew everyone my age in our village. Then, when I was nine, I got sent to a private school in a nearby town and everything gradually changed. I clung on to a few of my old friends for a while: Nick Middleton on Queen's Street, whose mum was friends with my mum; Simon Ashby on Tey Road, who won a racing bike in a raffle and whom I'd go on cycle rides with.

Then, aged thirteen, I went to boarding school and my

ostracism became complete. My friends in the village became fellow exiles returning home from various educational outposts with their social lives packed into their school trunks, padlocked shut, ready to be resumed with the start of term. I am still in touch with several of them today, but they are scattered all over the place now. Just as we were then.

Our parents continue to live where we grew up and, friends or no friends, I liked the idea of our boys being close to their grandparents. Yet Essex and Yorkshire are half a country apart, and choosing one would inevitably mean rejecting the other. The potential for a snubbed set of grandparents seemed high.

Other question marks hung over returning to our childhood homes. In the case of my parents, it was their proximity to London. Being within an hour by train from the capital put house prices way out of our budget. For Emma, it was the weather: she wasn't sure she could face another Yorkshire winter.

Added to the mix was an urge that had been slowly growing in me for a change of scenery. I had lived in cities ever since leaving school, and so much brick and concrete was getting to me. I fancied living somewhere with open skies and fresh air; somewhere I could strap on my walking boots and head out for a hike; somewhere alive to the sound of birdsong rather than bus exhausts. I envisioned the same for the boys. Growing up in wellies and with muddy knees. Weekend camping trips. Swimming in the river. Somewhere like Pen Ithon.

In this respect, Yorkshire's empty enormity fitted the bill far more closely than the overpopulated flatlands of Essex. This attraction to the countryside and the outdoors is more mine than Emma's, however. I could see us living in a remote spot in Nidderdale, say, or on a protected patch of moorland in the Cleveland Hills. Emma's natural inclinations are distinctly more urban. She feeds off cities and their endless possibilities. Buenos Aires, with its sleepless nights and its creative madness, kept her well sated.

There is much that Emma and I disagree on. Yet on the big-ticket items, the stuff that really matters in a marriage, we're of one mind. One of our core mutual convictions is that an interesting life beats a secure one. Life is short. More than half our three score and ten is already behind us. We'd rather risk the unknown than keep to the same. That's what excites us, pushes us to grow, keeps us learning.

It's for this reason that I felt I could moot the idea of Radnorshire and harbour a modicum of hope that Emma might agree.

I brought up the subject casually, all the same. And with various caveats too. For starters, instead of the relatively restrictive confines of Radnorshire, I proposed Powys as a possible location.

Long and chunky, Powys's eastern frontier runs beside the perimeter fence of the English border. Officially, the uncluttered bulge of Radnorshire, squashed between flat-pan Herefordshire to the east and coast-bound Cardiganshire to the west, was subsumed into this larger administrative unit in the mid-1970s. Bundled in along with it were its neighbours Montgomeryshire and Brecknockshire. Today, Powys's far-reaching boundaries cover much of what is popularly referred to as the Welsh Marches.

Remarkably, Emma proved receptive to the idea. Despite having a Welsh grandmother, her emotional ties to the country are almost non-existent. The pull is all mine. Yet to her, Powys represented a completely blank canvas. That was its great virtue for her: an opportunity to start afresh, to invent anew.

The Welsh word for Wales, Cymru, derives from the Brythonic term *combrogi*, meaning 'fellow-countryman'. For all my strength of feelings towards Radnorshire, my actual genealogical kinship with Wales is no stronger than Emma's. Our nearest fellow countrymen both lie at least one generation removed on our maternal side. Her grandmother was from Cardiff while my mother's paternal ancestors hailed from the market town of Abergavenny, which likes to champion itself as the 'Gateway to Wales'. Today, my ancestors are all resting together just outside the town, beneath dilapidated gravestones in Llanfoist village church.

The Steels were mostly medical folk. It was Owain Steel, my mother's grandfather, who made the big move north from Monmouthshire to Radnorshire. He landed a job as a doctor shortly after the Great War. The post was based in the remote but beautiful Ithon valley. My brother carries his name, although my parents opted for the anglicised version, Owen. He never uses it nowadays, preferring his second name, Robert, or his childhood nickname, Bo.

It is to Owain's son that I owe my lifelong connection to Pen Ithon. As a young officer in the Royal Artillery regiment, Eustace Steel met and married an elegant young visitor to the Haig estate. Her name was Patience Bell, known to everyone (for reasons lost in time) as Perd. She was from a coal-owning family in Northumberland. Today, the couple lie buried together in an overgrown patch at the back of Llananno churchyard. They abut the Ithon's bank, listening to the gossip of the river as its gabbling waters rush by. Or so I like to think.

It would be too much to say that my grandparents called me back. Yet knowing that their remains lie on the Silurian rock of Radnorshire eased our transition from Buenos Aires to the Welsh countryside. It robbed the idea of its randomness. In some small way, too, it felt as though I was reconnecting, retreading old ground. For me, this was enough.

Having quickly assimilated the prospect of Powys, Emma made the idea her own. She surfed all the relevant property websites and quickly identified three possible houses. Two were holiday lets deep into mid-Wales. Another was an old worker's cottage in a village called Clyro, located on the easternmost fringes of Radnorshire, a mile outside the market town of Hay-on-Wye.

We spoke to my parents. They were heading down to Pen Ithon the following month and agreed to visit the three potential properties on our behalf. Their verdict was less than positive. The holiday lets were too small and too remote, they said. Clyro they thought a better option. The village had a small primary school, a shop, a pub, a community hall. The downside was the house. Four hundred years old, it was showing its age. The roof buckled and the rooms smelled of damp. Needed a lot of work, my dad reckoned.

An appealing factor of the Clyro cottage was its proximity to Hay-on-Wye, or simply 'Hay', as all the locals call it. With around 1,800 residents, this miniature market town is more than twice the size of Clyro. Even so, it feels more like a township than a town. A rural hub, perhaps.

Hay's size may be small but its ambitions are not. Today, this small border settlement enjoys an uncontested reputation as the nation's 'Town of Books'. The title owes its origins to Hay's penchant for second-hand bookshops, which first began springing up in the mid-1960s and which today number more than two dozen.

In the late 1980s, Hay embarked on its very own book festival. Over the decades, it has grown into an annual literary love-in. Every town seems to have a book festival these days, but Hay's ten-day jamboree stands out as one of the country's largest and most iconic. With each passing year, the town's bookish status becomes that bit more cemented.

Emma and I had been to Hay once before. As with many other visitors, it was the festival that drew us. We had only just started dating and were too wrapped up in one another to pay much attention to our surroundings. The vague recollections I had of the town were all broadly positive: bright sunshine, stripy deckchairs, fresh-cut grass, new books, second-hand books, young novelists, old novelists, first love.

Having Hay on the doorstep appealed especially to Emma. She needs the movement and energy that busy conurbations bring. In Radnorshire, such opportunities are slim. Even by Welsh standards, the now defunct county is judged 'out-of-time', to quote the biographer and academic Peter Conradi. As with frontier states the world over, it suffers from being neither in nor out, neither one thing nor another. '[It's] ignored or forgotten by the English as too remote, and by the Welsh as too English,' Conradi writes. Its demographics seem to back this up: at 26,000 people, its population is a mere one per cent that of Greater Manchester, despite both covering an equal area.

Given our respective tugs towards the rural and the urban, Clyro struck us as a rare middle ground. Removed, but not too removed. One foot in the countryside, one in a town (of sorts).

A steady flow of new arrivals has found its way here over the centuries. First came the Marcher lords, sent by William the Conqueror to quell the troublesome Welsh. Then the hill farmers and the drovers, the merchants and the landed gentry, the artists and the hippies. Folk 'from off', as the vernacular has it. If the area remains true to its past, we wouldn't be the only new guys in the village.

A few background enquiries reinforced our expectations. Although Hay's name derives from *haye*, the Norman word for 'enclosure', it sounded like the kind of place that would be open to fresh faces. In the months before we moved, Emma's hesitations about rural life were further alleviated by her close reading of Life in Hay, a well-informed blog by an idiosyncratic local bookseller. The site includes a profile picture of the author in historical re-enactment garb as well as links to websites such as Hay Feminists, Brilley Buddhist Retreat and Cosy under Canvas.

Aside from the desirability of Hay and Clyro, Emma liked the house, which she thought quirky and brimming with potential. It once belonged to Adaš Dworski, a Croatian ceramicist of Polish descent, a memory kept alive in the first line of its address: Pottery Cottage. Some of the potter's glazes still adorn the exterior wall; a twinkling star, a colourful jester, a crescent moon.

The house sits beside the Hay road amid a cluster of mostly modern houses on the eastern fringe of the village. Immediately opposite is a heavily wooded hillock, home hundreds of years ago to a defensive fort. Locals, we'd later learn, refer to it as the 'castle tump', or simply, 'the tump'. Today it's overflowing with brambles and nettles and trees of all types; oak, ash, sycamore, yew, hazel, rowan, alder, beech, field maple. From the back garden of the cottage, it looks as though a jungle is sprouting through the roof.

Despite the work it would require, Emma's mind was set. As part of the renovations, she reckoned we could make an office for me out of the garden shed. I was sold and we started packing.

*

Several months after we move, I receive an invitation to contribute to an evening discussion at The Globe in Hay. A former Congregational church on Newport Street, the venue is now reinvented as a popular spot for live music and cultural events.

The topic for debate centres on the impact of digital communications technologies on rural communities. Are they welcome? Do we need more or less of them? On the platform with me is the local Welsh Assembly member, an academic in urban studies from Cardiff University and a film-maker for a media firm specialising in rural issues.

We meet backstage in a temporary yurt, where a young assistant fusses over our clip-on microphones and briefs us on the format. As he speaks, we surreptitiously weigh one another up. I feel distinctly ill-equipped. Removing myself from my fellow panellists, I find a seat to the side and go through my notes. They are sketchy but I hope their underlying argument is sound.

The main thrust links to the idea of belonging and place, two themes of abiding interest to me. The American novelist John Updike captures my thinking best. I'd been listening to the radio before leaving Argentina when a clip came on from an interview Updike had given in 1970. He was discussing the arrival of his second child and his subsequent decision to leave New York, the advantages of the Big Apple 'counter-balanced' by his new responsibilities. So the couple sold up and moved to Ipswich, a small coastal town in upstate Massachusetts.

The scenario felt familiar to me. You leave college, go to the big city, get a job, live it up, fall in love, make a home, tell yourself, 'This is it, this is us.' Then kids arrive. Your job gets tougher. And slowly everything begins to change. The nights out become more infrequent, your friends begin to spread out, your world begins to shrink. Somehow, time shortens; your days are spent chasing your tail, bemused, fraught.

If your income allows it, then you can sail through. You have a nice house in a safe neighbourhood with good schools nearby. For you, city living remains good. If not, if every spare penny you earn is going on childcare and the only green space you have is littered with dog mess, then it's demonstrably worse. Soon you're thinking it's so much worse that anywhere might be better. The burbs. Upstate Massachusetts. Even the countryside.

Surprisingly to me, Updike didn't lament leaving the big city behind. The throb of the streets, the energy of the crowds, the thrill of the new: their appeal seemed to weaken as this leading light of American twentieth-century intel-lectualism stumbled on something else. A replacement, just as rich and seductive, yet almost unknown to urban life.

He had found a place where people knew each other, he explained in the interview. Not just to share a 'hello' at the bus stop or a smile at the newsagent's. People who *really* knew each other. Knew one another's name and the names of their dogs. Knew where one another lived, where they took coffee, what they did at weekends.

This information came to them not because they spied on

one another or because they were busybodies. They knew it because the residents of Ipswich, MA, numbered in their hundreds rather than their tens of thousands. Their paths crossed more often. And when they did, they'd stop and share the time of day, asking about friends or Aunt Maud's operation.

A few of Updike's phrases had struck a particular chord with me and I'd scribbled them down. Now, transposed into my notebook, I reread them as I sit in the yurt. The first quote runs:

> It's a kind of community really in what I take to be the classic sense. In that if your child has a toothache on the weekend, you can call up the dentist you personally know. There's that kind of knit.

This idea of 'knit'. It resonated with me powerfully. I loved Argentina, loved it passionately, but I was never fully *part* of it, and it dawned on me that I probably never would be. It was the little things that made me realise. The subtleties of topical jokes that I didn't quite catch, the children's TV shows I had never watched, the football chants I could never remember. These kept us on the margins. Embraced, but never quite integrated.

This didn't bother me especially. I accepted it as inevitable. What's more, I found it immensely liberating. The ties that bound us back home – the cultural mores, the family expectations, the relational obligations, the social pressures – undid themselves. At the same time, we weren't beholden to their equivalents in Argentina. We could make our own rules, chart our own path. If we wanted to take the kids out to dinner with us at midnight, we could. No one would scowl. For seven sweet years we were footloose, unencumbered, floating free.

The more my mind turned to the prospect of returning, the greater the appeal of Updike's picture became. I liked the idea of finding a place where I could truly belong. It would be good to be on the inside for once, to be a thread or stitch in the social fabric. I wanted to live somewhere I could walk down the street and know the grocer and the postman and the café owner. If it turned out to be claustrophobic or insular, as well it could, then we could always move on.

Updike's observation didn't end there. In the interview, he went on to elaborate on the benefits of this 'knitted' community that he had stumbled upon beside the sea. As the next quote in my notebook read:

> And also you're exposed to people that aren't in your game. In the city I think there's this temptation to see only people who are very likeminded. In a sense for a writer, it's good to live between a widow and a plumber, and in a sense love your neighbour and know your neighbour in the old, old sense.

The five words, 'people who are very likeminded', are underlined in red. It is this phrase that had stopped me short when I first heard the radio clip. Within it is a subtle yet clearly discernible criticism. But of what? Surely building a friendship group around people you like and who have the same broad outlook on life is the most natural thing in the world?

To a certain extent it summed up our social circle in Buenos Aires. We had what might be called a 'crowd', a gang of friends with whom we got on well and who got on well with us. We had a lot in common; similar ages, similar education, similar politics, similar incomes, similar world-views. All of us worked, although none of us in conventional office jobs.

We lived in the city's less salubrious, more edgy neighbourhoods, making sure to shop in the corner store where everyone else shopped, to drink our *café con leche* in the pavement cafés where they drank, to ride the same cramped and creaking buses that our neighbours rode.

More important than where we lived or what we did, we desired to integrate. We wanted to speak the language, imbibe the culture, make friends. In truth, the latter is no great trial in Argentina, as gregarious and generous-spirited a nation as you can hope to find, a country of much cheek-kissing and unexpected kindnesses where it's never difficult to fill the house for an *asado* or bag a weekend invite.

Even so, without family links or cultural ties, I couldn't escape the feeling that we never quite fitted. Alongside thoughts of moving home, I became increasingly beguiled by the notion of living in a genuinely enmeshed community. The Spanish have a word for this kind of social interweaving, *convivencia*, which literally means 'together-living'. The emphasis in Spanish is on the '*con*', the together part.

It suggests a mindset as much as a place; an attitude of being that opens people up to mixing together, talking together, drinking together, gossiping together – fighting together, even. Whatever the activity, the point is that they do it together. It's this sense of *togetherness* – of life being a social exercise rather than a private pursuit – that so captures my imagination.

The problem comes when this togetherness is forged through our own selection and bound by our own terms. A

community that rests on mutual similarity and mutual like-
ability is certainly a good foundation for a life well lived, but
maybe, just maybe, it falls short of the best.

For the gain of shared understanding is offset by the loss
of diversity and difference. Conversations in such milieus
serve to affirm existing beliefs rather than challenge them.
Surprises are thus fewer and opportunities for learning
more scarce. It is the friendship equivalent of always reading op-eds from the same newspaper; a means of entrench-
ing the engrained, not opening up to the new.

I don't doubt that 'together-living' in its truest sense is no
easy task. If it were, the burgeoning worlds of gated communities and immigrant ghettoes would not exist. Such
phenomena are far from new, of course. Today's retirement
complexes and bijoux beach communities serve the same
purpose as the monasteries and garrison towns of antiquity.
They create protective fences, establish rules of entry and
design codes of common behaviour. In doing so, they help
us stay safe and keep us from feeling threatened.

Yet to live in such a place is to inhabit a demographic
desert where everything is homogenous, monocultural, the
same. We had moved to Argentina in part to seek out an
alternative. Could we try to do the same now we were moving back? When Updike spoke of rubbing shoulders with
plumbers and widows, he was thinking primarily in his
capacity as a writer. But surely the knock-on benefits go
beyond art. Could they not flow into the living of our everyday lives as well?

I was ready to bet they could. Or at least that they might.

Of all the factors that made me think the Welsh Marches
might work for us, this idea of *convivencia* was the most
compelling. It was not an especially good time to return to

Britain: the economy was flatlining, the government's deficit cuts were at full tilt, the weather was as bad as ever.

The possibility of finding our own Ipswich, MA, kept me upbeat and excited. The little we had gleaned about Clyro and the surrounding area gave me encouragement. The population was small enough to be familiar, but large enough to harbour all sorts. The area was remote, although not cut off. The culture we could only guess at, but we hoped it would be open and friendly.

This hope also forms the backbone of my argument for the evening event. The community experience I have come in search of depends on real-life interactions. People have to be out and about, calling in on one another, shopping in the local stores, filling the same spaces, attending the same functions.

An internet-based society would mean the end of all that, I tell the audience. Everyone would stay at home and start shopping online. Kids would disappear into their rooms to game with their Minecraft buddies in Hanoi or Snapchat their pals in Hamburg, while parents would be glued to Netflix or Skyping far-flung family. People would be on their phones constantly. Scrolling, Tweeting, messaging, WhatsApping, searching, crushing candy. Anything but talking face to face, anything but living cheek by jowl.

I fully expected this to land me in the minority. Faster internet connections will revitalise small businesses locally, the other panellists were bound to say. Inner Mongolia has faster dial-up speed than the Marches. Becoming properly wired-up would enable us to engage the world, to stretch our horizons, to overcome the limitations of rural life. And they would be right, of course, I admit, getting my retaliation in first.

But at what cost to society? The whole social media circus perpetuates the likemindedness point that Updike disliked about cities. Only with Facebook, Twitter and so forth, the effect is amplified exponentially. If someone posts something we disagree with, we defriend them. If a Twitter feed starts annoying us, we mute it. The digital 'echo chamber', the *Financial Times*'s Gillian Tett calls it. The result is the virtual gathering around us of friends and followers whose views we approve of, whose jokes we laugh at, whose lives we recognise. People, basically, who are just like us.

In case a mauling awaits me, I've brought back-up. The Reverend Francis Kilvert or, more specifically, his diary.

Published as the nation was on the verge of war, the simple Arcadia evoked within was lapped up by British readers. *Kilvert's Diary* quickly became a minor classic in the flowery canon of Victorian pastoralism.

Read today, the entries remain fresh and compelling, skipping as they do between anecdote and history, reflection and fact. A Romantic man in a Romantic age, Kilvert would take himself off on long all-day walks into the hills, returning in rhapsodic mood to share with his diary the sound of the year's first yaffingale 'laughing in the dingle' or the sight of fawn-coloured turkeys 'mourning in the stubbles'.

Emma had bought me an abridged copy of the *Diary* shortly after moving to the area. It covers the years 1870 to Kilvert's premature death in 1879. In sympathy with its contents, the cover of my edition carries the sun-dappled image of a rustic church. Beneath the branches of an ancient chestnut is a wooden lychgate, which gives way to open fields beyond. A brown heifer stands alone, grazing. In the foreground, a mother with three girls, all in Victorian frocks, sit around a picnic basket in the long grass of the graveyard.

I devoured the *Diary* greedily, particularly the Clyro sections. Kilvert's descriptions of the landscape speak forcefully across the centuries, but it's his depiction of village life that totally absorbed and entranced me. The Clyro women who 'stride about the village like storks'. The industrious blacksmith who chinks away at his forge night and day. The 'harvest man' absented by grog. The mole-catcher drunk on folklore.

Equipped with a university education and a common touch, the affable curate was uniquely positioned. Every layer of society lay open to him, and he submerged himself in each. One minute he's sitting in a pauper's hovel, the next he's playing battledore and shuttlecock at Clyro Court. The result is a pen portrait of remarkable breadth and intimacy.

Eccentric and ordinary, rich and poor, old and young, characters of all colours spill from the page. Real people. People with future hopes and worldly worries. People who mourn and sob as readily as they sing and feast. People, above all, who inhabit a vital, interwoven, living community. Not a perfect one by any means. Poverty and privilege were too common. But a living community without doubt. And one not at all dissimilar to the one I had envisioned for ourselves.

In preparation for this evening's debate, I have bookmarked a passage that I hope will offer a flavour of the above. Intentionally, I have steered clear from overt 'community' events, of which there are many. Such as Easter Sunday, say, when children in new clothes 'bright as butterflies' filled the churchyard, or Clyro Feast Ball, when Kilvert sat in his lodgings listening to the 'scraping and squealing of the fiddle' and the 'heavy tramp' of dancers' feet.

Instead, I have selected a passage from an unexceptional Thursday in the village. The morning sun had decided to flash a rare springtime smile, but otherwise the entry captures nothing out of the ordinary. It is as typical a day about the parish as I could hope to find. I read it in conversational style, in the way I imagine Kilvert would have written it.

. . . A heavenly day, lovely and warm, real spring. People busy in their gardens planting and sowing. Everyone rejoicing in the unclouded splendid weather, and congratulating each other on it in their greetings on the road. The roads lively with market women riding to Hay. A woman on a cream coloured horse with black mane and tail riding past the school and alternately in sunshine and the shadow of the Castle clump . . .

By 'clump', Kilvert meant 'tump', which I have no time to explain since the moderator is keeping strictly to the clock. Still, I say most of what I want to say, which cheers me. Less encouraging is the look of puzzlement on some of the faces in the audience. Their sympathies definitely fall more with the other panellists, whose claims that countryside dwellers are being 'left behind' and that our youngsters are being denied opportunities hit home with enviable effect.

Legitimate though their positions are, their efforts to contrast the lot of the countryside by portraying city-living as some sort of wired-up, interconnected nirvana strike me as somewhat exaggerated. I do my best to burst this bubble. Has anyone read Robert Putnam's *Bowling Alone*? Are they aware of the staggering levels of depression and loneliness in the atomised cities of today? Do they really believe the adverts for The Gap that show all those young hipsters hanging out in happy interracial harmony? A few heads nod. One or two grimace. In general, the audience remains unmoved. Their minds are set.

On the drive back, I play over how it went. As I pull into the driveway, a wave of gut-wrenching doubt pours over me. I sit in the car for a moment, gripping the steering wheel tight. Am I fooling myself? This 'knit' that Kilvert experiences so tangibly and that holds such appeal for me, is it still obtainable in twenty-first-century Britain? Or is it an anachronistic fantasy?

Calming myself, I remove the key from the ignition and step out. As I walk towards the house, it occurs to me that I have forgotten something. I turn back, unlock the door and reach over to the passenger seat.

Retrieving my copy of *Kilvert's Diary*, I clasp it close and head inside.

PART I

Locals

The Clyro Tour

In the afternoon Mrs. Bevan, Mary and I drove to Clyro.
As we passed along the old familiar road that I have jour-
neyed over so many times a thousand memories swept
over me. Every foot of Clyro ground is classical and sacred
and has its story.

Kilvert's Diary, 23 March 1874

The village tour leaves from the steps of the Baskerville
Arms pub.

We number about twenty in total, an even split between
women and men. Most of the women are wearing dark
glasses against the glare of the Saturday afternoon sun. The
men are dressed uniformly in plain, long-sleeved cotton
shirts, staples of their working wardrobes now redeployed
for retirement. They are white-haired and stiff-gaited.

But they are all smiling. For the members of the Kilvert
Society are a contented, amicable bunch. And, with the
curate's former stomping ground beneath their feet and a
steel blue sky above, today is a happy day.

Of the nine years covered in Kilvert's *Diary*, only the first
two and a half encompass the young curate's time in Clyro.
Yet it is during these years that we find him at his happiest
and most effusive. A zesty, enthusiastic tone courses through
his earliest entries.

The images he paints carry a palpable vividness. The clamour of geese, twinkling leaves, old-fashioned September fog, keepers' cottages, orchard banks, freshly dug red potatoes, crimson ball sunsets, melting hoar frost, trees thickening with bursting buds, dazzling snow, cider presses, purple grasses billowing like the sea.

The scenes feel very different from the output of a disciplined diarist who sits down at the end of the day to set down with diligence what's gone before. They are too bright and bubbling for that, too sprinkled with the present.

It's as though he has dashed to his desk direct from sleep, pen working furiously, grasping at the lucid fragments of a dream as they swirl around his head before the dawn light swoops in and snatches them away.

Kilvert's world-view leans undeniably towards the rose-tinted and poetic. Even accounting for his florid style, the picture he paints of Clyro is enticingly dreamy. A rural idyll tucked away on the Welsh borders, protected by the mountains and cushioned from the present, a private garden of calm in tumultuous times. As a reader, it is difficult to resist the enchantment of it all.

The tour group moves off in a north-easterly direction along the sinuous main street that divides the centre of the village.

Behind us the square stone tower of St Michael and All Angels rises above the pub roof, the bronze of its cockerel weather vane transformed into dazzling gilded foil by the sun. A bank of low-ceilinged cottages huddles around the churchyard's outer wall. Scattered among them is a collection of newer brick buildings, which grow in number as the village spreads outward.

Two primary features define the topography of Clyro.

The first is the precipitous hill at its back, which rises with a slag heap's sudden steepness directly behind the church. The hill is lush and green and populated by grazing sheep. Along its western flanks, a brook cuts down through Pen-y-lan Wood before coursing wilfully through an array of villagers' gardens.

Halfway up the pitch stands a pair of wizened oak trees, their upper sections bent over in a courteous, wind-blown bow. At either end of the village, two narrow country roads wind off into the hills; one to Cold Blow and the heart of Wales, the other to Newchurch and the fertile soils of Herefordshire.

The village's second defining detail is its bypass. Built in the late 1950s to divert traffic from the centre of Clyro, the now busy extension road cuts a straight path along the village's eastern edge. In Kilvert's day, open fields would have stretched out beyond it all the way down to the River Wye and the bridge into Hay.

Shortly after the bypass's arrival, an enterprising local farmer saw the opportunity to sell off some of his land for development and now two small housing estates occupy the far side of the road. The effect has been to divide the village between old and new.

Pottery Cottage finds itself on the new side despite being one of Clyro's oldest properties, an anomaly of uneven stone and timber amid an abundance of right-angles and red brickwork.

Across the bifurcating bypass, back in the heart of the village, the main street is quiet enough for us to ignore the pavement and stroll along the tarmac road. An archivist from Llandrindod Wells, a sprightly man with rolled-up sleeves and a knapsack on his shoulder, is leading the way.

He stops briefly by the pub car park and points out where the blacksmith's workshop would once have been. The smithy's fire and anvil are long gone, replaced by a square of asphalt and a pub garden with picnic benches and a child's slide.

I fall into step with a gentleman called John, a retired English teacher who lives in Bristol. Bespectacled and pale-faced, he sports a wispy white goatee beard and the whiff of academia. To quote the society's current chairman, John is the group's 'star turn'.

We had met briefly at the annual general meeting several months beforehand. The event was held in the timber-framed chambers of the Radnorshire Arms hotel in nearby Presteigne, a historic market town further up the border.

John had delivered the keynote lecture, a lengthy exposition of Kilvert's interest in mineralogy. It went down a storm with his fellow Kilvertians. He tells me he is currently putting together a paper about the diarist's religious beliefs, and touches the side of his nose. He is, I should know, a 'bit of a controversialist'.

The main body of the group has drifted off ahead. To the left of us is a row of bungalows, single-storey toadstools at the foot of the towering grassy bank. To the right is a short modern terrace and beyond it a collection of new three- and four-bedroom homes built where an orchard once stood. They are all inhabited by newcomers to the village. At the rear of their neat fenced-in gardens runs the busy bypass.

After about 400 yards, the village proper runs out, splitting between the hilly back road to Newchurch and the main road to Hereford. A clutch of brave cottages cling to the slanting sides of the former, which is known locally as Thomas the Cutter's Pitch, or simply Cutter's Pitch. The name is a throwback to a Mr Thomas, who used to live at the bottom of the hill and who earned a living as a castrator of rams and bulls.

A little way up the steep slope, the road is joined on the left by a threadbare tarmac track that wiggles back above the village and then away into the distance along the contour of the hill. The lane leads up to the ancient farmhouse of Penlan, which sits on the ridge line almost directly above the church. A whitewashed aerie, it is one of Clyro's most striking buildings.

Our friends Mary and Chris Bird live there now. They have two boys, similar in age to Seth and Bo. Mary grew up in the house, which was a working farm for generations until her father retired and passed it on to his son. He then sold it to Mary, who, like many young people born and brought up in the area, had moved away in her twenties. She worked as a nurse on film sets before returning home to start a family. Chris is a Londoner and a lighting technician for television and films. They met on location.

From Penlan's eagle vantage point, Pottery Cottage seems squashed and flat, an oblong waymarker dug into the ground at the exit to the village. Beyond, the rumpled bedspread of the Wye valley expands in sandstone lumps and bumps before ceding to the pretty pillowed foothills of the Black Mountains and their arching headboard peaks behind.

Kilvert often admired the view from here too. Once, while visiting 'old Meredith' in Bird's Nest Cottage a little up the way, he found himself taken back by the 'sublime spectacle' of a white and golden cloud on the far horizon, before checking himself and realising that the cloud was actually the 'long white rampart' of the mountains, their slopes bathed in snow and lit up by the setting sun. The snowfall so stilled the countryside that the church bells in

Hay could be heard from across the valley.

I like looking up to Penlan almost as much as down from it. The farmhouse's square front is so intensely white and the grass around it so strikingly green that it stands out with the stark intensity of a lighthouse on a cliff. Kilvert recalls waking up and admiring how the sun's early rays 'struck red' against its whitewashed walls.

At the bottom of the pitch stands another white, square building. This used to be the New Inn, a notorious drinking spot until its licence was revoked in October 1871. Between the Baskerville Arms (which Kilvert insisted on calling by its former name, the Swan) and the New Inn, Clyro was not without its night-time rowdiness. More than once, he observed a parishioner the morning after with a cut lip or swollen eye.

The tour group stands across the street from the former New Inn in an untidy semicircle as the archivist recounts a story about the gipsy Henry Warnell, who once ran cursing and blaspheming down this same stretch of road. A poacher from up on Clyro Hill, Warnell had recently been jailed for six weeks' hard labour after kicking the New Inn's publican in what Kilvert prudishly describes as 'the bad place'. The fast-moving innkeeper had moved just in time to save his corduroy trousers from being torn.

Today, the New Inn is a private home. The Baskerville Arms remains open for business, although it's far from the drinkers' pub it once was. A steady flow of ploughman's lunches and bed-and-breakfast guests makes up most of its trade nowadays, not barrels of beer or whisky shots. To drum home the point, the publican often calls time at nine o'clock.

*

The group turns on its collective heel and makes its way slowly back to its starting point.

There is much chattering. To my right, a gentleman in a light flannel blazer remarks on the fine weather. 'Uncle Francis smiling down,' a man with a West Country drawl replies with a chuckle.

Behind me, a pair of elderly ladies are trying to recall the parish to which Kilvert was assigned before Bredwardine. Despite their best efforts, the name escapes them. One declares herself to be having a 'senior moment'. The other, who says she has always had a terrible memory, gets as far as 'St Something'. John cannot restrain himself. 'St Harmon,' he tells them, his tone paternal as though instructing a young child. Their faces shine with glee. 'Of course, of course.' John's stature as the society's Kilvert expert edges up a notch.

Soon we are back at the Baskerville Arms. Our attentions are directed not to the pub but to an austere, awkward-looking three-storey building across the street. Set back behind low metal railings with looping paper-clip tops and a narrow front garden, Ashbrook House stands withdrawn behind a rash of ivy stubble. Four stone steps curve up towards a gunpowder grey door. The property is empty.

We wander through the gate and poke around. To the right of the house, beside a little lane, runs Clyro Brook. It gushes noisily in joyous infant bounds. On the other side is a lawned garden with thick hedges that provide privacy but steal the light. The building's most remarkable feature is set within the north wall, a huge Gothic window once thought to have graced the village church.

I'm presuming we have permission to be snooping on private property, but it's possible we may not. A wealthy

London couple own it, according to Ted, an accountant from Buckinghamshire who retired to Clyro about a decade ago. He references a dispute that upset the neighbours. It involved a rampant Russian vine, apparently.

The editor of the society's journal chips in. He too has found them awkward. The Interiors section of *The Sunday Times* recently ran a feature on the house and he is hoping to republish some of the photos from the shoot. Gaining permission to use the images is proving devilishly difficult, however. The society's members tut censoriously.

Our trespassing, if that's what it is, has its reason, for this is where Kilvert lodged during his seven-year sojourn in Clyro. The house was called Ty Dulas back then, John explains to me. Kilvert had the two corner rooms on the north-west angle.

He sketches out the household at the time: Mrs Arabella Chaloner, the widowed landlady; her invalid daughter Elizabeth; Catherine Wiles, a young live-in maid; and Arthur Clark, a fellow lodger who worked at a solicitor's firm in Hay and who vexed Kilvert with the smell of his tobacco smoke. There was also a house cat called Toby.

Kilvert doesn't refer to the lodging house very often. When he does, it's invariably from the perspective of looking out, rather than in. The hooting of the owls 'across the dingles'. The merry tunes of the volunteer band as they practised. The nattering of housewives on their way back from the market. Kilvert would not have taken well to the modern introduction of soundproof windows.

Life inside Ty Dulas isn't entirely shrouded in darkness. Despite the size of the house, every indication is that the home was a modest one. Insulation was minimal, a layer of single brick behind the grey stone exterior. Bare floorboards ran through most of the rooms, a mix of oak and deal. The house lacked a central meeting place and the bachelor clergyman appears to have taken his meals alone.

In comparison with the living conditions of many of his parishioners, Kilvert had it good in Ty Dulas. Downstairs there were two lodgers' sitting rooms, the scene of his diary-writing and thus a hallowed space for the society.

Above, he had his own living room. I imagine the gentle-spirited churchman sitting here daydreaming by the fire. Perhaps a much-leafed compendium of William Wordsworth's poetry open in his lap, the Bard of Rydal Mount's soft lyricism wafting up off the page, intoxicating the devoted admirer with its pastoral fumes.

His private bedroom was located in the attic, through the window of which swallows would occasionally come 'dashing . . . and rustling round the room'. There was no bathroom in the house, a fact borne out one chilly Christmas Day when Kilvert trudges outside with his towel and discovers his bath frozen over. He breaks the surface and climbs in, bravely ignoring the sharp edges of ice that continue to jut out from the tub's sides 'like chevaux de frise'. Even by the standards of Victorian grit, Kilvert has to admit that the experience was 'not particularly comforting'.

Such hardships did not put off a keen Kilvertian from taking up residency in the same house a century later. Mr A. L. Le Quesne, a schoolmaster from Jersey, had stumbled on the *Diary* in a second-hand bookshop during a lonely posting in Hobart, Tasmania. For the homesick teacher, Kilvert's beatific descriptions proved 'one of the shaping encounters' of his life.

So much so, in fact, that a little over a decade later, Mr Le Quesne, by that time a teacher at Shrewsbury School, decided to actually move to Clyro. His timing was well chosen. The year was 1970, exactly a hundred years after Kilvert started his diary and thus the marker for a number of centenary celebrations.

As serendipity would have it, he found Ashbrook House on the market. The avid Kilvert fan took a look round but was left sadly disappointed. As he recorded in his own diary, he found the property 'big, grim [and] shabby'. Still, the temptation to follow in his hero's footsteps proved too great and he bought it all the same.

Le Quesne ended up staying several years, an experience he recounts in an intriguing book called *After Kilvert*. In it, he spends much of his time tracking down places referenced in the *Diary* and the account is at its best when he's sniffing around old cottages or retracing Kilvert's routes across the hills.

All is not what it was, he quickly discovers. Buildings have been lost, paths ploughed up and woodlands cut down. Yet he pursues his quest earnestly and with great enthusiasm, and the result is a touching homage from one diarist to another.

Le Quesne's encounter with present-day Clyro lacks the passion he harbours for yesteryear's version of the village. His disaffection starts with Ashbrook House, which he quickly realises is in even worse repair than he first thought. The plumbing is primitive, the proportions 'all wrong' and the air damp. 'Awkward looking', 'desolate' and 'socially abnormal' feature among his summary adjectives, with the best he can dredge up being the house's 'fascinating varieties of level'.

He is no less disappointed by the village as a whole. Far from the rural Arcadia conjured up in the *Diary*, he judges

Clyro bereft of either coherence or character, 'a ragged street of odds and ends' in which nothing relates and the buildings ignore each other.

Revealing a latent snobbery, the public-school educator looks with particular distaste at the sight of retired Birmingham businessmen moving into the area and building themselves 'lavish, suburban-looking bungalows'.

Although Le Quesne couldn't have known it at the time, these incomers from the West Midlands were but the early pioneers of an urban exodus that would see Clyro's boundaries spread. Today, the electoral roll abounds with surnames 'from off', names unheard of in the parish until now. Januszewski, Littlefair, McNamara, Doyle, Balch.

＊

Leaving Kilvert's lodgings behind, the group begins to drift off along the road in the direction of the church. Opposite the little side lane beside Ashbrook House stands Bridge Stores & Post Office. Petite and pokey, it occupies one end of a twin-roofed stone cottage. Notices advertising plumber services and dog trainers fill the large square window at the front. A 'Closed' sign hangs on the door. It won't be open again until Monday.

Mrs Hood, a stalwart of the Women's Institute and fount of information about all local goings-on, has run the shop for close to thirty years. Every weekday morning, at about ten minutes to nine, a cluster of old ladies gathers on the doorstep. Ostensibly they come to buy their daily newspaper, but the ritual is really about sharing news among themselves. For some, it may be the only interaction they have all day.

Despite their loyal custom, business is slow these days.

There's a Texaco filling station on the bypass road that now stocks newspapers as well. Mrs Hood is an indefatigable woman but retirement inevitably looms. When that day comes, Clyro's only shop will almost certainly close and the ladies will lose their excuse to meet.

I stroll along at the back of the group. Immediately on the right, beside the pub, a road leads up the hill along the bank of the brook to a small close of about six family homes. One belongs to a young couple with children. The rest are occupied by retirees 'from off'. Back down on the village's main strip, there are a few stone cottages pressed up against the road. They are similar in style to our place; thick walls, small windows, squat roofs, bombproof.

Behind the last is the wooden lychgate into the churchyard. The wych elms under whose splayed boughs Kilvert would have passed thousands of times are no more, replaced by an entry guard of tall, stiff-backed yews. Close-pressed and unwavering, they man the initial section of the pathway towards the church.

A stone wall, about shoulder high, runs along the two sides of the graveyard that abut the road, protecting the rest of the church's 'sleeping folk', as Kilvert calls those buried beneath Clyro's consecrated ground.

On a triangle of grass in front of the gate is a framed information stand supported by four metal legs. Bearing all the hallmarks of a local tourism initiative, the rectangular message board provides blurb about the village's history and an illustrated map of suggested walks.

'Croeso i Cleirwy', the banner at the top reads. 'Welcome to Clyro'. The etymology of the village's name is disputed, but it's thought to mean 'shining' or 'clear'. The discovery of prehistoric flint arrowheads and a stone axe-head suggests there's been a human settlement here for several millennia. The signwriter laments the loss of the castle, but dates the overgrown earthworks opposite Pottery Cottage to the late eleventh century.

In a separate column, a short section is dedicated to the village's famous curate. Its tone is laudatory. As a landmark of social history, Kilvert's practice of documenting daily life compares to that of Thomas Hardy's novels. The last line makes me wonder if Hay's second-hand booksellers might not have had a hand in financing the message board. The *Diary* is still in print, it states, and, to quote the marketing trope, available 'in all good bookshops'.

The society's schedule will see the tour group circle back to the church at the end, so the members don't tarry and instead continue on their way down the main street.

A little in front of me is the Kilvert Society's chairman, a good-humoured man from the Vale of Aylesbury. He is describing to the elderly man next to him the plans for a 'do-it-yourself' church service tomorrow morning. A retired clergyman from the tour group has volunteered to lead it, while Mrs Hood and her fellow parish ladies will lay on tea.

His companion thinks this a splendid idea, although he wonders if the congregation might turn out to be a bit thin. A light breakfast might be best, the chairman sagely advises. Leave some space for the sandwiches and cake.

John, whose learned coattails I am still clinging to, points to a short row of terraced houses on our left. There are four in total, each two rooms wide and two deep. They are fronted in grey, uneven stone and look directly onto the churchyard. A horizontal ribbon of brick divides the top from the bottom floors. The same brickwork is etched around the doors and windows, only this time the design is erratic and uneven, creating the effect of glue squeezing out beneath an envelope flap and then setting hard.

The properties were slung up quickly and on the cheap shortly after Kilvert left Clyro, John informs me. On a brief return visit, the long-bearded cleric found them 'hideous' and 'huge'. They dwarf and spoil the village, he writes in his diary. If Kilvert had had his way, they would have been built further back from the road and equipped with 'pretty little flower gardens'.

We continue on, past the former police station (now a private residence) and the former milking sheds of Stock's Farm (now the vehicle service and repair workshop of Ashbrook Garage), until we reach the end of the squiggly main street. Here the road curls sharply left, while the pitch to Rhosgoch branches off to the right, first hugging the western edge of the churchyard wall before swerving away up the hill.

On the south corner of the junction sit two of Clyro's oldest cottages. The Historic Settlements Survey for Radnorshire defines the semi-detached pair as 'cruck-framed hall-houses'. Dating back to the Wars of the Roses, the buildings were heavily modified in the nineteenth century. Gabled fronts now point towards the road, jutting forward at an angle perpendicular to the original curved timber roof.

Unlike the Victorian terrace, the semi-detached houses have space for a modest front garden. Shrubs sprout up from behind a low fence of blue railings, one of which has beautiful leaves of heraldic purple and sprawling, overexcited stems. Beside it, a magenta pink rose is just coming into bloom, its petalled puffball buds the match for any knight's fleur-de-lis. A collection of hard-wearing pot plants occupies three tin buckets laid out alongside the steps. Kilvert would have approved.

Two signs attached to the wall identify the properties as No. 5 and No. 6 The Village. Next to No. 5 is a second sign that reads 'Ty Melyn'. The habit of christening homes with Welsh names is common across the village. One of the new builds on the former orchard is called Tan Lan, for instance, meaning 'Under the Bank'; a suitable counterpoint to Penlan ('Top of the Bank'), which peers down from above.

Though clearly not Welsh, Pottery Cottage also marks a recent addition. The official address is No. 1–2 The Village. As with Ty Melyn, the number of the house is followed simply by 'Clyro', as though the road name were superfluous. On reflection, I'm not sure if the road running in front of us even has a formal name. I think of it as the 'Hay Road', but there's no sign to that effect and the maps refer to it merely by its official road number (the rather uninspiring B4531).

This proves confusing for our guests, of whom there is a regular stream thanks to a small Bed & Breakfast business that Emma has set up at the far end of the house. The guest room is located in what used to be Dworski's pottery workshop, which after his departure was converted into a warren of dark and dank cubbyhole rooms. On exchanging contracts, Emma had these later additions removed to create a sun-dappled space with a pitched roof running up to the rafters and an exposed oak crossbeam spanning wall to wall.

When our time at the farm cabin came to an end, the former workshop was the only habitable space in the house so we moved in there. For six months we cooked on a camping stove outside and washed up with hot water from the bathtub. The boys adapted quickly enough to eating outside and sleeping head to toe on a single mattress that we stored against the wall during the day and laid on the floor at night.

One place that has never changed its name or questioned its status is Clyro village hall. Built in 1929, it sits upon a low bank opposite Ty Melyn. A stout rectangular building with a grey tiled roof, the hall is positioned side-on to the main street and consequently looks askance at the village as though it would rather peek out on Clyro's residents than look them straight in the eye.

The bottom half of the village hall is kept hidden by a neatly trimmed hedge, behind which rises an unruly cherry tree, its wild tentacle branches aiding the hedge's camouflaging mission.

Several of the tour group have crossed over the road junction to the main entrance gate of the churchyard. Digital cameras appear from bags and are pointed inexpertly towards the bucolic scene in front.

Of all the possible perspectives, this is the one that reveals St Michael and all his angels at their finest. The crenellated tower imprinted on the deep green canvas of the hill. Sheep encircling the belfry like Velcro stick-ons. The cockerel suspended in surprised flight just above the ridge, a strip of powder blue beneath his feet.

*

As they take their visitor snaps, I head across to the hall. Access is via a gate on the road, which leads to a ramp up to the entrance door. Inside is a rectangular room with wood-panelled floors and an elevated stage area at one end, the scene of primary school concerts and junior nativity plays. At the other end is a small kitchen alcove, from where tomorrow's tea will be served. The door is locked.

Back on the road, there's a community bulletin board. Directly opposite it, as though in opposition, stands the church noticeboard. The latter includes the name and phone number of the vicar followed by several spaces for information about the upcoming services. A piece of white paper is pinned to the wooden board in the 'This Sunday' column. The page carries the word 'NONE' in bold black capitals.

In Kilvert's time, Clyro's resident vicar was a Mr Richard Lister Venables. He was a man of private wealth and owner of a large estate at Llysdinam, near Newbridge-on-Wye. As such, he had the means to employ his own curate to help him officiate at Sunday services, as well as taking weddings, funerals and baptisms. In return for his efforts, Kilvert received the less than princely stipend of £100 a year.

Still, even with two full-time clergymen serving just the one parish, church attendance was slipping by the time Kilvert became curate. With the second Industrial Revolution in full swing, confidence in scientific modernisation abounded. Steel railway tracks were being laid and the first battleships built. Intellectually and politically, meanwhile, continental Europe was seething with a spirit of modernism and revolution.

Much closer to home, the Church of Wales was facing serious competition for the first time. Since the Methodist revival of the previous century, Nonconformist chapels of all hues had sprung up throughout the length and breadth of the country.

Our corner of the Welsh borders crops up early in that story. While preaching in the open air behind the Old Black Lion pub in Hay in 1740, the Methodist evangelist William Seward was struck by a stone, causing his death several days later and thus providing the movement with its first martyr. Other free church proselytisers followed in his wake. Not just Methodists, but Baptists, Congregationalists and Unitarians too. As their popularity spread, so the pews of Anglican churches like St Michael's began to empty.

The *Diary* sometimes carries a lament about low numbers in church. 'Sadly few communicants,' Kilvert wrote after one Holy Communion service. The Sunday in question happened to be his birthday, a factor that perhaps compounded his disappointment.

Even so, when he picked up his sermon notes and climbed into the pulpit, Kilvert could still probably reckon on a hundred faces or more looking back at him. All of them dressed in their Sunday best, all schooled in the liturgy, all suitably deferential to the young cleric in his flowing robes.

If Nonconformism dented the dominance of the established Church, then secularism today has almost flattened it. As with rural parish churches across the country, Clyro church counts on a faithful few to keep its doors open. Elderly folk mostly, drawn by faith and habit down the churchyard path and in through the chancel door.

One of Kilvert's contemporaries developed a canny solution to the problem of falling audiences. The Reverend Jon Price, MA (Cantab), acquired the living over the hill at Llanbedr in 1859. The church was in a 'ruinous state' and had been without a vicar for almost a decade, an indication of its spiritual as well as geographic remoteness. There was no vicarage, so the new incumbent took to living in three bathing machines that he had delivered from Aberystwyth. When these accidentally burned down, he moved into a decrepit hut next door.

Kilvert paid a visit in July 1872, providing one of the *Diary*'s best known passages. On being welcomed inside, he took a seat in the 'strangest interior' he ever saw. The 'foulness and wretchedness' of the place left the visiting clergyman boggle-eyed. No grate by the fire. The table covered with crumbs and dirty cutlery, leftover meat and a 'huggermugger confusion' of discarded cups and saucers. Broken bricks and dust mixed with the cold peat ashes on the floor. 'A faint ghastly sickly light' stealing from the open chimney. Amazingly, the so-called 'Solitary of Llanbedr' would live amid this 'wild confusion of litter and rubbish' for another quarter of a century.

Today, Clyro's vicar lives outside the parish and is responsible for not one but five churches. He is, to put it mildly, stretched. Once every couple of months he arranges a family service in the village that we try to attend in a show of solidarity. There's no Sunday School, although once a quarter the church organises a child-focused 'messy church'. Numbers differ, although the general marker for success is if the children outnumber the adult volunteers.

Over the decades, the village hall has gradually replaced the church as the nominal centre of communal life. No longer do the residents of Clyro gather for Advent communion or to lay flowers on the graves at Easter. If they can be persuaded out of their homes, it's for the Chinese auction in aid of the hall's upkeep or the annual Macmillan coffee morning.

I say 'nominal' because such occasions are sporadic and support for them variable. I scan the community bulletin board, which is encased behind glass in a wooden frame. No upcoming events in the hall are mentioned. There's a notice about a history weekend at the end of the month across the river in Hay. In England, on the other hand, Brilley village hall is putting on a play, while Clifford has a concert planned.

As I scan the other announcements, I wonder if I'm not looking for the wrong thing.

Community-wide events are rare, yet special interest groups abound. Take volleyball, which boasts a practice session in Three Cocks every Tuesday. Or T'ai chi classes in Cusop village hall. Choirs, Bible study, mums and tots, Pilates, table tennis, badminton, local history clubs, the University of the Third Age: all are there on tap for whoever wants to go.

Although it's not advertised, Clyro village hall plays host to a life-drawing class on a Monday and a willow-weaving group on a Thursday, as well as providing a regular meeting space for the Community Council and resident groups such as the Women's Institute.

My own introduction to the life of the hall came via the Monday-night bowls club, which I went along to at the invitation of my neighbour Ann, a buxom, chatty lady who lives on the estate opposite our cottage. The experience proved fun even though I was the youngest by about thirty years and by far the least expert.

*

With their photographs now taken, the members of the Kilvert Society reassemble and begin to move away from the church in a southerly direction. Ahead, at a distance of about 200 yards, lies the bypass. The passing cars are more audible now that we don't have the houses on the main street as a buffer.

Three relatively modern detached houses occupy the left-hand side of the road, the last of which has a brace of shiny black solar panels on the roof. Dominating the opposite side of the road, meanwhile, is one of the largest properties in the village.

Built in a Regency style typical of the early nineteenth century, its two-storey bulk has dual roofs; one seemingly flat, the other shaped in a spiky 'M'. The house is painted completely white, bar the eaves, window frames and masonry blocks along the building's edge, which are black as creosote. Embedded into the garden wall is a rectangular slate on which the property's name is etched in a gold calligraphic font: 'The Old Vicarage'.

In this slightly grandiose abode lived Mr Venables, Kilvert's boss. Widowed just before Kilvert's arrival in Clyro, Venables was childless, although the household included five or six servants, so it was far from empty. Kilvert was a regular visitor, especially during the initial years of his curacy when 'Dinner with Mr V' and equivalent entries often appear in his diary.

On one memorable occasion, Venables tried to cure his youthful aide of 'face ache', a malady of which the diarist frequently complains and which medics now think was probably a severe localised migraine. Whatever Kilvert's precise ailment, the effects of Mr V's prescription of four full glasses of port were short-lived at best. All the next day, poor Kilvert suffered a 'bursting raging splitting sick' hangover.

The vicar proved a better counsellor and adviser than he did a physician. Kilvert clearly looked up to him as a dutiful son might his father. Mr Venables cut something of a patrician figure. Well intentioned but removed, he appeared to get along with his new appointee well enough. 'He seems to be a gentleman,' the vicar wrote to his brother soon after Kilvert started in post. And, although he identifies him as 'quite young' (Kilvert was twenty-three at the time) and still awaiting formal ordination, he believed the task of finding a curate was firmly settled.

The letter contains a rare physical description of Clyro's famous curate. As a writer, Kilvert had an uncanny gift of capturing people in a few well-chosen words. Etty Meredith Brown, with cheeks 'the dusky bloom and flush of ripe pomegranate'; Mrs Stone of the 'fierce eyes and teeth'; the 'thin grey-bearded nutcracker face' of old Hannah Whitney. It is one of the frustrations of his genre that the fêted diarist never turned the same skill on himself.

Venables's account is precise, if less poetic. The new curate, he tells his brother, is 'tall with a black beard and moustache'. Kilvert's facial hair we know about because of the cameo role it plays in various scenes. Such as the time a bee stung him between the eyes, only then to buzz around in his beard in what Kilvert regretfully assumed was the insect's 'dying agony'. Or the occasion when he walked through a snowstorm that caused his whiskers to grow stiff with ice and his beard to freeze to his mackintosh.

Kilvert's hair colour and physical size, meanwhile, are confirmed by the only known photograph of him. The image shows him seated in a chair looking square on to the camera, a book open in his lap. Dated to around 1875, the portrait shows him to have a good head of hair; thick, neatly cut and with the tiniest hint of a curl. The beard is long but orderly, as though recently trimmed. Although the picture is taken against an empty background, an indication of his height can been gleaned from the way in which his body envelops the chair, the back of which ends well below his shoulder blades.

His precise features are difficult to make out from the surviving photograph; the nose is enviably well proportioned, the eyes slightly hooded beneath heavy brows, the forehead flat. Reading anything into his expression is impossible as it's set firm for the camera. Even with no knowledge of his diary, however, it's a face that looks generous and well-tempered.

Three years into his curacy, Mr Venables married a second time. This time his wife was twenty-five years younger than he, so far closer in age to Kilvert than the vicar himself. In as much as the social mores of the time would allow, the curate and the new Mrs Venables became good friends. The vicarage was no longer the lonely widower's home it once was, however, and Mr Venables's time for fireside chats was understandably diminished. Indeed, one popular theory has it that Kilvert started keeping a diary as an effort to replace his lost confidant.

As well as his employment, Kilvert had his boss to thank for his introduction into rural 'society'. As a pleasant, university-educated clergyman, Kilvert may well have found his way into the country set anyway. Having Mr Venables, who wore a second hat as Chairman of Radnorshire Magistrates, verify his gentlemanly credentials certainly helped.

The Revd and Mrs Venables aside, it was possible to number the landed gentry in the immediate area on one hand. In Clyro itself there were the Baskervilles of Clyro Court and the Morrells of Cae Mawr, two houses whose drawing rooms and croquet lawns Kilvert visited frequently. Below the lip of the hill between Clyro and Hay lived the Crichtons of Wye

Cliff, while a couple of miles downstream on the banks of the Wye were the Hodgsons of Lower Cabalva.

Further afield were the Thomases from Llanthomas in Llanigon, whose daughter, Daisy, Kilvert was to fall head-over-heels in love with. Her father refused to countenance the match, however, marking one of the deepest sadnesses in Kilvert's life and the subject of several particularly melancholic sections of the *Diary*. 'The sun seemed to have gone out of the sky,' his pen would confide.

Another family that moved within this inner circle of minor gentry was that of Archdeacon William Bevan, vicar of Hay for over fifty years. Throughout his incumbency, the long-serving cleric lived in the town's castle, which was the property of his uncle, Sir Joseph Bailey, Baron Glanusk, a wealthy ironmaster.

A mishmash of Norman, Jacobean and Victorian styles, the building was as structurally dubious as it was architecturally unorthodox. By Bevan's time, the outer walls and keep already lay in ruins. Much of what hadn't collapsed would later burn down in two major fires. Today, the gutted remains of the embattled castle sit rather forlornly above the town, its gap-toothed turrets and fat-fingered chimney stacks silhouetted against the mountains behind.

Rarely does a week go by without Kilvert receiving an invitation to a dinner party or luncheon at one of the large houses in the district, although summer was when the social calendar really switched into gear. From July through to September, the pages of the *Diary* skip to the sound of fruit-filled wine cups clinking and silk dresses swirling, to jolly quadrilles and 'flying fiddle bows'.

*

The lunar-eclipse party at Clifford Priory on a fine day in mid-July perfectly captures the mood of the season's encounters. To reach the early afternoon event, Kilvert strolls several miles across the fields with friends, enjoying a pleasant conversation about Tennyson and Wordsworth as he walks.

On arrival, their host comes out to greet them and ushers them into the drawing room, where Kilvert finds 'the usual set that one meets and knows so well'; the Dews, Thomases, Webbs, Wyatts, Bridges, Oswalds, Trumpers, '& co.'.

The party moves from the house to the lawn, where they have 'great fun' playing six simultaneous games of croquet and sending 'balls flying in all directions'. High tea is served at seven thirty, with more than forty people sitting down to eat. The iced claret cup catches Kilvert's eye, as do the 'unlimited fruit' and enormous strawberries.

Their stomachs full and their heads a little dizzy, the partygoers drifts back to the lawn to admire the eclipse. Some of the young men take turns racing up the slippery terrace bank, while the ladies walk around arm-in-arm like 'tall white lilies', their summer dresses looking ghostly pale in the twilit garden.

Two features of the account jump out at me, both small asides amid the jovialities. The first is the date: the party took place on a Tuesday.

In defence of the hosts, eclipses keep their own calendars. Unlike debutante balls or wedding parties, they cannot be booked for an August weekend. For the Crichtons and Thomases of this world, a Tuesday is as any other day; twenty-four hours to be filled with their artistic pursuits and charitable endeavours, with hobbies and house visits. Such was life for the Victorian rentier classes, a people who flaunted their free time and luxuriated in leisure.

Today, it is markedly different. The majority of us still work nine-to-five, five days a week. By necessity, employment and the constrictions of office hours govern our time. Prize them though we may, our social lives come second, a few precious hours snatched at the end of the working day or squeezed in at weekends between domestic chores and kids.

Everyone aspires to a 'work–life balance', but few achieve it. Even if you negotiate every Tuesday off, the chances of swanning around at a garden party remain slim because, unlike you, everyone else is still in the office working.

The exceptions, I suppose, are the retired and the unemployed. Around here, the former dominate. They are the early twenty-first century's pastime generation. While many take a well-deserved rest to write that book, go on that trip, learn that instrument, a good number throw themselves into civic life. Sitting on committees, organising events, attending meetings, jollying people along. In many ways, the baby boomer demographic comprises the dynamos of contemporary community life.

Retirement's leisured hours lie a long way off for me, if they ever come at all. The days of fat final salary pensions are over for most of us. Certainly for me. Downsizing and digging in, that's about the sum of my long-term financial planning.

I am not complaining. I had a well-paid job and I chose to give it up. In exchange, I have a working week that is mine to do with as I wish. Freelance journalism pays my bills and, in theory, leaves me time for my other passions. No waiting until retirement.

With this in mind, I decided to embark on a doctoral programme in Latin American studies shortly after we moved back to the UK. My idea was to keep a toe in a part of the world that continues to fascinate me. The course is compelling but time-consuming, and I find myself at my desk more than my free-floating plans first envisioned.

On the upside, my daily commute is minimal. Emma delivered on her promise and had the tool shed in the garden converted for me. As a work space, it has everything I need; a phone line, internet (like most people, I am an exception to my own rule) and an electric heater for when the winter cold creeps under the door.

The furnishings are simple and functional, which suits me just fine. A few bookshelves along the walls. A filing cabinet in the corner. A large wooden table, complete with a view onto our vegetable patch and through to a wild flower garden that blooms into bright oranges and pinks in the summer.

Pleased as I am with how the shed has turned out, it will not help me integrate into community life. Indeed, its galvanised walls are positively prejudicial to such a quest. I cannot follow in Kilvert's footsteps ensconced in my office chair.

So I set about cutting back my workload. I tell my editors that I'm no longer as available and ask my PhD supervisor if I can go part-time. Neither objects. Nor have the fears that all freelancers face when turning down work been realised: the world hasn't fallen in. That said, neither has my invitation to a Tuesday afternoon garden party arrived yet. If and when it does, however, I shall be ready.

The second thing that catches my attention in Kilvert's account of the eclipse party is a remark that he makes about his fellow guests. They are all very pleasant and friendly, he notes, before going on to say that they meet 'almost like brothers and sisters'.

It's the word 'almost' that brings me up short.

One of six siblings, Kilvert enjoyed a close relationship with his family. As the *Diary* reveals, he writes to all of them regularly and thinks of them often. Occasionally they visit him or he travels back to his parents' home in Wiltshire. Most of the time they were absent, however, and it is out of this relational void that a sublimated desire for a surrogate family appears to grow. If true, it seems to me to be an entirely natural urge.

Finding a replacement for familial warmth among the local aristocracy was never realistic. Throughout the *Diary*, there's a niggling feeling that Kilvert doesn't quite belong. He speaks frequently and in affectionate terms about Mary Bevan, for instance, daughter of Archdeacon Bevan, yet her references to him in her own extensive diaries are scant and cursory.

In reality, Kilvert, a vicar's son without a private income, was destined to be the nearly man: always the guest, not the host; forever the welcome visitor, never quite the full insider. Final proof of his almostness is seen in Mr Thomas's rejection of the curate's request to court his daughter Daisy. Kilvert's prospects and position, he is led to understand, are unbefitting.

In many ways, the position of impecunious clergyman must have been a tricky one to hold in the Victorian period; too poor for the nobility, too removed for the masses, and very possibly too religious for many of the businessmen and professionals who made up the early ranks of the middle classes.

Kilvert's closest ties appear to be with the laymen who shared his faith, such as Hope Morrell, the young, evangelically minded owner of Cae Mawr, or the clergymen who shared his cloth, like Andrew Pope, the curate in Cusop, who suffered the embarrassment of having himself confirmed by the bishop in a case of mistaken identity that had the whole congregation tittering.

*

Pondering Kilvert's exact place in society, I follow the tour group as it moves on from the Old Vicarage towards the bypass. Walking in twos, we stretch out in an elongated crocodile.

'So are you new to the area?' an elderly lady with grey curler-set hair asks me.

I tell her I am. She thinks it must be very exciting, 'living where Kilvert once lived and that'. She once thought about moving here herself, in fact. Then – she waves her hand at the busy road and the estate houses opposite – she decided against it.

Up close, the village's imperfections are hard to hide. The unsightly amalgam of old stone and new brick, of aged wood and uPVC. The sprawl of the garage workshop. The fluorescence of the Texaco garage with its luminous fuel prices. The sheer existence of the busy bypass and its surfeit of signage.

Observed from a short distance, however, Clyro is as picturesque a place as you could hope to find. Pointing down the bypass towards the Cutter's Pitch end of the village, I tell her about a run I have recently discovered.

Just beyond the most recent of the two developments in 'new Clyro', there's a stile half-hidden in the hedge. Go through there and it brings you out into an open meadow that brightens with buttercups in the spring. Below on the left is the old mill pond where Kilvert would come looking for primroses in the hedge before Easter, and where he and the pub landlord once saw a white-bellied shrew darting and tumbling about in the reeds.

If you were to carry on up along a claggy path alongside a corn field, I explain, then over some sloping grazing land just above Tirmynach Farm, you'd eventually come out on the crest of a humpbacked hill.

'Is that Boatside?' she says, familiar with the surrounding geography from the *Diary*.

That's right, I tell her. 'Used to be a Roman camp up there as well,' she adds. I'm not sure, I confess, although it would certainly make sense. Perched above the Wye valley flats with a horizon-stretching blaze of colour and country-side running north and south, the soldiers would certainly have had a commanding view.

The Wye is at its nearest to the east, huddled in the dip below two rippled fields of honeyed wheat and brilliant yellow rapeseed, its emerald-green waters rushing fast above the reeds. For sheer handsomeness, Wordsworth's 'wanderer through the woods' is a match for any river in the British Isles.

Burrowed among the trees above its far bank stands Hay, a blue-grey patchwork of tiled rooftops amid a swathe of sylvan green. Poking above the tree canopy is the castle, a wonderfully hotchpotch emblem of the town's borderland confusions. And then beyond, of course, the barren bouldery bulk of the Black Mountains. Implacably wild. Their beauty hard, unremitting, almost brutish in their bluntness.

Looking back west to Clyro, the view is altogether different. Softer, kinder, lusher. Scattered rooftops breathing trails of chimney smoke. Forested hillsides swooping down together, backs arched in a springboard dive. The church tower cushioned by a tree-softened vale beneath an ocean of sky. Kilvert thought the village at its prettiest from this same spot too, its dingle sides shining with 'gleams of green' and the dotted houses washed by a 'tender blue haze'.

I do my best to describe the scene to the lady, who tells me she can well imagine it. The Kilvert Society's outings used to involve a fair amount of walking. 'Not that you'd believe me to look at us now.' Overhearing, an elderly lady beside her jabs her arm and the two women share a laugh. No, but seriously, she says, in their younger days they would follow Uncle Kilvert up into the hills. 'Visit his old haunts, we would.'

I remark on Kilvert's pastoral work around Clyro. 'Villaging' he called the practice. The 1871 census shows 130 families living in the parish, putting the total population at over 800. It amounts to almost the same today. The young curate would aim to get round every household once or twice a month, making for an impressive workload.

'Villaging in the morning,' he sometimes writes in his diary. Or elsewhere, 'Been villaging all day.' Sometimes he provides a fuller itinerary, such as this entry for late January in 1872:

> Visited Edward Evans, old Price the paralysed keeper, Mrs. Lacy, Catherine Ferris, James Smith, and Mrs. Price of the Swan who showed me preserved in a box part of one of Price's whiskers pulled out by the Clyro women in the late row at the Swan.

It's Kilvert's memorable first-hand accounts of these visits that explain much of the *Diary*'s enduring appeal. Flesh-and-blood characters step off the pages, every one of them deftly described, all of them bristling with life.

Such as 'old Witcombe', the deaf, helpless and nearly blind ninety-year-old, who leaned on the friendly curate and fondled his hand, 'talking earnestly but incoherently and repeating himself almost every moment'.

Even those at life's end gain vibrancy under Kilvert's pen. Edward Evans with his 'ceaseless moaning' is one such luckless character. Catching him at death's door, the curate's eye is drawn to the 'gaunt ghastly' cat waiting at the end of his bed as though ready to 'begin upon him' the moment he breathes his last. Another bedside visitation was to the dying William Meredith, who lived beside the tump and whose eyes 'rolled . . . wildly in the darkness' as a fierce storm shook his old house and roared in the roof.

Of the dozens of villagers mentioned by name in the *Diary*, two stand out in Kilvert's affections. Both are elderly, hospitable and God-fearing. John Morgan, an octogenarian soldier who saw action under Wellington in the Peninsular War, is one of the few residents ever to have left the village. Kilvert would often make his way up to the veteran's modest cottage at Cwmbythog to listen to his stories, about whispered conversations with night sentries in France or scaring off marauding wolves with the flash of musket powder in Spain.

Hannah Whitney, she of the nutcracker face, was his other favourite. She lived alongside the stream by Ashbrook House, the water rushing in the gutter at her door. On sunny afternoons, she'd often sit on her front step, 'cloaked and with her rusty black bonnet fiercely cocked and pointed, crown uppermost', doing her knitting or just watching the world go by.

Even older than Mr Morgan, this elderly parishioner would turn her 'withered grey face' towards the attentive curate and, with shining eyes, share 'her reminiscences and tales of the dear old times, the simple kindly primitive times "in the Bryngwyn" nearly ninety years ago'.

It's easy to picture Kilvert seated at her side, listening intently as she tells of the ghosts that once haunted 'sheep cot pool' just beneath Cold Blow or the fairies who were once said to dance at night to 'sweet fiddles' at Rhosgoch Mill.

Quaint and colourful as many of the *Diary*'s entries are, they are not without a hard edge. Beyond the gilded drawing rooms of the gentry, day-to-day life for most of Kilvert's parishioners was one of abject poverty. Consider old Laver. 'Shaggy and grey like a wild beast', Kilvert struggled to say which was the more unkempt: the man himself, who was 'swarming with lice', or the 'filthy den' he called home. The dying Edward Evans was no better off, his 'hovel bedroom' in the attic 'almost insupportable' because of the 'close horrid' stench.

I mention to the lady the grim conditions that Kilvert encountered around the village. Clyro may have changed, but not altogether for the worse. She accepts the point, noting that the most precarious of the village's housing stock would have been demolished long ago.

Talking of housing, she asks where I live. I point across the road to Pottery Cottage. 'The white house,' I explain. Looks old, she notes, and asks if it's mentioned in the *Diary*. Not as far as I know, I have to admit. She gives me a pitying look.

Directly in front of the house, across the entrance road to Castle Estate from the tump, is an allotment. The lady comments on the triffid-like sunflowers that look out onto the road, their smiling paper-plate faces towering above the cabbages, carrots and runner beans behind.

They belong to my neighbour, Elwin, I explain. He regularly puts second-hand bikes and gardening equipment out on the main road, propping up a 'for sale' board beside them on the fence. Although they often take weeks to sell, no one ever thinks to steal them.

The archivist begins a patter about the former village school, which was decommissioned some time in the 1960s. From my shed window, I look out onto the square lavatory block at the back of the low-rise stone building, now renamed 'Kilvert's School'. This flat-roofed rear extension acts as the boundary line for the front part of our garden. Emma has attached two wooden trellises to the wall and is urging a combination of fig trees, rambling roses, sweet peas, vines, honeysuckle and a clematis to grow up it. I enjoy watching their progress from my office chair.

During Kilvert's curacy, responsibility for instructing the children of the parish fell to Josiah Evans, a man of whom we learn little other than that his violin suffered from a broken string, In Kilvert's opinion, the instrument had 'something wrong with [all] the others' too. As the school's only master, the faceless Mr Evans was assigned a modest house next to the school, the back of which I can also see peering up over my garden hedge.

Never a parent himself, Kilvert was fond of children – overly fond, some modern readers might think. Reading the diaries today, some of the language he uses to describe the prettiest of his charges is certainly 'florid', let's say.

Kilvert saves his most amatory ink for the 'darling child' Elizabeth Harris ('Gipsy Lizzie' to the diarist), whose drooping white eyelids and exquisite little mouth he finds of 'indescribable' and 'unsullied' loveliness. If that doesn't raise eyebrows, then his confession to have walked six miles to kiss the 'sweet face' of little Janet Vaughan may well do.

According to Kilvert's biographer David Lockwood, this is the poetically minded diarist engaging in literary dramatisation. The language, he suggests, is 'pure Pre-Raphaelite', more an idealised benediction inspired by divine beauty than the sordid confessions of a clerical paedophile.

I am prone to give him the benefit of the doubt and I take it from the Kilvert Society's general silence on the matter that they are too.

Whatever the case, Kilvert's life was very much intertwined with that of the village school, although how much of the actual burden of teaching sat on the curate's shoulders isn't clear.

One occasion when he really did pull out all the stops was in the run-up to the government inspector's visit in July 1871. For weeks, Kilvert had the whole school cramming intensively, turning up in person three times a day to ensure that no students were slacking.

On the big day, thirty-five of the school's fifty-one 'scholars' turned up. The attendance rate brings to mind one of the *Diary*'s most poignant vignettes. That of little Mary Thomas sitting on the floor at home with a broken piece of slate and a stick of chalk 'trying to think she was at school'. She was unable to attend school, Kilvert laments, because the ground was wet and her boots were full of holes.

In this context, he judged the turnout commendable. He cannot resist a tiny boast either, pointing out that Hay's school was only able to drum up seven more pupils despite having twice the number of children on its books.

Once the students had sat their examination, Kilvert retired to his lodgings with Mr Shadrach Pryce, the inspector, who had been joined for the day by his wife. The curate pressed various 'substantial' offerings of food and drink on them, but the couple contented themselves with a glass of wine and a biscuit each.

Whether it was Kilvert's hospitality or the students' scores that swung it we shall never know, but the next month the inspector delivered a 'capital report' from the Education Office. With it came a much welcomed grant for £36 10s.

At the mention of the cash, Ted the accountant whistles loudly. He wishes Powys Education Department was still as quick with its chequebook, he says.

He is a governor at the current primary school, he explains to the group. In response to a question about its location, he points towards the southern edge of the village.

'Ysgol' shouts a red-rimmed road sign along the pavement, 'School'. Further along, another triangular sign depicts an elderly couple crossing, the taller of the two clutching a stick, while the second grabs at the other's elbow. No explanatory text is provided, the inference being obvious. Further into Radnorshire, there are similar signs for sheep, though without sticks.

Government cuts mean a couple of smaller schools in the hills nearby have recently had to close. Class sizes at Clyro Primary have consequently swelled. Resources, however, have not. Bo and Seth are both pupils at the school, so I listen with interest as Ted describes ambitious plans laid out by the local education authority to build a new campus. Construction is set to begin in two years' time. Ted's manner suggests a healthy degree of scepticism. Similar promises have been made in the past, he notes.

Emma and I would welcome better facilities, of course, but the children seem happy enough. The ethos is inclusive

and the teachers attentive. Our two boys head off enthusiastically on their bikes in the morning and return tired but
happy at the day's end. Both appear to be making progress
in the classroom and with friends in the playground. As
parents, we couldn't ask for much more.

If there's one thing I could change, it would be the school's
homogeneity. Every morning, the entire student body
gathers for assembly in the main hall. Scanning the hundred or so pupils, there's not a single non-white face among
them. Diversity is having freckles. It's no good complaining.
All the other village schools hereabouts are the same. They
merely reflect the Marcher population as a whole, which,
like its sheep, happens to be very white.

For parents of young children, the school gates are where
many acquaintances are made and friendships struck.
Typically, I accompany the boys in the morning and Emma
shepherds them back in the afternoon. We live about 500
yards away, making us the closest household to the school.
We're also among the least punctual. With everyone rushing to get started with their days, morning interactions
don't often get beyond a quick 'hi' and 'bye'. Pick-up, in
contrast, is more relaxed. You find people, to steal a
Kilvertian phrase, 'in full chat'.

Keen to get into the hills soon after we arrived, I suggested to a couple of the dads at the gate that we should go
for a hike. The tradition has stuck and every other month or
so we pick a route in the mountains and head off together
for the afternoon. The group includes an electrician, an
insurance expert and a manager in the forestry department.
Men 'not in my game', in other words. By Updike's measure, I feel this is progress.

My attentions are drawn back to the old school. 'We did

a penny reading there once,' the lady says, pointing her fore-finger across the street. Her voice is hushed as though their reading of poems and their singing of songs were in some way shameful.

John, who has rejoined us after a lengthy conversation with the retired vicar, overhears. Popularised by Charles Dickens, penny readings were first introduced to Clyro in Kilvert's day, he clarifies for me. Mr Bevan in Hay was very keen on this chaste form of evening entertainment, which he thought a far more edifying alternative to the pub.

A report in the *Hereford Times* from February 1871 pro-vides a brief description of one such event. Held in the 'National School Room, Clyro', the article records. The Reverend R. Lister Venables is cited as 'kindly presiding' over an audience of some 250 people.

Among the highlights was Mrs Partridge's and Mrs Haines' 'rendering of *The Barber of Seville*', which was judged to be 'everything that could be desired'. The choir's rendition of the part songs 'Hail, Smiling Morn' and 'The Carnovale', meanwhile, was singled out for the 'capital pre-cision' of their execution. Both performances would have been repeated were strict rules not in place against encores.

I suppose the nearest equivalent of the penny readings today might be open mic night at the Globe in Hay. Pitched as an opportunity for amateur poets and musicians to test out their material, the evening tryout takes place on the first Tuesday of every month and attracts a small but faithful crowd.

Before the group wheels around and heads back to the church, there is one more landmark to see. Unfortunately, Cae Mawr, the seat of Kilvert's friend and regular walking companion Hugo Morrell, resides behind a barricade of

Leyland cypresses that screens it almost completely from the bypass.

We walk up a tree-shaded driveway that runs off the main road just beyond the bus stop, our path lit by a luminescent strip of lichen running right up the middle. At an inhospitable set of mechanical gates, we stop. An oval blue plaque on the stone post declares that the invisible residence beyond belongs to the Historic Houses Association. Shame it's not winter, John laments. We'd have been able to peer through the foliage.

The owners once arranged to put on a Victorian tea for the society, he recalls. Back in the late 1980s. They ate sandwiches with the crusts cut off and listened to Gilbert and Sullivan. Various pupils at Clyro Primary School performed readings. Each one was a descendant of a villager mentioned in the *Diary*. A generation on, John wonders aloud how many candidates there would be now. Not as many, I suggest. Regretfully, he agrees.

Arriving back on the bypass, I say my goodbyes. I had promised Emma I'd be home in time to take the boys swimming.

As I watch the elderly Kilvertians stroll back towards the churchyard, I realise my question about the curate's place in the community remains unresolved.

Pinning him down to one single group certainly seems problematic. Kilvert spread himself widely. In contrast to the prevailing social prejudices of his day, he talked to anyone, anywhere. His ear always cocked, his eyes ever open, his diarist's pen never far from hand.

His approach struck me as a sound one. But where to start? My thoughts turn to the faithful guardians of the diarist's memory and their rendezvous in the pub.

2

The Rhydspence Inn

The night was cool and pleasant as I walked home under the stars. About midnight I passed over the Rhydspence border brook, and crossed the border from England into Wales. The English inn was still ablaze with light and noisy with the songs of revellers.

Kilvert's Diary, May Day, 1872

'What've we got?' the landlord repeats back to me. 'Bitter, you said. Well, there's the Bass or there's the Otter.' He lays a hand on each pump. 'Otter's a good beer.'

'I'll try the Otter, then,' I tell him, and wait as he pulls the pint.

The lounge bar is empty except for five men huddled around the circular table nearest the fire. Two of the drinkers are pressed shoulder to shoulder on a wooden bench. Positioned tight against the wall and with high sides at either end, the piece of furniture resembles a truncated church pew.

The bench is designed for two, yet one of the occupants is unusually large, which makes the arrangement look rather cramped. Neither man appears to mind. Truth be told, they look rather snug. The three others sit around the table opposite, the trio evenly spread at three points of the compass. Their chairs are of conventional pub design. Dark varnished pine, thin cushions, a slatted semicircular back.

Five pint glasses line the table's rim. They are filled to various depths and all within easy reach of their owners. In the grate beside them a gnarly log smoulders, its steady heat giving the room a tea-cosy warmth. The drinkers' cheeks are ever so slightly aglow.

Around retirement age or a little younger, the men are entirely without haste. Sitting there, they seem cushioned against time. Periodically, one of them will push back his chair and head outside for a smoke or go to the gents. Otherwise, they remain stationary, as if cemented to their seats.

A sense of acute self-consciousness washes over me at having disturbed what feels like a private gathering. In a way, trying to settle into a new area marks a string of long awkward baptisms like this one. A succession of walking into unknown places, encounters with group after group of new faces.

So the first kids' birthday party, for instance: parents already locked in their friendship huddles, jabbering away among themselves, me loitering by the cupcakes and jelly hoping for a stray smile or a welcoming word. Or the running club, which I joined a few months after arriving: heading off in the dark along routes I didn't know, with people whose names I couldn't remember, wondering if this was really something I wanted to do.

Unsure of the best step to take, I focus on the landlord and watch as the beer shoots from the swan-neck tap into the base of the empty pint glass. The liquid strikes the bottom in a puddle-brown swirl, muddying a little more with every pull of the landlord's arm. The publican wheezes as he tugs the baton-shaped tap. As if in sympathy, the pump system wheezes along with him in a low-pitched, hydraulic gurgle. To the sound of their gasping duet, the beer bubbles and pushes its way towards the brim. A sudsy cap layers the surface, a million pin-head eddies all awhirl in the froth.

'There you go, young man,' the landlord says, his accent unadulterated Derbyshire. He places the foamy-headed pint on the bar. 'That's two pounds eighty, please.'

I hand over a five-pound note and he steps across to the till, his movement stiff and rheumatic. In his late fifties, the landlord is dressed in a check soft-collared shirt and tie, over which he wears a V-neck jumper and on top of that a quilted gilet in hunting green with square, buttoned pockets. He looks somewhere between a country squire and a gamekeeper.

Picking up my pint, I steal a quick glance over to the table of drinkers. Tony, who owns the holiday cottages we rented, is the only one among the five I recognise. He gestures for me to join them. 'Pull yourself up a chair, man. You don't want to go standing there all night.'

Still nervous, I edge towards him, the sight of my approach promoting the conversation around the table to halt abruptly. I hope the smile on my face appears congenial.

'Evening,' I venture.

'Ev'ning,' everyone replies, their tone if not unfriendly exactly, then cautious and perhaps even tinged with an edge of suspicion.

Tony and the other two men in the chairs shuffle round to allow me space. Gingerly, I put my pint on the table and take a seat.

Their muted reaction does not surprise me. This is Tony's Wednesday-night drinking group. It is made up of men he has known for years, in a place they consider their own.

Such groups evolve organically over time. They are born

from common bonds of friendship and trust, of mutual interests and shared experiences. For a novice such as myself, initiation is far from straightforward. I need my own Reverend Venables, someone who will open the door for me and vouch for my credentials. I was banking on Tony filling this role. A hobby farmer with a permanent limp, he's the owner of the cabin we rented and the very first person I met on moving to the area.

'This is Ollie,' runs Tony's laconic introduction. 'Him and his missus stopped at our place for a while, in one of the cabins, like.'

I smile. They nod. Feeling the weight of their collective gaze, I study the back of my hand and pick up my glass. I take a sip and put it down again. I return to looking at my hand, all the while silently willing someone to say something, anything, wishing that I could merge into my seat, that I could sit among them invisibly.

Then, for the briefest of moments, I wonder if I haven't made a mistake. It hadn't occurred to me until this very second that everything might not turn out well. Tony had mentioned to drop in if I happened to be passing, but in an off-the-cuff kind of way. What if they didn't really want me there? Even with Tony's fragile endorsement, I am still intruding. And no one likes an intruder.

I start thinking I might have been better off choosing another pub. The Boat in Whitney, say. Or the Roast Ox in Painscastle. Both are village pubs, both relatively close and popular with locals. Maybe I'd have been less of an outsider there. Mixing in among the crowd a little, taking my time to find my feet, getting myself established. Yet this is where Tony drinks, and Tony is my unwitting sponsor, so the Rhydspence it has to be. I determine to stick it out and make the most of it.

The Clyro sections of the *Diary* offer little by way of advice on how to act in such situations, for Kilvert is already ensconced in the community by the time we meet him. This is a shame, as we are not so different in personality, I suspect. In the company of others, I always feel more comfortable on the edge looking in, rather than at the centre holding court. Kilvert's writing leaves a similar impression. He listens more than he speaks, watches more than he participates.

All the same, Kilvert clearly enjoys socialising, although his opportunities to do so tend to be concentrated around either the soirées of his aristocratic hosts or communal events linked to the church. Comfortable turf, in other words. His interactions with his village parishioners, in contrast, are predominately private and pastoral. In his day, it probably couldn't have been any other way.

As for frequenting the pub, Victorian social mores would have made it out of the question. Not that Kilvert was the puritanical sort. 'Hot coppers, too much wine last night and an ill temper this morning,' reads one confessional diary entry.

Nor should his dog collar suppose a naivety about the ways of the world. Listening from afar to a wedding party at the New Inn, he observes how the girls squealed 'as if they were being kissed or tickled and not against their will'. Most weekends, meanwhile, he'd watch from his window as Clyro's heavy drinkers stumbled into the street from the Baskerville Arms, 'drunk, cursing, muttering, maundering and vomiting'.

Kilvert definitely had a gregarious and fun-loving spirit, although the social strictures of Victorian society meant he kept this mostly between himself and the pages of his diary. We're offered a rare glimpse of his lighter side during a birthday party that he organises for the schoolmaster's young daughter, Boosie. Feasting on buttered buns and mugs of tea, the birthday girl and her friends giggle as Kilvert recounts stories about wolves and Sowar horsemen and joins them in games of bagatelle and fiery snap-dragon.

At the end of the party, after the children have played with his tabby cat and marvelled at a lock from a lion's mane that Kilvert acquired during a visit to Clifton Zoological Gardens, he is left alone and happy, thinking to himself how pleasant was the company of these 'little gentle-women'.

I suspect retelling a children's story or suggesting a party game might, in my current circumstances, be an ill-advised method of inculcating myself into Tony's drinking group. Instead, I remain silent, and take another sip of my Otter, which, as the publican promised, tastes good.

*

A classic timber-framed coaching inn from the late fourteenth century, the Rhydspence is a delightful muddle of warped beams and slanting windows, of wobbly chimney stacks and lime-washed walls.

Among its various remarkable features, my personal favourite is the single-room Tudor extension, which wobbles on stilts directly above the main entrance door and which looks so off-kilter that you expect it to topple into the gutter at any minute.

Fortunately, someone later on had the good sense to construct a much more conventional extension at the pub's northward end, whose solid brick bulk provides a stabilising anchor onto which the louche and liver-pickled inn can now cling for balance.

Set up on a lawned bank, a matter of yards into England, the border pub is attractively situated at the base of a steep grassy pitch that leads directly into the hills. Scattered houses surround it, although these quickly thin out as the gradient steepens and the sheep pasture descends.

In front lies the expansive Wye valley in all her silvery, flat-bellied glory. A mile or so up the road is an old toll bridge. A mechanised gate permits motorists safe passage in exchange for eighty pence.

The main trunk road between Brecon and Hereford passes at the bottom of the pub garden. It's the same road that a few miles further on bisects Clyro so neatly. The road earns the briefest of mentions from Kilvert, who happens to be passing one time when he spots a 'deadly sick' man being carried to the roadside from the pub.

Another time, he writes about a flash flood that sweeps down the valley, ripping turnips from the ground and reducing the roadways to their rock base while leaving a muddy deposit four inches thick on the Rhydspence's floor.

Inside, the pub's virtues become less immediately obvious. The thick oak entrance door opens into a carpeted hallway with a staircase in front and toilets to the left. To the right lies the main bar area, which opens into a smaller adjoining saloon bar at the far end.

Beyond the lavatories to the left, meanwhile, is a large restaurant lounge and a connecting breakfast room. Upstairs, a rickety hallway leads the way to seven guest rooms, all of them sizeable and most with a view of the river.

The decor is that of a traditional rural pub: landscape prints in un-fancy frames on the wall, black-and-white photographs above the fireplace, a crooked constellation of bronze pots hanging from the ceiling, a stuffed pike in a glass-fronted box.

Little has altered over the years, which the regulars probably view as a virtue rather than a drawback. As they do the absence of a television, pool table, dartboard, juke box or anything else that might disturb a peaceful pint.

The bar itself is relatively small, about the size of an old farmhouse larder. It is split into two serving areas, with a main counter to greet customers as they arrive and a hatch into the overspill bar next door. The bar counter measures the length of a park bench and has a hinged section at one end to enable the landlord to get in and out.

Behind the counter, the bar is clean and well-stocked for its size. In addition to the Otter and Bass there's a lager on tap and two choices of cider – one sweet, the other dry. An assortment of upturned spirit bottles lines the wall, their necks tied tight with bow-tie optics. Above, peering down from the low ceiling, is row upon row of glass tankards, a crowded colony of crystalline bats hanging on their screw-hook perches.

There are nibbles as well. Kettle Chips bunched on a shelf just beside the bar counter. Packs of peanuts dangling from a cardboard sheet. A few ageing bags of pork scratchings.

Only one thing is missing: customers.

In truth, the pub has been quiet for years. Tougher drink-driving laws have hit it hard. So too has the so-called 'off-trade' market: the bulk-buying muscle of the supermarkets and their multipack deals mean that pubs can no longer hope to compete on price. Hence the general move to hot meals, pub quizzes, music nights, televised sport, anything that will pull in the punters.

The Rhydspence appears strangely adrift from this trend. Its restaurant is never full, its chef underemployed. Its single concession to modern entertainment is a portable CD player. The plug-in machine plays the part of resident drunk, propping up the end of the bar and repeating itself ad nauseam. It starts with some early Presley, moves on to a touch of Chubby Checker, Al Green, Etta James, then a tribute to Buddy Holly maybe, some Sinatra perhaps, before returning to more Presley, and so it goes on, playing and replaying endlessly in the background.

It wasn't always this way. For centuries, the inn was a popular stopover point on the Black Ox Trail, the legendary drovers' route from the valleys of Wales to the markets of England. Even after the railways came and the drovers swapped their walking boots for cattle trucks, the Rhydspence remained noisy with revellers, as Kilvert himself bore witness when walking past one May Day at midnight.

Back at the table, Tony breaks the silence with a brief round of introductions.

'So, this is Les . . .' Tony says, pointing with his pint glass to a tall man in a thin yellow jumper across the table from him.

'Hello,' I say, as warmly as I know how.

The man tips his glass. 'How d'you do?'

' . . . and this is Peter.'

'Hello,' I repeat to the man immediately beside me, my eye drawn to his mop of carefully brushed white hair.

'Pleased to meet you,' he says, his vowels redolent with the privilege of a very particular English upbringing.

'And this here is Geoff . . .' The man on the bench with the rugby-player's physique gives me a warm smile and half-raises his glass. ' . . . and Mike.' His smaller companion echoes my 'hello' back to me.

'Mike and Geoff both live in Clyro,' Tony explains. 'Up on Begwyns Bluff.' As well as being neighbours, they are also brothers-in-law, a fact that Tony doesn't think to explain and that would take me a month or more to realise.

Geoff follows up on Tony's invitation by asking where I live and how I'm finding the village and telling me that if I need anything then to be sure to ask. I like him immediately. Then Mike mentions all the building work on my house and asks which builder I got to do the job and says, 'Oh, aye, the Greenow boy,' when I tell him who it is, and then assures me that I'm in good hands there.

The subject of my house renovations occupies the conversation for the next five minutes or so. I mention the huge cost of redirecting the drains to the main sewage system and they offer me their sympathies.

Between the five of them, they cobble together a chronology of the house's owners since the war, recalling with particular affection the old school nurse who used to live there when it was still two separate cottages.

The property theme continues. Mike has heard that a plot of land is coming up for sale close to Tony's farm, prompting Geoff to ask about the auction date, to which Tony says that it'll happen 'as soon as someone's daft enough to pay nine grand an acre', causing everyone around the table to laugh.

I watch gratefully as the group's focus moves away from me and back onto one another. Soon, the conversation has returned to its natural patter. Who might buy the farmland? Tony isn't interested, he says. Enough of a headache managing the fifty acres he already has. Les asks whose place adjoins the land. There's Carol opposite at Corner Cottage, Tony says. Then Angela and Ian on the one side. All along the bottom is Theo Leighton.

'Apart from my two fields, all the rest of it, right from Pent-y-cae down that block, except for a small bit that Angela's got, it's all Theo's,' continues Tony. 'Except for Jean's got one or two fields opposite her house. And Cwm-Yr-Eithin bungalow's got a couple of fields. But otherwise, all that block is part of Llwyngwilliam.'

And then some confusion breaks out. Is it Dol-y-caddy that's on the market or the land down at the Dol-y-cannau turn? From how Tony is telling it, it sounds to Mike as if he's referring to the first, but his understanding had been that it was the second that was up for sale.

None of it makes any sense to me. Not just the thread of the conversation, which I lost at Corner Cottage, but even the basic dynamics of the evening, like whether the men buy drinks individually or in rounds, or when they arrive, or how they get home.

Yet here I am, with a seat around the table, which for now seems achievement enough. So I sit back and listen, the conversation unfolding around me, me biding my time, not rocking the boat, hoping my silence will admit me to the Rhydspence community.

'So you turn right towards Crowthers' Pool, as if you're coming from Clyro. Right, you with me?' We all watch as Tony draws an imaginary map on the table with his fingers. 'Now if you're going towards Cwm-Yr-Eithin, it's on your right from the second gateway. Tump Hill, it is . . .'

He prods the surface, leaving a thumbprint smudge.

*

My initiation apparently successful, I start going to the Rhydspence most Wednesdays. I generally arrive around nine o'clock after putting the kids to bed and having a bite to eat. Tony and the rest of the group are already there, pints on the table, almost as if they haven't moved since the week before.

With time, the rhythm of the place begins to grow more familiar. The glowing of the fire, the tinny hum of the CD player, the soft talk of the men. Winter gives way to spring and then summer, but little inside the pub ever changes.

The landlord, whose name I learn is Paul, takes up model-making at one stage, the evidence resting at anchor on a table by the bar. A three-foot balsawood replica of an English galleon. HMS *Victory*, he informs us. Rigging, masts, deck, captain's quarters, cannons, all cut to size and delicately glued in place.

We never order anything to eat. Someone might buy a packet of crisps, which they'll spread open on the table and share. Paul recently tried advertising a cheap pie-and-gravy night to reinvigorate the restaurant, but it didn't take off. Last month, he cut back the chef's hours. He's thinking he might have to lay off the kitchen staff altogether if things don't pick up.

No one in the group drinks excessively. The men consume their beer as they conduct their conversation, methodically and without haste. Consequently, Paul often vacates the bar for long stretches at a time, sometimes settling into an armchair on the far side of the room with a small bowl of ice-cream and a glass of crème de menthe. Then his eyes will droop and he'll be asleep. Other times, he heads outside for a smoke or to work on his wood carvings in the log shed. He spends months on a huge winged dragon, which he paints red and hangs at the bottom of the garden by the road. If someone wants a drink in Paul's absence, they serve themselves and leave the money on the counter.

The months pass. Numbers fluctuate from week to week. Of the five, Les and Peter are the most consistent attendees, except for three weeks over Christmas when Les goes to Cyprus on holiday. Geoff and Tony miss the occasional week, usually because of work or family commitments. It's uncommon to see Tony during lambing, for example. Mike is the least regular, his attendance motivated in part by whether or not Geoff twists his arm to come.

Wednesday nights are not exclusively the reserve of the drinking group. Occasionally, a bed-and-breakfast guest might pop in for a nightcap, although Paul's bookings mostly fall on weekends. One time, a group of Dutch off-roaders holed themselves up in the bar next door and drank triple whiskies all night. Paul, for once, seemed happy.

Every now and then Jean, who lives up the pitch with the one or two fields, calls in for a half of cider, although she hasn't done so for months now. A farmer from the neighbouring parish of Brilley once came down with his family, but they sat by themselves in a corner and never returned.

Another infrequent visitor is Tom the Otter, who lives in a storybook cottage right at the top of the hill behind the pub. He specialises in surveying bats, newts and other endangered species after people submit planning applications. It's a profession that wins him plenty of fans among the wildlife but few among his neighbours.

For a short time, a retired Londoner called John used to stop by too. He lived in a rambling house up near the Begwyns and as a young man had spent time in South America, which we talked about at length. Tragically, he died. In a flash flood, of all things.

The drinking group does have two loose affiliates. One is Kiron, a man of unidentifiable age and limited wardrobe. He owns the filling station in Whitney, which has a zero-frills convenience store and a forecourt cluttered with beat-up cars for sale.

Kiron was born in Tanzania, grew up in India and emigrated as a young man to the UK, where he made a home for himself in Luton.

Hindu, dark-skinned and a non-drinker, Kiron is something of an enigma in the Marches. As the story goes, he saw the petrol station advertised, liked the price and bought it in an online auction. Only it wasn't Witney in Oxfordshire as he thought, but Whitney-on-Wye in Herefordshire. I've no idea if the story is true, although it's plausible as Kiron neither reads nor writes.

He generally arrives at the pub just before ten o'clock, once he has closed up the shop and eaten his dinner. He orders a Coca-Cola for himself (no ice) and insists on buying everyone else a drink. He pays from a plastic money-bag bulging with pound coins that he pulls from the pocket of his scruffy coat. He comes because he knows Tony and likes Paul, and because his wife is still in Luton.

The group's other affiliate member is Clive, an assured and affable man who is as local as Kiron is not. The son of a keen racehorse breeder, he grew up at Clyro Court Farm, opposite where the village primary school now is. As a younger man, he had a spell as a jockey until he injured his neck in a bad fall at Worcester races and had to give it up. Today, he plays golf instead. Past retirement age, Clive still turns up to work every day at the haulage firm he owns. His blue-and-yellow lorries regularly trundle through Clyro on the way to his depot across the river in Llanigon.

Over time, I slowly get to know the members of the core group. My closest connection continues to be with Tony, who has a dry sense of humour and a reputation as something of a wheeler-dealer. Outside the confines of Wednesday nights, I sometimes go along with him to a farm sale or to the livestock market in Hereford. One time he drove me into the Radnorshire hills to show me where the salmon come to spawn up the River Edw. I think he sees a need to educate me, as though I were a slightly witless child or an orphan bereft of parental instruction. In matters agricultural and rural he's not far off, and I gratefully take on board whatever he has to share.

An inherent kindness lies beneath Tony's transfer of knowledge, which I appreciate as much as the information itself. He has helped me out more than once. Such as the time my tyre burst and he arranged for his neighbour to come and fix it for me. Or when I ended up in a ditch on the Begwyns after sliding on the ice and he drove across the hill to pull me out.

As for the others, my initial affection for Geoff proves well placed. He has that soft, gentle nature sometimes common to bear-like men, coupled with a wonderful belly laugh. If anyone is going to ask me how my week's been or what I've been up to, it's generally Geoff. Mike strikes me as a practical, level-headed man, the kind of person who is good on a committee or handy with a drill. He's friendly enough, but I sense he harbours doubts about me that he's reluctant to relinquish.

Les is the liveliest and the most loquacious of the group. Blessed with a quick wit and a comic's timing, he has us all leaning in to listen to his stories, the vast majority of which derive from family life growing up on a hill farm in Brilley and carousing in the local pubs as a young adult. If a tale doesn't feature Les playing quoits or tickling trout, then it invariably sees him causing mischief at a summer fete or staying out late at a village dance.

The veneer of rustic naivety to Les's storytelling is a narrator's ploy to some extent, a theatrical device to give extra punch to the climax of his tales, which typically arrive wrapped in mild illegality or abject drunkenness, such as the time he picked up a ten-bob fine from Doctor Jack the Magistrate after Gastor the Gamekeeper caught him shooting his pheasants ('Fair dues, it was two o'clock in the morning'), or when he volunteered one year at the Young Farmers' dance and dropped a skinhead at the door with a single punch.

Peter is the only one not born and bred in the area, and he's also the hardest to read. He'll chip in with his opinions from time to time, so I know he thinks immigration is perilous and that rising sea levels are 'complete poppycock', but otherwise he keeps his cards close to his chest. One evening, when the men started reminiscing about various misdemeanours from their youth, he leaned over and whispered quietly in my ear, 'Lucky they don't know anything about us, eh?' as though this gap in the group's knowledge was a huge positive, a protective shield between us and them. Yet I had reached precisely the opposite conclusion. From where I was sitting, on the edge looking for a way in, I could only view this lack of a shared past as a lamentable chasm. Here we both were, Peter and I, facing an historic void that no amount of time or information would ever truly fill.

Peter isn't the only one reluctant to air the details of his private life. References to the men's wives or children are almost always fleeting and rarely elaborated upon. Talk of health matters or private finances are equally taboo. Sex, similarly. Work is about as personal as the conversation gets, and then it's generally little more than an anecdote about a colleague or a complaint about a client.

I piece bits together over time. I learn that they are all married, for example, although Peter no longer lives with his wife. All have children. Tony's son, who does the occasional shift as a washer-upper in the pub kitchen, is the only one still at school. The remainder are either at university or have flown the nest. One of Les's two student-age boys regularly wins cash playing computer games, which is a total marvel to his technology-averse father.

I never discover my companions' exact ages, but all are over sixty, except for Tony, who is in his early fifties.

Les has a job at an engineering firm in Hay, where he's been on the books for most of his adult life. Mike used to work as an electrician and Geoff at a plastics factory in Hereford, although both are now retired. Peter, it turns out, ran the Rhydspence for many years and is now renting the place to Paul. There's no great love lost between the pair, which, given that Paul still has eight years left on his lease, creates a slightly testy dynamic.

Other than Peter and Les, who live in the nearby villages of Whitney and Glasbury, respectively, we all live in Clyro parish. Most of Tony's family still live locally too. His mother, who is in her late seventies, still keeps sheep on a farm two miles outside the village. His brother lives next door to her. Geoff's family roots run deepest into Clyro soil. He's an Anthony, a clan whose flaking gravestones spread here and there throughout the village graveyard.

The Anthonys crop up regularly in Kilvert's diary, too. It was the curate's descendants, in fact, who moved into the terraced houses that he so disliked (Geoff and his brother still own most of the row).

Several Anthony children gain specific mention. Gussena features among Boosie Evans's birthday party guests, for instance, while an attack of rheumatic fever earns 'poor young' Harry a bedside visit from the diarist. On another occasion, Kilvert requests some strips of wood from their father Henry, the local wheelwright, which the curate manufactures into crosses and then gives to Mrs Evans to cover in moss so they glow bright green during the grave-dressing ceremony at Easter.

Although we all live relatively close, the group isn't in the habit of dropping in on one another at home. Kiron once called by with some Easter eggs for my boys, and Clive kindly donated me some golf balls so I could practise my chipping, but on both occasions I was out and they left the gifts at the back door. They were probably relieved to have missed me. To step across our respective thresholds, it feels, would somehow breach the comforting distance created by the Rhydspence.

As a consequence, Tony is the pub's only regular who's actually been inside our house. We invited him for dinner when his wife was away in America. He came in an ironed shirt and brought some freshly picked field mushrooms.

Gifting foodstuffs represents a commonplace gesture of goodwill in the Marches. One memorable Wednesday, our numbers were augmented by the presence of two pheasants at the table, both neatly plucked and ready for the pot, the denuded birds a repayment by Tony for a favour Les had done him.

Just as the personal is kept at bay, so too is anything that might be interpreted as serious or controversial. Wednesdays are for relaxing and shooting the breeze, not re-righting the world. So religion, race, education, terrorism, global poverty, you name it, all are given a wide berth, in the main.

This never ceases to amaze Emma, who finds it inconceivable that we can sit for two or three hours and discuss nothing of substance.

This isn't strictly the case, I tell her. There's a lot of talk about farming, for instance. The cost of feed, the price of land, the Single Farm Subsidy, the pencil-pushers in Brussels, the NFU, avian flu.

'Bad week for cull ewes,' Tony will say, as part of his habitual report on that week's livestock market. Or, 'Good trade on store lambs.'

Then someone else will shake their head and say how they can't understand how these boys can pay twelve or thirteen hundred quid for store cattle and hope to make their investment back, to which Tony will say that there's serious money about, and everyone will agree that the market's owners are sitting tidy.

'And what else?' Emma will ask. Politics. We discuss politics too, I say. Politics with a small 'p', that is. Government policies are largely ignored, except for an occasional swipe at 'stupid' health-and-safety laws or 'clueless' environmental requirements.

International affairs are dealt with summarily too. 'So, looks like it's all kicking off in the Middle East again,' someone might say, to which someone else will reply, 'Aye,' and another might mention boots on the ground or, more likely, bombing the lot of them.

In the same way, parliamentarians get short shrift, tarred as 'power-hungry second homeowners' who would no more know how to fix the deficit than they would a tractor tyre.

Tony has a simple if somewhat blunt solution: go to Westminster and sack every other one of them. 'There's your bloomin' deficit sorted, right there.'

Mostly, it's local politics that occupies them. Petty bureaucrats in County Hall. Tinpot dictators on the Town Council. How did such-and-such a farmer get permission to put up a huge poultry shed? Why can't Highways pull its finger out and stop cars cutting the corner by the bus stop in Clyro? These are the political concerns that matter to them.

Emma will raise a sceptical eyebrow. We also talk about property, I add, a rejoinder that merely sets her expression in place.

Which houses or farms have come on to the market, who might be looking to sell up, where house prices are at, these are perennial themes as well. Who owns what now, and who might come to own what in the future, carries great import for the group. The answers locate their fellow residents and, indirectly, they place the Rhydspence crew too.

It's only after many months of going along on Wednesdays that this realisation hits me. And with it comes another insight that helps explain the limited purview of the group's conversation: the men are, it gradually dawns on me, only cursorily concerned with the present. In the peace and quiet of the Rhydspence, it is not the here and now that counts. It's the past.

Not the distant past of history books. Rather, it's their past, the recent past, the past of yesteryear. This is what captures their imaginations and loosens their tongues. The past of Sunday best and rationed meat, of marching bands and top-of-the-milk, of trouser braces and May Day rides, of Old Knowles the Schoolmaster and his holly-stick cane.

This is how most evenings roll, with dusty memories dug

up and dusted down, with former friendships remembered and regaled, with old rivalries relived and re-won. A mere nudge of the lock-gate and out from the sluices of their memories it floods. So Mike, say, will have been waiting for traffic at Crow Turn junction and will have got to wondering if there wasn't once a cottage directly opposite, and Geoff will be darned if he can remember, and Tony will think there might have been because he remembers talk of a lorry driving into it, to which Geoff will recall a similar incident at the Baskerville Arms but not a cottage at Crow Turn, and finally Les will settle the matter by recalling not only the cottage but also the driver – 'Dennis Burton, it was' – behind the wheel of the lorry, and Mike will say, 'Gert away,' and Geoff will say, 'Well, I'll be damned,' and that will be that.

For me, there's something mesmerising about this group retelling, the way the men skip between past and present, present and past. Magic lives in these gaps, I swear.

Because no one has a monopoly on the past, events gather pace and grow as they bounce between the men. The winter of '62 provides just such a case, when the snows fell and fell and Les was shut up at home for six weeks solid and Geoff swore the snowdrifts were up to the roof and the sheep took to eating holly. Pigeons froze on the wires, Mike adds, while Tony remembers his father telling him about an old boy who slit his horses' throats rather than witness them starve.

Part of the pleasure of Wednesdays comes in connecting people to other people, and other people to places, and places to other people. It's as if the world outside the Rhydspence represents one giant community crossword book that waits for midweek for a few more clues to be solved.

Take the school minibus run, which Tony does because his brother owns a coach company and Tony can do with the extra money. He goes up to the Begwyns, past Rickettes's place, he says in answer to someone's question about his route. No sooner has he started than Les interrupts to ask if it's the Wern he's talking about, and Geoff starts tapping his temple and repeating 'Now, what's the name of the place?' Williams, at Vrondee, chips in Les, apropos of nothing, while Geoff is getting there with Scavin, Salvin, Scalding, *Scalding Farm*, that's it.'

The conversation about the route continues in this vein, me cruising along on the cushion of the pub seat, silent, listening as Tony's imaginary school bus driver passes Dai Stephens's place with the new bungalows and some kids called Jones, and down the back lane to Llanstefan and then right at Ceri Owens's, who is in a bad way with cancer ('Hell of a good bloke, Ceri Owens'), and switches back to Glasbury when the weather is bad, before turning up via the waterworks and back down over the brook, where the floods can be a bugger but the fishing is good.

Eventually the minibus reaches the school gates and that week's crossword is finished. Someone jokes they should join Tony one morning and see the route for themselves.

For now, everyone is content exactly where they are, comfortably ensconced close to the fire, in an empty ancient pub, beer within reach, and nothing but their memories and a softly snoring publican for company.

*

I find Geoff sitting alone nursing his pint. He drinks lager, with a splash of lemonade on top. No one ribs him for the lemonade. With a smaller man there might be some ribbing. Not with Geoff, though; he's too big a man for that.

And too kind. He wouldn't know how to give it back.

Top-up? I ask. He's good for now, he says. He tells me to pull up a chair and asks how I'm keeping. I don't think he really understands what a freelance journalist does, but he listens politely when I describe my week and he nods from time to time and says it sounds like I've got plenty of work on and that's certainly a good thing in times like these.

I enquire after Les, who is recuperating at home after a knee operation, and from what Geoff understands he's doing fine. Mike can't make it tonight because he's got something else on. He doesn't know about Peter or Tony.

Paul wanders in and, on seeing that it's just Geoff and me, wanders out again. The dragon is long finished. He's on to an owl now, I believe. And then Geoff gets talking. It's the old stone cottage with the new double-glazed windows opposite the post office in Clyro that starts him off. He remembers when the house came up on the market, back in the 1960s it would have been. He was working for Bryan Jones at the time.

'You know Ashbrook, the garage? Well, that used to be a dairy farm.' It was his first job. An old woman called Davis used to work there and when she died Bryan tried to persuade Geoff to buy it. 'Well, I hadn't got, what, two bob.'

The house ended up being sold at auction in the Crown in Hay and made £350. '"You want to buy that place, boy," Bryan said to me. And I said to 'im, "Well, I haven't got no money." And he said, "Well, I got some money. I can lend you some, no problem, if you want to buy it." I swear to you, as sure as I'm sat on this seat here, that's what he said.'

I smile, occasionally interjecting on a point of clarification or just to show I'm still listening, but otherwise only too happy to sit and listen to Geoff reminiscing.

'Where my house is now – exactly where my house is – there used to be a big rock there. Come soaring right out the ground, it did. One of the first jobs I did when I started work was I ploughed that field. With an old Fordson Major tractor, a trailer plough hitched on the back. We edged from the top end right down to the road at the bottom. And there was this rock. And we used to sit on that rock and have our bait, you know. Cor, I tell you, what a view that was.'

I stop him to ask what 'bait' means. Food, he tells me. 'Bait time, grub time.' Slab of cheese, hunk of bread, an apple maybe. None of them had flasks back then, so they'd put their tea in a bottle and wrap the bottle in newspaper to keep it warm.

Post office field, they used to call it, he continues, picking up where he left off. Best field for miles around for catching rabbits. Old Tom, who used to milk the cows up there, would run a net right down the one side.

'Then they used to get a line, a long line, and drive a peg in up the top corner. They'd walk down round with this line and pull all the rabbits out of the squats so they'd run into the net.' Someone would then follow up behind with a wooden stick, sort of a truncheon shape, and knock the rabbits on the back of the head. 'Dozens and dozens of them, like. Aye, there were rabbits about then. Kept the country alive.'

People turn their noses up a bit at rabbit nowadays, Geoff says, shaking his head, but there's a good bit of meat to be had on a rabbit. 'The saddle, two fat rolls of meat like that.' He locks his fingers in a small circle to illustrate its dimensions.

As he does so, I notice he's missing the top half of two fingers on his left hand. I want to ask what happened, but I don't feel I can. Then I wonder if I'll ever know Geoff well enough to ask, and it saddens me to think that perhaps I never will.

Keeping to his theme, he tells me how rabbit is best eaten roasted, although he wouldn't criticise anyone for putting rabbit in a casserole. Then he asks me if I've ever eaten pigeon and when I say I haven't he rolls his eyes and says how they used to eat a lot of roast pigeon when he was growing up.

Elwyn Sheen, now there was a man who knew his pigeons. Used to shoot them as they came in to roost, up in Lloney Wood. 'He'd feather one while he was waiting for some more to come in. Drop it into his pocket, like.'

Not for the first time, I find Geoff's recollections dislodging fragments of Kilvert's *Diary* and setting my imagination whirring: pictures of Pentwyn, a rambling old house up by the old post office field, for example, filled with swarms of flies on a summer's day. Or of John Morgan, the 'little Welshman' from Cold Blow, pulling down the property's old cider press, while Miss Bynon, the owner, peered out of her windows nursing fears about India's 'Musketoos'.

With Geoff's talk of pigeons, it's the reddened face of Gipsy Warnell, the poacher, who jumps most clearly to mind. The shouting, the angry words, the trousers so nearly torn. How different the Rhydspence is by comparison. Just the two of us, quietly nursing our pints, far from the fracas of that night in the New Inn.

Which in turn leads my thoughts to the drunken wild man, whom Kilvert describes stumbling out of the New Inn one breakfast time with a steeple-crowned hat on his head and waking the village with his droning bagpipes while the children danced to his tune as though he were a modern-day Pied Piper.

Geoff's thoughts run away with him, back to a time when the land opposite Pottery Cottage was all open pasture and the tump his outdoor playground. There was a big gang of them when he was young, he tells me, a touch of wistfulness in his voice. 'We were nine. The Harleys were eleven. The Griffithses, six.' All holiday, they'd spend up on the tump, larking about, making dens, building tree houses. 'Oh, we had these beautiful tree houses, we did.' Geoff emits a throaty chuckle, his eyes dancing brightly in the light of the fire.

We talk late into the night; about his memories of the old school by my house; about Cae Mawr, and how his mother had come to work there for Lady Baskerville as a mere fourteen-year-old; and about Clyro Court, the big country house on the edge of the village, where Kilvert used to go for dinner and croquet games, and where Geoff's grandfather, the estate manager, used to start the oil engine every night to bring light to the building, and where the beaters on shoot day would walk down through the wood and the guns below would blast the pheasants from the sky until the keeper's cart creaked under their feathery weight.

Eventually, a beam of headlights through the window signals Geoff's lift home and, downing the dregs of his beer, he reaches for his coat.

'Been good talking,' he tells me, patting me on the shoulder as he walks towards the door. 'See you next week, then,' he says, turning briefly before he steps out.

A few minutes later I'm behind the wheel as well, driving along the same stretch of road as Geoff back to Clyro. It's half past ten and although the darkness has long since settled the night is clear and the moon bright. Arboreal giants, stretched thin by the moonlight, march beside me along the tarmac, while the mountaintops dance with troupes of shimmering stars. Having sat and listened to Geoff all night, I'm struck by how different everything already looks, how different it already feels.

Over the coming days, as I stare out over my garden or past the Texaco garage as I accompany the boys to school, I attempt to see the village through Geoff's eyes. I try to picture the timber yard behind our back hedge, try to evoke the smell of the lime pit next to it. The practice serves to lengthen my perspective. Everything begins to take on a fraction more depth. Shadows appear. My vision becomes more layered. Try as I might, however, I can get only an inkling of the past; I can't see it as Geoff sees it. Not as any of the Wednesday-night crew do. I struggle to envision people whom I've never met or see empty fields where houses now stand.

I look at the garage and I see the garage, not Bryan George's milking parlour. To me, Begwyns Bluff is an amalgam of red bricks, tarmac and vertiginous lawns. There are no rabbits there, no protruding stone. Yet these things exist for Tony and his friends, exist in a material sense, which is what surely draws them back to the Rhydspence. It's more than simple nostalgia, more than recollecting the 'simple kindly primitive times', as Old Morgan or Hannah Whitney were wont to do when Kilvert came calling. Wednesday nights provide them their opportunity to rearrange, to reconstruct, to almost resurrect what was but is no more, or what still is, yet is strangely altered.

This sense of rupture hit me powerfully during the summer. I'd joined the Kilvert Society on an annual pilgrimage they make over the hills from Newchurch to Llandewi Fach via Llanbedr. On the way, we cast stones to raise the bog above Pontvane Farm and stopped for readings from Kilvert and Housman, Eliot and Rossetti.

Does the road wind uphill all the way?
  Yes, to the very end.
Will the day's journey take the whole long day?
  From morn to night, my friend.

I went with Seth, whose little legs kept pace with the pilgrims as far as lunch, which we ate under the ancient yews of Bryngwyn.

The day had commenced with Morning Prayer at St Mary's church, where, daydreaming between the various hymns and readings, I found myself scanning the memorial plaques on the wall. My gaze eventually settled on the embossed epitaph of Major Samuel Beavan, from Ty'n-y-cwm, onetime home of the rector of Bryngwyn. He died in 1836, the tablet informs me, his remains then interred at Hereford Cathedral. 'At his death,' the inscription finishes, 'Ty'n-y-cwm passed to strangers.'

'Strangers', two simple syllables that bring so much upset, such disorder. Past and future severed.

By piecing together the links between people and places, it feels as though the Wednesday drinkers are doing their bit to refasten what's been loosened and patch what's been torn. And the Rhydspence is the place to do it because it's the one place that does not change. The one place that resists the need to move on, to reinvent itself, to redecorate, even. The men enter on a Wednesday knowing everything is more or less as it's always been. 'Always' being relative, of course. 'Always' being as long as they can remember, which, for them, is as long as anything really matters.

None of the five is ever going to buy the pork scratchings. Yet to remove them would be to overlook their function.

The group knows that the pork scratchings are there and available to buy *should* they ever choose to do so. That's the point. Take away the pork scratchings and that possibility, that eventuality, disappears. So it is with the chairs, the fire, the patterned threadbare carpet, the songs on loop. They act as ballasts in a changing sea, a mooring line in a choppy tide.

This is what keeps them coming back, this is what anchors them to where they are and who they are and where they're from. For me, in contrast, it holds no such associations. Would that it did.

*

It transpires that Paul is dying.

He tells me just as I'm leaving one evening, grabs me at the door as I'm putting on my coat. 'The others know, so I just wanted you to hear it from me.'

He has pancreatic cancer, he explains. He's going to Cheltenham oncological unit every morning for chemotherapy. The cancer they can cure, he hopes. 'It's the other two gonna kill me.'

The doctors have diagnosed him with the cerebral small-vessel disease and pernicious anaemia. His tone is matter-of-fact. Five years, the doctors tell him. 'So I'm not sure what we're doing yet . . . so, yeah . . . maybe eight years at best.'

I thank him for letting me know and tell him I'm terribly sorry to hear about it and to advise me if I can do anything, and then I leave. No one has ever told me that they've been diagnosed with an incurable disease before and I don't know what to say or how to act. I think about his words as I climb into bed that night. I can't sleep. I keep turning over what he must be going through, over and over.

Terrible, that's all I can think. Terrible and terrifying.

For several days, I feel thrown. We don't do personal, that's how Wednesdays work. Life, however, operates differently. It has its own rules, rules that even time can't bend.

The next Monday I drive over to the pub after dinner to see Paul and ask if there's anything he needs. I have never been to the Rhydspence other than on Wednesday nights. Stepping over the oak-timber threshold, I'm hit by how deeply familiar and yet oddly alien it feels, as if I've been there before but at a different time, in a different life.

'Hello?' I call. Nothing. The room is empty, empty as only a public place can be, emptier than ever.

A few steps to my left, our table sits devoid of drinkers, its surface dishcloth-clean, the smudged rings of beer-glass bottoms wiped away. The CD player is switched to 'Off'. There's no Paul at the bar, no noise from the kitchen. Is this what happens when the latch is left off the hook and the world slips in?

'Hello?' Once more, nothing. Not a sound but for a whispering echo and the knowing presence of the old timber beams.

I stand there, in the middle of the room, unsettled, waiting, feeling ever more like a trespasser. To shake off the silence, I wander over to the fireplace and examine the pictures on the wall. In all the times I have been here, I realise that I have never thought to look at them before. Romantic landscapes abound. Turreted castles in heraldic pose, peasant cottages with Hobbit doorways, each scene green and mountainous and lit by moody skies.

The photographs I find more compelling. Set at head height, their black-and-white faces stare back at me from inside the frames, looking at me eye to eye, meeting my gaze. Each image is born of commemorative intent: friends out fishing on the Wye, a rugby team preparing to take the field, a troop of young conscripts heading off to France. I wonder what, if any, their connection is to this time-worn pub. No one lets on. They are silent to a man.

I return to the bench by the door, weighing up whether to stay or go. I'll give it five minutes, I decide. I rest my feet on a stool and tilt my head back, fixing my gaze on the tobacco-stained ceiling above, tracing the edges of the porous discolourations, imagining the smoke-filled nights that went into its creation. My mind drifts to the drinkers who must once have sat on this self-same bench, puffing at their cigarettes, drinking from their personal tankards. The Rhydspence knows their names. Its floor recalls the pattern of their dancing. Its beams, the timbre of their voices.

''Allo there,' says Paul, pushing through the door. 'Y'ur all right, then?'

He rubs his hands together. He has been outside, working on his latest carving. It's another Welsh dragon. 'Coming out nicely, it is.'

'Oh, hi, Paul,' I say. 'I was wondering where you'd got to.'

I stay until late, listening to him speak. He tells me about his past, his career 'making machines that make machines', his broken marriage, his new love, his search for a pub that would see him into retirement, and, finally, about the uncertainties now surrounding him. He rasps as he talks, his breathing more laboured than usual. He's going to break his lease. No choice, really. 'Take some time to think, reassess.'

Kiron has offered him the flat above his garage. He and his wife will stop there for a while; they're not planning to head off anywhere immediately. We'll see each other around, he's sure.

And we do. I pop into the garage from time to time to see how he's faring. I'd once mentioned in passing that I had a record player and he calls in with some old LPs that he thought the kids might like. One summer evening we go up to Hay Bluff to test out some model aeroplanes he has built. We prop up each plane in turn on an old advertising bill-board from the Rhydspence, attach it to some elasticated rope tied to a gardening fork, and then let it go. He has built six in total and we record six near-immediate crashes.

*

I never saw Paul in the Rhydspence again. Peter couldn't find anyone else to take it on, so he reluctantly stepped back behind the bar himself.

The clever money, Peter figured, was in the B&B trade. So the beer selection quickly slimmed and the kitchen closed. Then the pub tables went, replaced by two arm-chairs and a sofa.

The drinking group got the hint. Mike was the first to leave, bemoaning the quality of the beer. Then Geoff fol-lowed shortly after. Les stuck it out, but then fell ill and took to his bed. In his absence, Tony decided he'd give the Boat a go instead. And that was it. Suddenly, no more Wednesday nights.

Instead, I decide to wind back the clock. If Wednesday nights are all about looking back at what has gone, then Monday nights are about starting out with what's to come.

Mondays are when friendships are struck and lifelong attachments made. Mondays are for learning life's lessons and sharing its early triumphs.

Mondays are when the Young Farmers' Club meets.

3

The Young Farmers

We came to the gate of the meadow where the rural festival was being held. A group of men whose clothes were splashed and dyed by the red wash were plunging sheep and lambs one by one into a long deep trough. The sheep . . . walked away across the meadow to join the flock, shaking the red wash in showers from their close-shorn fleeces.

Kilvert's Diary, 26 July 1873

A leather halter fixes fast around the muzzle of the dappled brown heifer. She is panting heavily, gulping down great chestfuls of air. With each breath, her nostrils flare open like fireplace bellows and then deflate as she exhales.

The farmer, a grey-haired no-nonsense man who has reared cows all his life, stands with rope in hand. He looks her straight in the eye as two wide, frightened pools of incomprehension look back at him. He pats her neck and, leaning in towards her, says, 'Come now, come now,' and, 'There's a good girl,' and, 'Don't be a dull bugger, now.'

All the while, Woko is standing at the rear of the four-year-old Hereford, his shoulders roughly at the same level as the animal's backbone. His jockey-sized frame is well within her peripheral vision, a foreign body, untrusted, unwanted.

Skittish by nature, the heifer nervously shifts her weight. Half a tonne of meat and muscle rocks from hoof to hoof in an awkward swaying four-step. A prelude to her death dance; the cattle truck pulling up in the yard, the cows bundled into the back, the latch clanging shut, the engine rumbling into life.

The farmer tries to calm her. Her low-gear ruminant brain registers the tugging rope and his gentle protestations, but she keeps with her ungainly shuffle, instinct telling her that the man in mud-stained overalls is not her friend. In that respect alone, she is not as stupid as she looks.

Woko begins the stock-judging class by thanking the farmer for allowing the group to visit his farm. The old man tips his cap. 'Ain't no bother at all.' The younger man continues with some introductory remarks, his broad Marcher accent as earthy as the oil-black peat on Twmpa Hill.

'Right now, listen up. What we've got here is butcher's beef. We're looking for width here now and meat cover, right? What we want here is an even balanced animal, see. A good piece for you young ones to look at is the width down the top line on the beef.'

He points a finger over the cow's flanks and then, stretching his arm out in front, traces the contour of her spine. The flat of his hand marks out a perfect horizontal in the air. I picture the animal hung out to dry on a washing line, each vertebra individually pegged and then pulled taut from shoulder-blade to tail stump.

At twenty-six, Woko is in the twilight year of his Young Farmers' Club career. He joined the Llanigon club aged ten, already handy with an air gun and competent on a quad bike. An only child, he was born into a long line of farmers. Watkinses ('Woko' deriving from 'Watkins', his family name) have worked these valleys and hillside slopes for the last three or four centuries. Very possibly longer.

There are no fewer than five different Watkinses listed as County Sheriff during the seventeenth century – one of whom, Thomas, heralded from right here in Llanigon parish.

The surname has deep local resonance. Kilvert ministered to several Watkinses in Clyro in the late nineteenth century. One, a certain John Watkins who lived at the Cwm, was reputed by his neighbours to be 'roguish' and given to 'shams'. The curate describes his condition as 'abject, wretched [and] pitiable' after one visit. There were Watkinses at Lower Cwmgwanon, too. The mother, a 'poor mad creature', had to be confined to an upstairs room for her own safety. Neither, I'm sure, bears close relation to Woko's Llanigon branch.

Bruce Chatwin also found space for a Watkins in *On the Black Hill*, his fictional tale about twin-brother farmers local to the area. The depiction is less than flattering. Tom Watkins, or 'Watkins the Coffin', as Chatwin sometimes christens him, is cast as a callous, rough-mannered man who seldom dipped his sheep and whose antics created a constant headache for Amos Jones, the book's early protagonist. ('Get ye away, Amos Jones' . . . Watkins shouted. 'That land belongs to we.')

Farming is what Woko does. It's what his people do.

As might be expected, he dresses the part. Not in all the country get-up, as the gentry farmers do at their summer shows, in their waxed Barbour jackets and worsted-wool shirts. Woko's uniform of choice is what he's wearing now: jeans as mucky as a car mechanic's, hard-toed working boots, a washed-out rugby shirt, a shapeless all-weather fleece and a rain-bleached baseball cap as ragged as an unshorn ewe.

As a look, it's practical, not polished. But polished, as

Woko would say, doesn't get fence posts fixed or lambs to market. Practical does.

Woko talks little and labours hard, two habits inherited from his chapel-going ancestors. Windburn turns the thin, freckly skin stretched across his cheekbones a permanent blister-red. Rarely are his lips unchapped or his knuckles free of boxer's bruises. Gleaming under every fingernail is a grimy crescent moon. Much like the battered mud-stained truck he drives, Woko looks beat-up and old beyond his years.

The assembled children are standing around the rear of the heifer in a wide semicircle, listening with varied attention as Woko descriptively dissects the animal in front of them. 'You can see how square and wide this one's back is, see? So that's what you want to look for, like. And you want a wide shoulder and good fleshing over it, see?'

It's Week Two in the Young Farmers' Club calendar and everyone is still finding their feet. Twenty-six youngsters are signed up this year, a record number for the small Llanigon branch. Most are between ten and fourteen years old and a good number of them are new recruits. When they're not out visiting a farm, club night is usually held at Llanigon's red-brick village hall, where parents dutifully drop their charges off at seven-thirty and return to pick them up at nine.

A co-ordinating team of about five or six Young Farmer veterans is charged with keeping order, all of whom are in their late teens or early twenties. Lauren, a blonde hair-dressing assistant from Glasbury, is this year's club secretary. Although responsibilities are supposed to be shared out evenly, the burden of managing the children seems to fall mostly on her shoulders. She wisely carries a whistle.

'. . . twenty-four, twenty-five, twenty-six,' Lauren counts.

Happy no one has sloped off, she turns her mind to the hubbub of whispers and giggles that has steadily grown during Woko's presentation. 'Now, everyone, listen up, please,' Lauren says firmly, before reminding those who brought writing pads with them to take notes.

'What should we be taking notes about?' a smart aleck at the back wants to know.

'Whatever you think is interesting,' replies Lauren, who has a teacher's ear for truculence.

The older cohort knows there's no test in the offing, so they don't bother with notes. Instead, the boys jostle and lark about, their hands thrust deep into the pockets of their branded body warmers. The girls, in contrast, pair up and feign oblivion to the antics of their male peers.

The younger contingent is greener and thus more pliant. They square their shoulders and furrow their brows, although full concentration appears to be beyond their gift. There is too much else new to look at, too many novelties to assimilate. The draughty barn, the sickly sweetness of fresh manure, the bleating lambs in the pen, the cold in their fingers, the prospect of a test at the end. It's not long before they are fidgeting too.

Woko persists nonetheless. He's nearly done anyway. After sharing some summary tips about judging squareness of ribs and straightness of leg, he's ready to wrap up.

'You want shoulder there,' he says, prodding the cow's upper flank with a finger. 'You want width of top line, then you've got your ribs, and finally your loin, hind leg down to the second muscle. And that there's your main parts on a beef animal.'

Two girls at the front scribble something down in their notebooks. The remainder stare dully.

Lauren steps forward. 'Thank you very much, Woko. Now, has anyone got any questions?'

Her high-pitched voice echoes off the barn's galvanised roof. The question elicits nothing but the scuffing of shoes on the cement floor.

'Oh, one last thing,' Woko says, recalling a potentially confusing point from Week One. 'Now, you don't want no big bellies on these beef animals. When you had them dairy cows last week, we was on about the deep barrels. Well, you don't want that on beef cattle. You want a good tucked-up animal, carrying no waste then. So you're killing out percentage, like.'

For a fraction of a second, the heifer stops her waddling jig and stands stock still, not even a swish of her tail.

'What's a barrel, again?' asks a girl at the front with a bob and thick-framed glasses.

'It's the ribcage, there, you see,' Woko explains, his enthusiasm for his subject unrelenting. 'Behind the joints of her legs, like.'

He straightens up and takes a step towards the group. 'There, so you're all happy now,' he states. 'You know what main points you're looking for, don't you.'

Both questions are presented as points of fact. It's a binary form of instruction: information given, assent received. It's the law of the farm, orders before understanding, cognisance before sentience, compliance before questions, two legs before four. Sheep and cattle understand it. If only the human yearlings did too.

Woko steps towards those in the front row of the crowd. He smiles encouragingly. 'Maybe some of you would like to take a feel? Come on up, now. Step up. A couple at a time maybe?'

No one is brave enough to volunteer, everyone shyly looking at their shoes.

Lauren repeats Woko's invitation in gentler tones. 'Come on, who wants to have a go?' When no response comes, she deftly changes tack and targets the teenage boys' sense of self-esteem. 'There's no need to be scared now. It's only a cow.'

The heifer moos and four lads put their hands up. 'Well, then,' Lauren says. 'Don't hang around.' They saunter forward, hands still glued to the seam of their pockets. The girls laugh teasingly behind cupped hands.

Woko tells the first of the volunteers to feel under the ribs. The boy is wearing white pumps and expensive skinny jeans. He steps forward, confident and cocksure.

'You can feel the meat on its ribs, see,' says Woko.

Gingerly, the boy reaches out a hand. His cockiness is swiftly disappearing, but his image is at stake so he persists, inch by slow inch, until finally human skin and cowhide touch. Woko nods.

'Good, now for the back end.'

That's enough grandstanding for the boy, though. He looks at the animal's hind legs and her stamping hoofs, and retreats towards the comfort of his friends. His lips purse in a sulky pout as though angry with Woko or the cow for having played a trick on him.

Woko points to one of the other boys in the gaggle. 'How about you?'

The replacement student, a square-set boy of about thirteen, steps forward. More confident and with less of a smirk than the first volunteer, he approaches the heifer in a way that suggests familiarity with livestock. He first touches her underbelly and then, at his tutor's instruction, moves his hand upward over her flanks.

The animal looks vast beside him, a tower block of a creature. Woko holds her steady as the boy steps onto the tips of his toes and runs a hand along her backbone.

'Feel that? Wide and flat, it is.' The boy agrees. 'You want a top like a table, see.' Woko projects his voice loudly to indicate that the observation is for the whole group.

Edging around the heifer's oblong mass, instructor and student step towards the cow's rear. Woko positions himself directly in line with her bell-rope tail, his feet set half a yard apart, his knees ever so slightly bent.

He looks set to leap, and for a wild moment I imagine him springing up onto the heifer's pommel-horse back and spinning around, legs and arms all akimbo. He doesn't, of course. Instead, Woko continues doggedly with his instruction. The boy stands at his side with a shepherd dog's attentiveness. 'Look from behind, see how wide she is,' the experienced YFC hand says. Width is all-important for Woko. Width means meat, and meat means money.

He moves on to the muscular curvature of the cow's hindquarters, which he compares to the muscled legs of a hundred-metre runner. 'The more muscle, the better.' He doesn't explain why, but the same two note-takers as before scribble down the adage regardless. A few others are now following their lead, concerned perhaps that a test might be coming after all.

'Now, have you ever heard of a rib-eye steak?'

For once, a large number of hands go up. Woko doesn't smile much, but a flicker of pleasure crosses his lips at the positive response. 'Good, well, next time you see rump steak in the butcher's, you'll know where it comes from.'

So they're absolutely sure, he points a second time to the

rounded upper section of the cow's hind. 'Look, see, no waste at all. Firm rump is what you got: here, no waste.'

A ginger-haired boy standing next to me pulls a biro from his pocket and writes a brief phrase in his booklet. He gives a conspiratorial nudge to the boy standing next to him. The two descend into muffled laughter, prompting me to peer over the shoulder of the redhead.

The incriminating page lies open. 'RUMP = ARSE!' it reads. He sees me looking and closes it quickly. The two stand stock still and stare straight ahead, their faces reddening as they try to gulp down their giggles.

In front of us, the heifer's tractor-like body suddenly stops shuddering and, with almost a comic's timing, she picks up the scraggly braid tip of her tail, gives it a swish this way and that, and then releases the most splendid jet of steaming gravy-coloured excrement.

Sailing through the air in a majestic rainbow arc, the hosepipe stream of runny undigested goop carries a good few feet before eventually petering out and plummeting downward, where it splatters on the floor in a magenta pool of oily slurry. And all done so nonchalantly, with such infinite finesse.

The class stand transfixed, their laughter stuck in their throats. They have all seen cowpats before, these discus-shaped fly feasts with their squelchy innards and their deceptively encrusted lids. Yet their genesis, their bringing into being, their original manufacture: this is something altogether new. All that grazing, all that chewing, all that grinding, and then to suddenly splurge forth in such a gush. We are all slightly awed.

The heifer at last looks fully content. For a while, she remains still, her dancing done. The children's full attention is hers. She can taste their respect. She can sense their admiration. The farmer leads her away, grumbling quietly. 'Come on, now, yer silly thing.'

Walking tall, she leaves the stage, a dainty tail-flick her curtain-call goodbye.

*

Touch rugby is on the agenda tonight. Spring is at last upon us and its gift of lighter evenings allows the children an escape from their winter's internment in the village hall. Lauren is bravely occupying the position of referee. A pile of jumpers defines the corner flags and two teams of seven youngsters are charging up and down the grass playing field, although not always in the vicinity of the ball. A third team stands on the sideline, waiting its turn. They make a fickle crowd, shouting support for their friends one minute and then heckling them the next. Tries are infrequent.

Rhys and Chris, two of the nominal organisers, are practising drop-kicks at the side of the pitch. Irritated that she's being left in charge as usual, Lauren suggests they might 'actually like to join in'. The two young men, both local farmhands, leave their ball-kicking and reluctantly enter the game.

The pair soon set aside their hesitancy and throw themselves into the play. With one on either team, the tempo lifts. Ball in hand, Rhys speeds along the touchline, shouting over his shoulder for his teammates to 'keep up, keep up'.

Next, Chris has control of the ball and is making great show of whether he should chip or make a pass. In the end, he does neither, dummying his marker and sliding through a tag-tackle before eventually laying the ball off to a tough-looking kid who is racing along beside him.

For the best part of ten minutes the girls and boys are running and panting and shouting, until Lauren finally blows her whistle and calls full time. Two tries to two, it's a diplomatic result.

'Good effort, everyone,' Lauren shouts from the centre spot. 'Right, Billy's team, take a break.' Billy, a lanky boy of about eleven, leads his fellow players off the field.

'Jill's team,' Lauren says loudly, signalling to the waiting side. 'You're up against Bronwyn's team.' The seven fresh replacements rush enthusiastically onto the pitch to shrieks of 'champ-yyy-ons' and 'no-oo prisoners' and other bellicose battle-cries.

'So you know what the rules are,' says Lauren. 'Try by the posts. Six touches and it's a turnover ball.'

Lauren is a member of the women's team down at Gwernyfed Rugby Club, so she knows the drill. 'And no kicking the ball, please,' she confirms, to which a boy on Bronwyn's team says it's unfair and that they should be allowed to kick after the fifth touch. Lauren consents. 'All right, kicking after the fifth tackle is okay. But not before. All of you got it? Okay, let's play.'

She blows the starting whistle.

Just as the match gets under way, Woko walks out of the shadows from the car park. I'm standing by myself on a raised bank just back from the touchline. We catch one another's eye and he wanders over. He's been busy lambing and I've had work commitments, so it's the first Monday night that I've seen him for a month or so.

'You all right, then?' he says.

'Hey, Woko,' I say, trying to sound cheerful. 'All good, thanks, yeah. Lucky with the weather, eh?'

It's an inane start, but I'm never quite sure what to talk to Woko about. I have learned a little about farming under Tony's tutelage and from general conversation at the Rhydspence, yet my grasp remains pretty rudimentary. I take some solace from the fact that Kilvert, who was always happier chatting with farmers' wives in their kitchens rather than with their husbands in the fields, appears to have little hands-on knowledge of agriculture either.

I sense Woko encounters a similar difficulty with me. As an incomer, I am a blank sheet: no background, no history, nothing for him to latch on to – a phantom, in effect. As a consequence, although he's always civil, we've never talked much.

'And you?' I ask. 'Done with lambing?'

'Yup, all finished up.'

'Go well?'

'Yeah, not bad. Well as to be expected, s'pose.'

'Still keeping busy though?' He doesn't reply. 'Must always be busy on a farm, I guess,' I say to fill the void.

'Yup, plenty to do all right.'

We stand in silence, both watching the chaotic game unfold on the pitch.

'One touch,' Lauren calls out. 'Two touches . . . no, Dylan, no pushing. Let him get up. Huw, on your feet now.'

As Lauren tries to bring some order to the match, Billy's team is growing bored on the touchline. Two boys are practising kicking, only they lack the skill of the older organisers and one of the two miskicks badly, the ball slicing off the side of his boot and rolling up the bank towards us. Woko scoops it up and expertly spin-passes it back to them.

'Play a bit of rugby then, do you?' I say.

It's an off-the-cuff observation rather than a pointed

question, but Woko replies with uncommon enthusiasm.

'Sure, I played a bit in my time,' he replies. 'Used to play flanker, down at Gwernyfed. Played over at Builth a bit as well, me and my mates. There was a bunch of us. Several of them are playing for the seniors, whatever, down there, like, you know.'

I don't know, but he waves a hand vaguely off to the right, over the humped outlines of the Radnorshire hills, which, as Chatwin describes them, recede 'grey on grey towards the end of the world'. Or, in this case, as far as Builth Wells.

I ask when he stopped playing, keen to keep the conversation going now Woko was on something of a roll. ''Bout five years ago, s'pose,' he replies. 'Maybe a bit longer.' He'd have been around twenty, he calculates.

Was he working on the farm then? He laughs ironically. 'Started working as soon as I left school at sixteen,' he tells me. 'I went to college, like. Got my certificates and all.' He complains how you need 'tickets' for everything nowadays. 'For your health and safety and what not, like.'

Woko has always had odd jobs in addition to farming. One of his neighbours has a small building firm, so he often helps him out as a day-labourer. For now, he needs the extra cash. His father is still working and the farm, which is mixed beef and sheep, isn't large enough to provide two full incomes. Woko is hoping that, as his old man approaches retirement, he'll begin to take a more active role, make a few more decisions around the place. 'Stepping up' is how he describes it.

Johnny, the current Llanigon Young Farmers chairman, finds himself in a similar situation. Gangly, good-humoured and just turned twenty, he has been working the family farm since his mid-teens as well. Part of him would love to have gone into acting or music, he confided to me once, before quickly dismissing the idea as a 'pipe dream'. Where would he start? He's never even met a jobbing actor or musician. Farming, in contrast, is there on his doorstep. The natural default.

Most of Johnny's school friends came from farming backgrounds. 'Joskins', the other children would label them. None of them studied much, content for the most part just to achieve the minimum GCSEs for agricultural college. A-levels or university were never really on Johnny's radar.

Opportunities to travel proved slim too. Because farm work rarely lets up and extra hands are expensive, Johnny's family was not in the habit of taking holidays, not even a bucket-and-spade mini-break to Tenby. He's only been abroad once in his life, he tells me a little sheepishly. That was to France, for four days with some mates. They took the boat. I ask if he's ever been on an aeroplane. He shakes his head.

One Monday night, while the younger members were occupied preparing pumpkins for Halloween, I fall into conversation with Chris and Rhys, who are killing time in a side room in the village hall. Both grew up locally, they tell me. As with Johnny, Rhys went to agricultural college straight after school, while Chris did a brief apprenticeship in carpentry, which he didn't like much so he took a job on a dairy farm instead.

The conversation turns to travel and Chris tells me about his various package holidays to Europe with his parents. He went on his first big trip by himself last November, to watch Formula 1 in Dubai. 'Eating out is dead cheap,' he enthused. 'It's all two for one out there.'

Rhys hasn't taken too many holidays, but he has done a few stints labouring in Norway, at a slaughterhouse that his uncle manages. His best mate spends six months in New Zealand every year as part of a shearing gang. Johnny and his peers, they don't backpack.

I ask if they have been to London, to which Chris says he has, once, and Rhys replies that he hasn't but that he fully intends to soon. 'Everyone is, like, "I've been to London, been to London." And me, I've hardly left the ruddy village.'

He'd like to go for a week, he says. Eat in all the nicest places, go to a cool club, 'do all those things I can't do here'. It's only fair to see how the other half lives, he thinks. 'I mean, they come up to our country here, don't they. Driving like tossers.' Chris strenuously agrees.

Woko hasn't been to London, either. It's rare for him to go even to Cardiff. He has been abroad, though; to Texas, on an exchange trip organised by the Welsh branch of Young Farmers. They visited farms, mostly.

Having a farm to inherit makes the decision to go into agriculture easier. In that respect, Woko and Johnny are one up on the likes of Chris and Rhys, who will be earning minimum wage or close to it. Not that the two farmers' sons collect a salary as such. 'Asset rich, cash poor' is how Johnny describes this lack of regular payment. Just as Woko does labouring, Johnny undertakes contracting work on neighbouring farms. It was this after-hours work that funded his Paris trip.

For farmers and farm labourers alike, working the land presents an uncertain future. Two generations ago, more than a dozen dairy farms dotted Llanigon parish. Today, there's one: Phillip Price, at Tynllyne Farm. Farmers are encouraged to grow their herds, increase their landholding and buy in new machinery to become more competitive, but not all have the means to do so. All the extra debt and risk and stress are hardly attractions, either.

At the same time, alternative opportunities for young people from farming families are limited. The more ambitious often end up moving away, attracted to better employment prospects elsewhere. Those who stay hope to find work with a local employer, of whom, bar the council, there are few. Without good contacts, most school leavers are looking at a low-paid job stacking shelves at the Co-op or waiting on tables in a café.

If they can acquire the necessary training, some might land on a trade that will permit them to set out on their own. The boom in house-buying incomers, for example, means the local business directory is now brimming with plumbers and decorators, roofers and electricians.

Even if the labour market were buoyant, which it isn't, young farmers still face the psychological and social challenges of cutting loose. Whatever farmers say to their children, however much they reassure them that their destiny is theirs to choose, for Woko and his ilk to become a policeman, say, or a teacher, is seen as opting out. Very possibly it means saying that the long line of Williamses at Penygenhill or Joneses at Llanthomas will be no more. For a young person, that's no easy task.

Fortunately for Woko, farming is not only in his genes but it's also what he loves best. He couldn't imagine another path. Barring an unforeseen calamity, his father can rest assured that there will be a Watkins at Caenantmelyn Farm for at least one more generation.

*

From where Woko and I are standing, the sloping sheep fields of Llanigon follow the gentle contours of the valley bank down to the Wye below, whose twisting metallic-blue form slithers and snakes its way downstream to the doll-house rooftops of Hay in the distance.

On the western edge of the town, right on the road junction up to Llanigon, a collection of white-roofed marquees glimmers brightly in a large rectangular field. The tented enclave signals the early preparations for Hay's annual literary festival, a ten-day jamboree of books and literature that brings hordes of bibliophiles flocking to the town every spring.

Woko has fallen back into silence and so, in an effort to move the conversation on, I point down to the canvas blobs below and enquire if he's planning to go to any events at this year's festival.

The full programme has yet to be announced, but he doubts it. In the twenty-five years the festival has been running, he's only ever been to one talk before.

'Oh, right. Who was that, then?'

'Adam Henson,' he responds. I was expecting Bill Clinton or Stephen Fry. My surprise evidently registers on my face because Woko repeats the name again as though I didn't catch it right the first time. 'Adam Henson. You know, off *Countryfile*, like.'

I offer a muffled response, unsure if I should admit that I've hardly ever watched the BBC's flagship rural television programme and consequently have no idea who Adam Henson is. A look of stupefaction lingers on his face. 'It's *Adam*'s Farm, right?'

It's clearly inconceivable to him that I don't have a clue what he's talking about, so rather than confess as much and have his opinion of me sink even further, I enquire about what Adam Henson of Adam's Farm had come to talk about.

'He was doing a thing at the Royal Welsh. Brecknock was hosting it and he was down there, like. And you could have this dinner lunch thing then up at a farm, not far from here. We had a bit to do with organising it, like. With the lunch ticket, you got into a talk he was giving after at the festival about his book, see?'

'So was it good?' I ask.

'It was all right.'

'And did you buy his book?'

'Mother bought the book for Dad, yeah.' It's on the bookshelf at home, he clarifies, although he's fairly convinced that his father has never read it. 'But it's signed 'n'all.'

Woko hasn't read Henson's book either, despite being a massive fan of the *Countryfile* star. That doesn't stop him filling me in length about Henson's career as a presenter, writer, brewer, 'big grain farmer too'. There's even a beer brand named after him these days, he tells me. 'He's making hay while the sun shines, that's for sure.'

Coming from someone so young, the saying sounds peculiarly old-fashioned, almost Kilvertian, in fact. It reminds me of stumbling on an obtuse word like 'wittan' or 'Thirza' or 'asplenium' in Kilvert's diary. A lexicographical fugitive from a bygone age, snuck quietly into Woko's phrase book, waiting for an opportune moment to relaunch itself on the world.

A piercing altercation on the pitch breaks off more talk of Adam Henson. Jill's team is protesting that they still have one touch in hand. Laying down the law, Lauren requisitions the ball from a boy with gel-spiked hair and places it on the ground. A girl from Bronwyn's team then steps up, rolls the ball backwards with the sole of her foot, and the game is back in play.

Aside from farming, I'm interested in what else Woko does with his time. Thoughts of Les spring to mind, with all his tales of youthful derring-do and narrow escapes. Here is Woko, supposedly in the midst of building his own story bank. What colourful episodes is he notching up beyond the farm gate?

I ask if he goes out much. He looks at me curiously. In the evenings, I clarify. Perhaps meet up with friends after work? Go to the pub maybe?

Not much, he says. The pub in Llanigon closed years ago. After club nights, they used to head down to the Three Horseshoes in Felindre, but it's shut on a Monday nowadays. 'If I go out anywhere during the week, it's the Griffin in Llyswen, likely as not.' The choice surprises me. Llyswen must be a fifteen-minute drive from where he lives. 'It's my missus's local, really,' he explains. 'She lives just up the road.'

This brings us into new and frankly unexpected territory. Woko had never mentioned a girlfriend before and I'd rather assumed he was married to the farm. Not that I should be surprised. Most of the older contingent at Llanigon are or were once going out with each other.

In this rural borderland, the range of Cupid's arrows stretches somewhat further than in the past, when the Young Farmers' Club effectively doubled as a matchmaking service. Today, the sound of blaring car stereos can be heard along the country lanes as youngsters head out to the bars and clubs of Hereford and Brecon, or even to the bright lights of Cardiff if their parents and their wallets allow it.

Woko's old stomping grounds fell a little closer to home, he tells me. In his late teens, a standard Saturday started in the rugby club bar after a match, then on to a local pub or two before ending up at the Wheatsheaf in Hay. 'Hell of a place, the Wheatsheaf,' he says, a look of youthful nostalgia passing over his face. Packed to the rafters. Bouncers on the door. 'Hell of a place.'

His mouth widens in a rare smile. From there, they'd catch a minibus to Clyro Court, where the old school gymnasium doubles as a nightclub at weekends. People came from all over, Woko recalls. Hereford, Kington, Bronllys, Talgarth, New Radnor, Brecon, Llyswen, you name it. A thousand people crammed in there on a Saturday, 'easy, like'.

'Sounds pretty crazy,' I say.

'It was crazy, all right.' He grins to himself at the memory. 'It used to be proper rough. There'd always be a massive punch-up. Full-on fighting, like. Them guys that came on the buses, they'd come just to look for a fight.'

The contrast between the genteel afternoons that Kilvert used to spend at the same venue, playing bowls on the lawn and admiring the 'beautiful orchids, lilies, & co., which Herbert Baskerville brought back from the Cape', seems extraordinary. That said, there's a ring of familiarity to his description too, what with Les and the tales from his pugilistic youth.

For all the bucolic imagery of the *Diary*, acts of thuggery and violence periodically appear in its darker margins. Returning from his Christmas break in 1871, for example, Kilvert stops by to chat with Lewis, the local policeman, whose wife is suffering from 'dreadful quinsy' (a complication related to tonsillitis). The officer fills in the curate on the details of a 'fearful fight' on Boxing Day between Clyro and Hay, which most folk agree was the fault of both sides but for which responsibility was pinned squarely on the Clyro contingent.

The real fighting at Clyro Court disco nights hit its peak before Woko's time, he admits. Scraps would still break out, but not with the same intensity or scale as before. He seems genuinely regretful to have missed out on the glory days.

'Do you still go out in Hay much?' I ask.

He doesn't, he says. None of his friends do. 'It's not like it was.' I ask him what's changed. He shrugs, his mood suddenly melancholic and a touch defensive. 'Just changed, s'pose.' I push him gently for more specifics. Is it the people? The shops? The houses? 'Bit of everything, I guess, like,' he says, noncommittal.

Falling into silence, we watch the toing and froing of the game once more.

The children are tiring now. Rhys and Chris have long given up, returning to their ball-kicking on the touchline. With the exception of a few of the older lads, no one appears especially interested in the result.

'Okay, next try wins,' Lauren declares, giving renewed impetus to the match as the players see the prospect of imminent release.

'About Hay and all, like,' Woko suddenly says, returning to the theme. 'It was mother's birthday on the weekend, right. So we went down to the Three Tuns, now, right, for a meal. And the place was full, like. It was absolutely full. And I didn't know one person in there.'

'Really, no one at all?'

'No, not one person, like,' he insists.

He shakes his head, bemused by the strangeness of the experience.

'And, hell, the whole of Hay was busy on the weekend, like. We walked down through town and the blooming Indian was all full. You could see them parked outside. And they were going in the Blue Boar. Hay looked real busy, like. Saturday night it was.'

Last Saturday was the first weekend of the Easter school holidays, a fact that I point out but which holds little interest for him. He's not after an explanation for the town's busyness. The essential point he wants me to understand is that Hay *was* busy, not why. And not busy as in Wheatsheaf busy, when he knew every face in the room. It was busy with strangers, with the faces of people 'from off' whom he didn't recognise.

The experience must have been quite weird for him, I suggest. An invasion of sorts. He lights up at the observation. It *was* weird, he agrees. He mulls over the word 'weird' and then says it again, quieter, as if almost speaking to himself. 'That's *exactly* what it was: weird.'

There is no anger in his voice, more bewilderment at the strangeness of it all. A marked difference separates the two. 'Weird' is coming home as a student to find your parents have rented out your room. 'Angry' is wanting to punch the new lodger on the nose. I am pleased Woko is not angry.

'And were they incomers, do you think?' I ask in a tentative voice. 'Or tourists?'

His answer feels desperately important to me. I long for it to be the latter. Every diner in the pub, every driver parked at the kerb, every drinker occupying a stool at the bar, I want them all to be tourists. It's not that I don't like tourists. They represent an essential economic asset for the town.

But if it's day-trippers and weekenders rather than incomers like me who are proving intrusive, then I can side with him. I can share his confusion, can offload my responsibility for arriving on his doorstep with my newcomer clansmen and bringing change.

'Yeah, I guess a lot of them were from out of town,' he says.

And there it is, as ambiguous an answer as it's possible to give, neither one way nor the other. I can't push him further. Biased though I am, I'm guessing most were tourists. As well as being a holiday weekend, the Three Tuns is popular with day-trippers and holidaymakers, what with its beer-battered fish, gastro refit and 4.0 rating on TripAdvisor.

Not that it really matters: incomer or tourist? Woko doesn't much care either way. To his way of seeing things, the distinction is nebulous. Both are out-of-towners.

Disappointed, it's now my turn to fall silent.

Anyway, the game is coming to a close. A dash down the wing by the tallest boy on Bronwyn's team sees the ball grounded over the line at last. The whistle goes and, to the sound of Lauren's call of 'Try', the victors punch the air and engage in bouncing bear-hugs.

Then the young recruits are ordered up to the basketball court and shepherded into a large circle. The court is up on top of the bank, just behind where Woko and I are standing. Our proximity to the action allows us no escape: we must take to the tarmac too.

I half-listen as Lauren explains the tenets of Fireball. It doesn't take long as there's only one basic rule: do *not* drop the ball. The penalty for doing so is to sprint around the outside of the circle while the other players pass the ball from hand to hand as quickly as possible. If the ball completes a lap before the runner, then he or she is out. That, in essence, is Fireball.

'Any questions?' There are no questions. Once again, Lauren's whistle sounds. 'Okay, let's play.'

The game begins at a sufficiently pedestrian pace to permit Woko and I to continue talking. He embarks on a brief monologue about sheep sales. Woko tends to avoid the livestock market these days and sell direct to the St Merryn slaughterhouse in Merthyr. I ask how many lambs he'll hope to shift this year. The question causes him to take a slow breath. Leaning his head to one side, he tells me it's right difficult to say.

Then follows a detailed explanation of his breeding strategy and the prolificacy of putting Texel ram on Welsh Mule ewes. 'You see, in an ideal world, all your ewes on the farm would have twins, see. You've got two teats, so you'd have two lambs . . .'

I find myself thinking back to Woko's reaction to the crowd at the Three Tuns. His lack of anger puzzles me. I suspected his reaction to be more proprietary, as it would if hikers trespassed across his land and a rambler's dog ran after his sheep. Yet his bemusement speaks of something else, of distance, of things lying outside his remit, of being beyond his control. Could it be, I wonder, that in some peculiar unexpected way, Woko fits the category of out-of-towner too?

The very notion seems outlandish. If being 'born and bred' means anything, surely it means ownership rights over your patch. Not just in terms of property deeds, which, in the case of Woko's farm, will pass down to him as the only son in due time. There's a more intrinsic, more elemental sense of ownership than that: the possession of a place's sense of self, its mores, its customs, its way of being.

Everything about Woko speaks to that person. The way he talks, the way he dresses, the way he spends his time, the way he views newcomers, each shouts loud and clear a deep and ingrained attachment to the place where he was born and schooled, the place where his opinions were formed and his character shaped. He is the undisputed owner of his world, no question, just as the Young Farmers' Club's current intake will one day come to own the same world too.

If Woko's universe existed in a vacuum, such reasoning would hold true. Only it doesn't, nor has it done for a good many years. Even in a rural parish such as Llanigon, along whose soft meadow footpaths Kilvert once ambled contentedly, waving at 'cheery looking' rustics as he went, other competing worlds now exist. Those of the schoolteachers and council workers on the cookie-cutter estate, the new-monied millionaire in Old Gwernyfed Hall (who, as it happens, also owns the Three Tuns), the retirees in their bungalows, the incomers in their barn conversions.

Many more such subworlds inhabit Hay, with its bookshops and its literary festival, its traders and its townspeople. For Kilvert a century and a half ago, a trip into town invariably entailed a visit to the post office or an appointment with the draper, a withdrawal from the savings bank or a trip to the doctor.

Farmers were part of that mix, of course. During Hay's annual fair, the town would become 'lively . . . with horses and sheep', its streets filled with ploughboys hoping for a hire, but at night the roads would empty as the farming folk would head back into the hills. Such as the old man whom Kilvert watched drive eight small white pigs back to Llowes, the next village up from Clyro along the Glasbury road, muttering all the way that his dogs were being too tender with their charges.

In Kilvert's time, the boundaries between these various worlds were kept more strictly than they are today. Now they mix and overlap constantly, in the market, on the street, at the bowls clubs, in the shops, down the pub. People flit between different groups, often with a foot in two or three at once. The retired smallholder who sings in the community choir, the incomer who sits on the Town Council, the shopkeeper who rides in the hunt.

By virtue of being the longest-standing, Woko's universe – that of furrow ploughs and shepherd's hooks, of quad bikes and tup sales – remains the most emblematic of the Welsh Marches. The rustic hill farmer is the common staple of popular perception and official myth, even though most residents would know as little as I when it comes to drenching a lamb or whistling instruction to a sheepdog.

On the farm, there is no doubt that Woko is master of his world, with his hoggets and his 'beef animals' and his lengths of gigot. Beyond the gate to Caenantmelyn, however, this total command inevitably loosens. Instinctively, I suspect he knows this. Which is why when a tapas bar replaces the Wheatsheaf, or when Lucy Powell is no longer landlady at the Three Tuns, it's not anger he feels but confusion. And it's also why he roots himself here, among fellow farmers, where he belongs and where everything makes sense.

So wrapped up am I in this notion that someone as seemingly authentic as Woko could also be, in some respects, an out-of-towner like me that I entirely lose the thread of his conversation. From sheep, he seems to have moved on to biodigesters (which stink, apparently, and, what's more, are responsible for pushing up the price of maize).

'So soon matey up here wants a hundred and fifty acres to feed his cows, look. And Joe Bloggs down there wants another hundred. They all want it like, so the price goes up . . .'

I lean in a fraction the better to catch what he's saying. My timing could not be worse because at that very moment, with my head turned askew, the girl to my right catches the ball, swings it across her body and releases it into the air in my direction. Only at the very last moment do I spot the rotating oval appearing at speed in my peripheral vision.

Swivelling round, I thrust out two desperate hands but I'm grabbing at air. The ball is already on me, colliding with my upper arm, then knocking against the side of my thigh as it falls, before quickly clattering to the floor and racing tip over tail into the middle of the circle.

'Run! Run! Run!' a roar of children's voices screams in my direction.

The noise, the clamouring: it's instant, incessant, insistent. I look at the ball. I look at the crowd. There's no means of escape, no exit, no plea bargain. Fireball's golden rule: don't drop the ball. I've broken it. I lose. I'm 'it'. Touched. Tagged. Cornered. Kiboshed. Round the circle it is. As swiftly as my legs will carry me. No delay. No hesitation.

And so I turn and I sprint. Fast as I can.

*

The lab-coated boy in the back of the horse-trailer is sitting on a chair with a blindfold across his eyes. Two official-looking women are standing beside a bare desk next to him. They are holding clipboards.

A third woman with a lipless grin is passing various objects to the boy. He looks frightened, as though the unseen items might bite. From the bottom of the gangplank outside, it's difficult to make out what exactly the objects are. I suggest to Seth and Bo that we climb inside.

They look at me as if I'm insane and impolitely decline. Rally Day has far more appealing activities to offer besides hostage simulation. The first lies a short sprint away and comes in the shape of eleven toadstool letters. Three feet high and carved from soft wood, they spell out the name of this year's host club. TALGARTH YFC. The boys disappear towards them, darting in and out of their upright stems.

Off to the left stand two sheep pens with a raised platform in between. One is empty. In the other, four flustered ewes are bleating and bumping into one another. A young, nervous-looking lad in a shirt and tie is preparing to give his summation in the stock-judging competition.

'Mr Judge, Mr Timer,' he starts, a picture of courtroom formality. 'I place the four Texel butcher's lambs in the following order: X, Y, B, A.'

He checks his notes quickly and then commences on a well-argued defence of his verdict. In his view, ewe X excelled in the class, having tremendous width and fleshing throughout. Fullest loin of the four by far, bulbous over the chump, good depth in gigot, 'all round a tremendous animal, Mr Judge'.

His second choice of lamb shares similar attributes. Same width and fullness over the top, tremendous squareness of the shoulder, carrying no waste. Just lacked the length compared to his first-placed lamb, he feels. Third and fourth are saleable lambs, but are slacker-coated and lack overall finish at present. 'And those, Mr Judge, are my reasons for placing the four butcher's lambs in the given order.'

The elderly adjudicator looks impressed and scribbles down a score on a card. Mr Timer checks his stopwatch, thanks the competitor and invites him to step out of the sheep-pen dock. The boy obliges, making way for another young farmer to take his place.

Bo and Seth are tugging at my coat. They are done with the letters. They have spotted a burger van inside the entrance gate to the farmyard where the majority of the rally activities are taking place. Can they have a hot dog? I'd like to wait to hear the judge's response, but know better than to fight the rumbling of small stomachs.

We pass through the gate and join the queue for food. The menu of the Welsh Venison Centre is painted on a chalkboard: steaks, burgers, bacon rolls, chips, wedges, chilli. An afterthought appears at the bottom: 'salad'.

Standing immediately in front of us is a mother-and-daughter pairing. The older of the two is wearing a fitted derby tweed jacket and wellington boots, while the younger is dressed in jeans, white trainers and a sweatshirt. 'I told you not to wear your new shoes,' the mother is saying. Her daughter must be around eleven, old enough to know what adolescent freedoms look like but still too young to taste them. She says it's fine. The mud will wash off.

The queue runs to about twenty people in total. Most of them are teenagers or on the verge of becoming so. Jeans, rugby socks, heavy boots, baseball caps and, among the cooler girls, spotty wellies prevail. A good number are dressed in branded sweatshirts too. 'Probably the best club in the world,' reads the strapline across one. Another has four boxes in a vertical column, each with a white tick inside.

Next to each box in a parallel column are the words, 'Eat. Sleep. Farm. Repeat.'

Right at the front, I spot a pair of young lads from Llanigon. They are tipping vinegar and salt onto a polystyrene bowl of hot chips. A picture of an upturned turnip is emblazoned across the front of their T-shirts. 'Toshing Swedes Since 1955,' the slogan proudly declares. I don't know what 'toshing' means, nor what doing it to a swede entails, but, conscious of the Young Farmers' penchant for double entendres, I think it might be best to leave off asking until Bo and Seth are out of earshot.

Beside the food van is a large barn. Once we're done with the hot dogs, the boys want to see inside. It's organised like an IKEA store, with a clockwise circular route marked out. Instead of flat-packed living spaces on show, however, there are rows of trestle tables laden with cakes, arts and crafts, and other assorted output from club nights across the county.

The boys sprint off, disappearing through the barn door marked EXIT.

I wait for them at the entrance. Within two minutes, they have completed a full surveillance of the place. Through gulps of delight, Seth conveys that he would like his face painted, while Bo is excited at having seen a group of supermen. He insists on the plural. It's definitely supermen, he says. 'And them is dancing.'

In the far corner of the barn, hedged in behind a wide semicircle of plastic chairs filled with camera-pointing relatives, there is indeed a troupe of dancing superheroes. To a thumping techno beat, eight of Erwood Juniors' best are racing towards the climax of their dance competition set. They kick their legs and jab the sky, flip over in cartwheels and then, as the music reaches its climax, they charge towards the audience and leap on top of one another in a choreographed heap.

The music stops, the audience claps and Bo removes his hands from over his eyes.

Next up is Talgarth Juniors, an all-girl ensemble decked out in purple gym dresses and waving fluffy pompoms. They spring out onto the dance floor to a speeded-up version of 'Mickey'.

Bo and Seth are rapt. I sit them on two plastic chairs and ask a responsible-looking lady on the end of the row if she could possibly keep an eye on them for a few minutes. No problem, she says. 'I'll be back in five,' I tell the boys. 'Don't move.'

The barn is busy with families and kids. An announcer is reading out competition times over the loudspeaker system. Groups of teenagers mill around in huddles, joking with one another and checking their phones.

Spotting an exhibit free of people, I wander over. A sign reveals it to be the Minutes Book Competition. Fourteen Black 'n' Red notebooks, A4-size and hard-covered, are lined up along a lengthy trestle table. A judge has ranked them, a speech card clipped to the front page revealing their score and overall ranking. First place goes to Troedrhiwdalar. Second to Sennybridge. Llanigon is tied equal in eleventh.

I pick up Llanigon's minute book to read the scrawled comments on the judge's note more closely. The adjudicator finds room to praise the write-up for the annual general meeting, which is rated as 'well-written', but the club's failure to provide updated accounts ('as per the rules') has earned them a major black mark.

I open the minute book at random, turning up the entry for 14 October. Lauren's rounded script covers the lined page. The entry is brief and bureaucratic. Written at the top is the name of the chairman, the date of the club night and the number of members present (thirty-one). Six numbered points follow:

1) Apologies: There were no apologies.

2) Minutes: The minutes of the last meeting were read, signed and dated as a true and accurate record.

3) Matters arising: There were no matters arising.

4) Correspondence: Members discussed the Brecknock YFC Harvest Festival. It was decided that Owen Watkins and Beth Jones would attend at Brynbont Chapel, Pontfaen on Sunday 20th October.

5) Business: Members discussed what they would like to do at the next club meeting and it was decided that Owen Watkins would teach members how to make sheep halters out of string.

6) Any other business: There was no other business.

The entry finishes with the time of the meeting's closure and the scheduled date of the next club night. Swirling across the bottom of the page in a blue pen is the aforementioned chairman's florid signature: *Johnny Davis*.

A similar laconic style characterises the remainder of the book, stiff sentences charting the club's year from the Christmas bingo and Halloween party through to the creative arts day in Llangynidr and the percussion class by Brecon's samba band. Each merits a single line under 'business'.

The only entry to run to more than one page relates to today's rally. It dates back a month or so and contains a list of names clumped into batches. Each batch is linked to a specific activity, which is capitalised and underlined in the left-hand margin.

The activities fall into one of three broad categories. There's the Agricultural, which covers the likes of Stock Judging, Wool-rolling, Setting a Stack Box, All Terrain Vehicle Driving, 'Junior Agri Challenge' and the 'Poultry Challenge'. There's the Physical, which ranges from Mountain Bike Racing and Woodwork through to the Wheelbarrow Obstacle and the Pedal Tractor Course. And, thirdly, there's what might ambitiously be defined as the Theatrical, which is made up of the Heroes Challenge, Dressing Up, The Voice, the Bake Off and the Senior Taste Bud Challenge. Toshing does not appear to be included.

Responsibility for the annual rally rotates among the different clubs. It will be Llanigon's turn to act as hosts next year. A few weeks ago I talked over the prospect with Woko, who is already getting excited. The plan is to hold it at Dan-y-Comin, Johnny's farm. Plenty to sort out, he mused ruefully. They'll need to wash down the barns, scrub out the sheds, arrange the parking, organise the toilet facilities, book the band. 'It'll be all hands to the deck.'

The rally marks the year's pinnacle, the Young Farmers' equivalent of the World Championships. For months, the clubs have been contending in one-off tournaments, but Rally Day is when the majority of competition points are on offer and so their performance today typically decides which club is crowned County Champions.

I return to the boys, who remain gripped by the dancing.

Troedrhiwdalar is now up, another all-girl team, this time dressed in silver-sequinned bodices and streaked in red war paint. I thank the lady for keeping an eye on them, and suggest to the boys that we move on. They are reluctant to leave. Then three words sound out over the loudspeaker – 'pedal tractor competition' – and they're done with the dancing.

We ask for directions from a man at the help desk, who points us to a patch of yard along the far outside wall of the barn. The race circuit is marked out by training-ground cones. It is oval-shaped, the main straight running to about fifty yards before hurtling into a sharp bend.

Competitors are already queuing behind the start line. I recognise a tall boy from Llanigon. He is up second. We cheer him on but his knees knock against the bonnet of the toy tractor, significantly reducing his pedalling power. I fear Llanigon won't be carrying the cup home tonight.

Once all the competitors have had their turn, the time-keeper lets Bo and Seth have a go. Clipboard and whistle in hand, he counts them down. 'Three, two, one . . .' They massacre the cones and career through a puddle, but cross the line elated. The timekeeper reads off their respective scores from his stopwatch. Seth finished marginally ahead, at thirty-two seconds. Bo clocks thirty-four and claims victory on the grounds that his number is greater.

Euphoric from their race, they prove amenable to checking out the wool-rolling, which is taking place in a marquee located on a patch of grazing land next to the farmyard. The field also contains a candy-floss stall, a craft tent and a bouncy castle, all of which we can return to later I tell the boys.

The wool-rolling competition is already under way when we arrive. The marquee is divided into two, with chairs and spectators occupying one half, and pens and sheep the other. A circular wooden platform stands in the middle of the room about two feet off the ground. In the centre of the platform is a curtained cubicle, out of which a series of bewildered-looking ewes will be periodically thrust into the custody of a series of brawny-looking men wielding electronic shearing clippers.

Sitting behind a flimsy desk close to the action is a white-haired gentleman holding a microphone. In a strong Radnorshire drawl, he reads out the name of the next competitor from a sheet on the table. 'Next up is Gwilym, from Pontfaen.'

A boy of about fourteen steps forward from the crowd. He is dressed in a green jumpsuit with a black-and-yellow trim and a John Deere logo affixed to the breast pocket. He looks a little lost inside it, as though his tangled teenage limbs remain a novelty to him.

'And we're away,' the commentator says, as a sheep emerges from the cubicle and the shearer grips the animal between his knees. 'There, up the neck he goes now. Shearing that awkward first shoulder, the most difficult part of the sheep.'

Bo and Seth look on, fascinated by the ewe's gradual denuding.

'Right down over the sheep now, one, two, three, short blows there, and then onto the long blow, right from the hip bone to the top of the head. And away he goes, round that last shoulder now.'

As the first shearer nears the end, another sheep is shoved out onto the boards and a second shearer gets to work. All the while, Gwilym is standing on the floor below the platform, waiting patiently for the first fleece to slip off the ewe.

When it does, he springs into action.

The expert's commentary begins to take on a more instructive tone. 'Wrinkle that one up, get any dirt off that's not wanted.' Concentration writ across his face, Gwilym pulls rapidly at the fleece, gathering the loose clumps of clean belly wool into a small pile. 'Now he'll be watching for the bits around the neck.' The teenage competitor wraps up the fleece as though it were a sleeping bag, scrunching it tight at the tail end and then folding it in on itself. 'Very good, he's rolling that sheep round in the classic Bowen style.'

With the fleece now bundled up against his chest, Gwilym steps away from the platform and moves towards a wide metal table that runs lengthways beside the commentator's desk. The table's surface ripples with a succession of horizontal, stainless-steel rolling pins, which are spaced out at two-inch intervals. Positioning himself at the head of the table, he briefly eyes its length, picturing his next action as a golfer might seek to envision the flight of his pending shot.

A vote of confidence sounds over the loudspeaker. 'It looks like he knows what he's doing, this young man. Let's see how he does.'

His fingers gripping hard to the tail end of the fleece, Gwilym throws his hands forward in a sudden, explosive motion that sends the sheep's ex-winter jacket unfurling through the air. It lands flat and uncrumpled, a woolly picnic rug covering the width of the table. Over the side flop four stumpy leg-warmers.

'Bingo, that's pretty good,' the commentator cries. 'Bit of wrinkle off the side, but that's not too bad at all. Now then, he's away.'

Suddenly, everything is happening very fast. Gwilym is

frantically folding in the outer parts of the fleece so he can start rolling it, while over his shoulder the second shearer is nearing the end, manoeuvring the ewe around on her hind-quarters as he passes the clippers over her back legs.

'Get it rolled up, there, turn the sides in real well. This second shearer now, he's coming down that far side. Three more blows and she'll be down the porthole again. Tuck it in at the neck there, Gwilym. Tidy job. Now give it a pull, that's it, good neck on it. Nice roll, well done. And he's straight on to the next fleece and we're in business again . . .'

The process repeats itself, the commentator's delivery growing increasingly staccato as the clock ticks on. Gwilym wrinkles up the fleece, dashes across to the table and unfurls it in haste, causing it to land less neatly than the first time. Quickly straightening it, he begins rolling it into a tight sleeping-bag coil.

'Any sweaty bits from round the neck . . . there you go, turn it in, so all the shoulder wool is showing . . . Tuck it in and he's away once more. Looks like he's done plenty of wool-rolling in his time this boy. That's it, yup, not bad at all. You could play football with that.'

Placing the second rolled fleece beside the first, Gwilym rushes back to the platform and starts clearing the woolly scraps left by the shearer with a plastic brush. After throwing the debris into two separate black bins, one for clean wool, one for dirty, he thrusts a hand in the air and the commentator calls for the timer to stop the clock.

Gwilym smiles modestly as the crowd claps and he walks to the back of the tent where his father shakes his hand, beaming with parental pride.

*

That evening, I'm back at Great House Farm in Talgarth, this time without my boys.

Everything is ready for the Rally Dance. The barn has been cleared. Gone are the trestle tables and in their place is a raised stage on one side, all set up for a DJ and band. The other side is occupied by a fifty-foot-long bar, stocked with 13,000 pints of beer and cider.

Separating the two is a high metal fence, at one end of which there's a narrow gap permitting access back and forth between the bar and the dance floor. Four beefy security guards check everyone in and out on the bar area. Access is conditional on showing the bouncers a fluorescent wristband, available only to those eighteen years old or over.

Having volunteered to help out for the night, I find myself assigned to the spirits bar, where I am kept occupied mixing Jägerbombs priced at £2.50 a pop. We sell hundreds.

Around midnight, our clientele begins to thin out or, in one or two cases, to fall over. I ask for a break. The music is pumping. The dance floor is heaving. Beyond the happy melee of dancers, however, off towards the back of the barn, I spot a scuffle breaking out. A young man with a scruffy beard and a barrel chest is throwing cartwheel punches.

I move closer to the action.

The aggressor hasn't picked his adversary wisely. His opponent is not only bigger, but moderately more sober. 'You want some? You want some?' he is shouting at Scruffy Beard, dodging side to side on his toes, easily evading the other man's flailing blows. 'Come on, come get some, then.'

So Scruffy Beard does. He drops his shoulder and charges at the bigger man, locking his arms around his midriff and driving him backwards with short pumping steps into the crowd of onlookers that has quickly gathered around them. Losing their balance, the two collapse on the floor in a jumbled mess. Rally night now has a full-on fistfight on its hands. The crowd starts baying.

Then security arrives. Six of them. These are the real thugs, shaven-headed bricks of men, their skills learned in bar-room brawls just like this one. They make short weather of the fighting pair, pulling them apart and forcing them into a hammer-lock before marching them out of the barn.

I follow. So too does a blonde girl in a short skirt, who, until then, had been standing close to the shoulder of the attacker and screaming at him to stop. Both men are drunkenly protesting their innocence and cursing the other for starting the fight. The security staff pay no heed to either of them.

Once outside, the contracted heavies troop across the yard and fling the scrapping pair unceremoniously through the exit gate into the field beyond. Over the course of the day, with thousands of people coming and going, the grass has become boggy with mud. The two trip over straight into it.

The more sober of the two gets to his feet and, holding his hands up towards the security staff, insists that he doesn't want any grief. Scruffy Beard obviously thinks otherwise. His trousers caked in mud, he scrambles up and charges once more at his rival.

'Billy, no!' his girlfriend wails, drunken tears splashing down her cheeks. 'Billy! He's not worth it, Billy!'

Bunched together at the gate, the security staff look on with relative indifference, even amusement. The mud-splattered car park isn't under their jurisdiction. Then one of them, perhaps tempted by the smell of violence, breaks the line and wades in. This prompts Billy to do something he would never have done in the sober light of day, however incensed: he lashes out at the bone-head security man.

The result is only a brush on the arm, but it proves provocation enough. In a flash, two of the other security men rush out and Billy, his legs whipped from underneath him, is instantly back on the ground again. This time, there is no getting up. One of the men has a knee on his spine and is wrenching back his arm in a wrestling hold. Another is standing on one of his legs. Billy's nose is bleeding and mud is dripping from his beard.

The police are called and a blaring siren soon comes into earshot followed by two flashing blue lights hurtling downhill through the parking field. The police car slithers to a halt a few feet from the action. Two coppers get out, bundle Scruffy Beard into the back seat and speed off as quickly as they came. Howling uncontrollably, Billy's girlfriend collapses onto the shoulder of a friend and sobs.

The victor waves a sarcastic goodbye and is led off by friends to a St John Ambulance station to patch up a bleeding gash across his cheek. A nurse ushers him up the stairs and into the back of the temporary medical station. As he goes in, another young man comes out, a blackish purple bruise over one eye and his arm in a sling.

At around 1 a.m. the bar closes and I make my way back to my car, my feet sore from standing and my fingers sticky with spilled Jägerbomb. The fight turns out to be just the first of many. There's more pouncing, arm-locking and frogmarching to be done by the heavy-handed security staff.

Meanwhile, minibuses queue at the top corner of the car park to take the ticket holders home. At one point, the passengers on the Brecon bus pile off and start laying into a small contingent of lads boarding the Talgarth bus opposite. Three more names join St John Ambulance's list for first aid.

I catch only brief glimpses of Woko and the other Llanigon crew during the evening. The times I do spot them in the crowd, however, they all look to be enjoying themselves. Certainly the banter on Facebook the next day seems to suggest a good night was had. 'Hellish tidy farm, impressive bar and a couple thousand Breconian swede kickers,' Rhys posts. 'Nail that and you've got yourself a very memorable night.' By the end of the day, he has more than 200 'Likes'.

Between the old boys at the Rhydspence Inn and the young farmers at the Llanigon, I feel a growing familiarity with the farming community. I now understand better who it encompasses and how it is faring. I also realise that I will never belong in the way they do. I cannot. Farming is not in my blood, nor is it a way of life I am about to embrace. Possibly my children could make the leap. It would mean joining the YFC and working their way up through the ranks. Given that they won't qualify for a number of years yet, I resolve to ask them nearer the time.

My kin, I suppose, are my fellow incomers. As a tribe, we are a mixed bunch, washed up on the banks of the Wye from all over. As well as Brits, I personally know at least four Americans, three Frenchmen, two Spaniards and one Hungarian currently residing in Hay. It is a mini League of Nations hidden away in the Welsh borders.

We are a loose agglomeration, a heterogeneous group. Yet many of us 'from off' are bound by similar motivations: a desire to start afresh, to reshape our lives somehow, to explore new horizons. Nowhere are the vistas more open than up in the hills. On the trail of one of Kilvert's favourite walks, I set off up Cutter's Pitch towards Little Mountain to meet a couple I've heard about with a majestic bus.

PART II

Incomers

4

The Majestic Bus

On the Little Mountain the gorse that glowed and flamed
fiery gold down the edge of the hill contrasted sharp and
splendid with the blue world of mountain and valley which
it touched.

Kilvert's Diary, 19 August 1870

Rob is kneeling on top of the bus, his arm lodged down the
top of a chimney flue. An aluminium ladder rests on the lip
of the roof, two or three feet away from where he is crouched.
These are the very last days of winter. A blanket of dewy
mist hovers beneath the undercarriage. Birdsong cascades
down from the trees. Jays, woodpeckers, blackbirds, all
beckoning spring from its slumbers.

The ladder slips down a few inches, causing the smallest
of scrapes to the paintwork of the static bus. A muffled curse
tumbles down from above. I move from where I'm standing
at the bus's entrance and put a foot on the lowest rung of the
ladder.

'Thanks,' shouts Rob. 'Pass us the pole, could yer?'

I hand up a stretch of copper piping. He takes it and
climbs gingerly to his feet. Edging towards the flue of the
wood burner, he thrusts it down the open vent.

Today is changeover day at the Majestic Bus. With the
latest round of guests due to arrive mid-afternoon, Rob is

doing odd jobs. Layla, his wife, has already stripped the sheets and replaced them with fresh ones. The room has been swept and the surfaces wiped until they shine. It falls to Rob to light the fire so the bus is snug and cosy for later.

It may be marketed as 'glamping', but spending the night in an old bus on an empty hillside still marks a bold step for many of their paying guests. The nearest street light is four miles away, down the hill in Clyro. Neither the electricity nor the water is on the mains. There is no TV, no internet and no mobile signal.

Typically, it is stressed city folk who book in, enthralled by the idea of escaping their fast-paced lives for a spell in the country. We'll immerse ourselves in nature, they tell themselves. Walk in the hills, read our books, sleep in, make love under the stars. It'll be blissful. And so it is. 'For most of 'em, anyway,' Rob says, his Suffolk upbringing declaring itself loudly in his long drawn-out vowels.

Even so, arriving along the steep country back roads and lurching down the final stretch of rutted puddle-pitted track must set even hardened stomachs fluttering. It helps settle them in if the bus is warm when they arrive.

Rob is a relaxed, forty-something guy with a witty tongue and a ready laugh. His balding pate is closely cropped and habitually covered with a hat of some description. As a young man, he used to wear his hair long and I sense the middle-aged Rob has never quite come to terms with his follicles' betrayal.

The ladder appears stable enough for now, so I leave him to his chimney sweeping and take a snoop around the site. The bus is located at the base of a sloping bank. Bedded into the turf are four squat tree-trunk stools that form a circular pattern around a sunken pit. Shards of blackened firewood rest on the pit's ashen bed. Curiously, the funerary scene speaks of happy times. Marshmallows on twig pokers. Campfire songs. Woodsmoke smells. Whisky warmth.

Further up the bank, pressed close to a perimeter hedge that divides Rob and Layla's one-acre plot from the farmer's field beyond, a water tank sits stout and silent, its contents generously replenished by an underground spring.

I wander across to the bathroom, which is separated from the bus by thirty yards or so. It is housed in a square, timber-framed room built on to the back of a Dutch barn. Wooden boards, a foot wide and cedar-stained, line the floor. On the side nearest the door, a deep roll-top bath hugs the wall. A grey-muzzled cat with yellow eyes looks down from a sheet-steel advertising sign above. Pure Matured Virginia Cigarettes, it promises. Ten for six shillings.

In the far corner of the bathroom, two bookshelves are nailed to the wall above a wooden chest, which is furnished with four plump cushions so as to double as a bench. A pile of board games rests beside it. The books above are pressed close on the shelves, their authors – Chimamanda Ngozi Adichie, David Mitchell, Chris Cleave, Penelope Lively, Sadie Jones – a cut above the usual holiday home hand-me-downs. Each looks diligently read, faint tracks furrowing their spines.

In the opposite corner sits a dinky wood-burning stove awaiting a match. An enamel bucket is stationed beside it, the kind that once used to hang in apartment corridors stencilled with the words 'FIRE'. Overflowing with firewood that begs to be burned, this one has clearly been appropriated by the other side.

Leaving the bathroom, I take a peek in the adjoining barn. The wall at the end facing the bus is clad in rusting corrugated iron, as is the long horizontal back wall closest to the bank of the hill. The other two walls are only partially enclosed, leaving space for the elements to enter.

The overspill of domestic life litters the floor: prams, furniture, a sledge, bats and balls, children's bikes, an old sofa, an electric radiator. Guarding the entrance is a Buccaneer caravan, which sits on bricks in the doorway, its brown curtains pulled tight, waiting patiently for blue summer skies and an open road.

Mixed in among it all are the tools required to tame their patch of arcadia and keep the wilderness at bay: mowers, trimmers, spades, pitchforks, half-empty tins of paint, boxes of screws and nails, sheets of insulation, piles of plywood, a chainsaw, ladders, a can of petrol, large red gas canisters, firewood, a wheelbarrow, straw bales, a filing cabinet.

The one-time hay barn has become a vast outdoor cupboard. The suggestion of so much maintenance exhausts me. I step back outside. As I do, I hear a shout from the bus. Rob has finished on the roof. I walk back over and retake my position at the bottom of the ladder, as he throws the pole onto the grass and climbs down after it.

'Bet that's made a right ol' mess,' he says. 'Amazing how much crap gets caught up them chimneys. Only cleaned the thing six months ago.'

Rob delivers the comments with typical good humour. He is not one for moaning. Nor does he begrudge the upkeep of the bus, which pays their way. They bought the plot eight years ago, emptying their savings account in the process. After the initial euphoria, the tedious reality of financial constraint sank in. Their initial plan had been to renovate an old stone barn that stands at the entrance to the property. It is in poor repair, but has planning permission.

The couple had bought and done up an old house before, a ramshackle sixteenth-century forge in a village just outside Ledbury. They purchased it close to the top of the market, against their bank manager's advice. 'A proper wreck it was,' Rob says. They lived in a caravan in the garden for the first six months, then gradually occupied one room at a time as Rob pressed on with the renovations himself.

Money was perpetually tight, especially after Rob's veg-delivery business collapsed in the wake of a supplier's bankruptcy. With characteristic grit, Layla took herself off to college and, after two years of gruelling study and part-time work, she emerged as a qualified horticulturalist with her own small business.

After six years, the house was finally finished and they put it on the market almost immediately. It sold quickly, and for enough to give them what they had always dreamed of: a deposit for a rustic smallholding in the wilds.

Tilda was three months old when they took possession of their hillside plot, and two years later her sister Goldie came along. Layla gradually scaled back her gardening business so she could spend time with the kids, while Rob found work as a handyman building sheds, fixing guttering, laying decking and so forth.

With the arrival of Tilda, time and money both became tight once more, so they decided to temporarily shelve their renovation plans and buy a large caravan, a twin unit which they parked up the slope towards the top of their plot.

As the name suggests, the mobile home came in two halves, each measuring about thirty foot by ten. A farmer friend hauled both halves to the entrance gate with his tractor, where they promptly sank into the mud. And there they remained, a sulking old couple sitting back to back, until

Rob laid his hands on a truck with a loading arm to lever them into place. In an act of heavy-handed marriage counselling, he then bolted the pair together. After adding a lick of paint and a new tin roof, the family moved in.

The spacious caravan has remained their home until today. Periodically it expands in width, filling out with the bulges of age. Tilda and Goldie have their own timber-framed lean-tos at the back. Rob recently put in a utility room beside the kitchen area so they no longer have to trek across to the Dutch barn to load and unload the washing machine. Following the birth of another baby girl four months ago, Rob is now busy planning Meri's nursery.

Two of the three girls had home births. Meri arrived so quickly that the midwife didn't get there in time. Layla took it all in her stride, according to Rob's version of events. 'Cool as a cucumber, she was.' A few days later he loaded up a picture of a tiny bundle of pink-nosed towelling on Facebook. 'Just call me Dr Rob,' his post read.

Kilvert records an extraordinary tale of his own about a home birth and a midwife. The story played out in a house called The Pant, a short way across the hill from Rob and Layla's smallholding. The house exactly straddled the national border and the attending midwife insisted that the baby be born on English soil. The poor homeowner was consequently shunted into the eastern half of the cottage, where she 'was delivered of the child standing'.

As for Meri's nursery, Rob has it in mind to knock out the side wall in Goldie's bedroom and build sideways into the bank of the hill. That would place the baby's room beside the main bedroom, leaving Meri's cot exactly a bed's length from where she entered the world. It strikes me as a wonderful idea, full of life-encircling symmetry.

We step into the bus. Rob is careful to clean his shoes on the mat and wipe his hands on his trousers before entering. He's wearing jeans and a T-shirt, which form his perpetual base layer, a sartorial second skin.

Accessories appear from time to time. He has a thick bedraggled coat that gets an airing in deep winter. For a short spate last autumn, he took to wearing a hoodie with Majestic Bus branding emblazoned across it. The only other wardrobe constant is his sludge-brown deerstalker, which he wears in all weathers and always with the basset hound ears flopping down. He plays bass guitar in a band called the Cherryshoes and the faux-furred hat provides his signature look.

Rob lays two sheets of newspaper in front of the wood burner and kneels down to open it. Inside is the charred mess he had warned about. 'Move that chair, could ya?' he asks, pointing to a low upholstered armchair resting against the wall behind him. He is bending forward to open the stove door. I guess he fears an ash cloud might envelop the room. The armchair has a circular orange seat and thin stunted legs that splay outwards. It's all very retro, very junk-shop Hay.

'Just put it over there. That's fine.'

He waves a hand towards the entrance area. I lift the chair over an L-shaped sofa that faces the fire and then edge it around a protruding cupboard that separates off the kitchen-dining area, which is located at the front of the bus.

The bus isn't much wider than a modern people carrier and measures about twice the length. It feels surprisingly spacious all the same, a sensation aided by the high roof. There's room to swing a cat, were cats allowed. Which they aren't; the Majestic Bus is a pet-free zone.

'It's a Bedford SB Plaxton Panorama.' Rob delivers the information with uncharacteristic seriousness. He pauses a fraction to allow the full weight of the revelation to sink in. '1968,' he adds, a look of beaming pleasure lighting up his face.

The vehicle used to belong to Brodyr Williams, whose name still adorns the side of the bus in an expansive blue, cursive font. Brodyr Williams is a bus firm based in the Carmarthenshire village of Upper Tumble, a fairytale name if ever there was. The company's vehicles still ply the roads of south-west Wales, although no longer in Panorama 68s. These bow-sided forty-five seaters left regular service decades ago, replaced by slicker, more reliable models.

I can't help but think that the world is poorer for the Panorama's passing. It might have belched diesel fumes and struggled up hills, but the 68 had pizzazz, with its chrome-striped trim and wrap-around windscreen, its Cape Canaveral radiator grille and its racy curves. Even the twin headlights – rounded, protuberant, bright as glitter balls – screamed cool.

So too does Rob and Layla's post-restoration interior. It didn't start out that way. Rob stripped it right back, redid the wiring, replaced the boarding and laid a timber floor. A photo montage on the wall of the outside lavatory block depicts the full transformation. The mini-exhibition is mounted beside a glass frame containing a pictorial 'Guide to the Bees of Britain' and above two potty seats which look like a pair of infant lifebelts, dangling in repose.

For someone like me who's never built so much as a rabbit hutch, the entire enterprise seems like an incalculable ordeal. In the pictures, the bank has none of the picnic-perfect grass or wild flowers that adorn it now. It's full of cable trenches, wobbly wood-plank paths and strips of plastic piping. It reminds me of a slurry pit.

Unimaginably, the sight inside is altogether worse. The first picture in the montage shows all the mouldy old seats still in place. Laced in cobweb netting and mildewy grime, they make for a noirish, macabre scene. By the fourth picture, the project is beginning to come together. The seats are gone, together with any skeletal remains once hidden beneath them. The walls are half-clad. The timber bones of the kitchenette and furnishings are taking shape. There's no mistaking it, though: it remains a coach crash on wheels.

All of which makes standing in it now feel slightly fantastical.

At the far end is a double bed that stretches from wall to wall. Plump cushions line up in colour co-ordination along an invisible headboard, which rests against a huge back window of clear glass. The effect is that of an infinity swimming pool, tempting guests to crawl the bed's length and spill into the night beyond. I find myself picturing the naughty schoolkids who must have once occupied the back rows, their faces pressed against the glass, blowing raspberries at passing motorists and smudging obscenities with grubby fingers on the pane.

Against the glass, a dried-flower wreath now hangs. It is perfectly centred. Observing the floral arrangement from the entrance door end, I experience a compelling sensation, as if the wreath were calling out, beckoning me towards it. Brindled with blood-orange berries and bubbling bright with purple-capped thistle heads, the floral halo has the semblance of an ancient bridal crown. I fancy the petalled headdress once belonging to a freckle-skinned silvestrian queen. Fair of hair and fair of hand, this temperate monarch passes unremembered in woodland song or Marcher lore, a victim of history's fascination with the victorious and vainglorious.

I picture her rustic kingdom quietly contained amid these neglected, Neolithic hills, a rare refuge of peace in tumultuous times. Her loyal citizens would not have minded that their queen lacked the bridle of fame or fortune, believing that to be graced by one so fine was the very best of grace itself.

Rob continues to brush out the fire, collecting the burned remains from the chimney in a coal shovel before tipping it into a plastic bag. He is careful that not a single speck should escape. So intent is he on the task that he doesn't look up. With nothing to break my daydreaming, I indulge my musings a minute more.

Stirred by the spirit of the place, the image of a bluebell palace pops into my head, the foot of the queen upon the threshold and her floral crown upon her head. I'd like to think her royal residence was housed upon the hillock behind, home to an ancient Iron Age fort and a panoramic view. Or else a fortress deep within a forest, in a glade beside a gushing stream. Wading the Wye and up into the hills her subjects would come, beating a path to its door. Men and beasts alike, striding along hidden pathways through the heather and purple moor grass, drawn onward by the sweet sound of merriment from its hawthorn halls.

I know Layla made the wreath. Another, larger version hangs in their living room. Until recently she was growing fresh-cut flowers to sell at Hay market. Large beds, now mostly gone to seed, continue to give their sledge-run garden its shape. Yet I prefer my imagined version of events. I relish the image of a woodland people once living harmoniously in these same hills. Just as I revel in the thought of Rob and Layla accidentally happening upon the crown of a long-forgotten queen. One of their girls stumbling across it while scrabbling under a hedge, perhaps. Or while digging for worms under a mossy rock.

Almost everything in the bus has a story to it. In that sense, its decoration could be considered organic. The cylindrical Timemaster clock by the reversing mirror, diligently calculating departure times and marking the march of the years. The key in the ignition, sparking the engine to life on a thousand wintery mornings. The peaked cap hanging from its peg, property of the German bus driver whose name adorns it: Herr Menke; employee number 54. The driving wheel, its rubber grip worn thin at ten minutes to two. The tabletops, salvaged from the wood pile. The tin kettle on the gas-stove, hissing with gossip once secretly shared. The original silver lettering above the windscreen – 'You Are Travelling Overland Majestically' – revealing the riddle of the Panorama's christening.

'Wow, Rob,' I splutter, forcing myself back into the present. 'This place is great.'

'Like it, do yer?' he says. 'Good thing too. You should!'

The boast is in jest and I laugh. Rob is a man blissfully devoid of arrogance. It's a rare and redeeming quality, and one that immediately warms people to him.

He beckons me to take a seat on the Majestic Bus's cushioned corner unit, and I return to the middle of the bus and sit down. The window opposite falls at eye level and offers an unbroken view. The panelled glass is new. It runs the length of what once were three rows of passenger seats. The width is inch perfect, the vista fully framed from eastern glen to western vale. It's as if the window were the permanent feature of the piece and the rolling landscape just a conjurer's trick to fill the empty glass.

'Take a look at that. Beautiful, innit?' Rob pipes up.

He is not wrong. Fields and trees, sheep and sky, fences and footpaths, all combine and coalesce on the window-pane's transparent canvass. By rights, the picture should be chaotic. Wild hedgerows make darting, squiggling runs towards the tree-crested horizon. The farmer's fields shrink and bloat, blindly led by the contoured countryside. It is all dips and folds. There isn't a straight line to be seen, not even a stretched telephone wire.

The disarray works, however, and does so wondrously. For out of the seed-blown bedlam, an uncommon beauty bursts. From anarchy comes structure; from clutter, compo-sure. Simple yet complete, it takes an artist's eye to know the hows and whys of such a marvel. Logically, computational-ly, such symmetry should not be. Unity of form should no more spring from so confused a composition than darkness should beget light. There it is, though, plain as day: a scene of consummate concord.

Signs of nature's febrile abandon do not disappear. Weeds grow. Trees tumble. Walls collapse. Yet somehow the win-dow glass blurs their edges smooth. All become one, a merged and magnificent whole.

I shift forward in the seat, rest the back of my head against the cushions and kick out my legs. For the briefest of moments, I wish for such a window, for such a view.

'We weren't sure about much at the beginning,' says Rob, looking up from the stove. 'I always knew this is where I wanted the bus to be, though. Right here, on this spot, so people could sit where you're sitting now and take in all this.'

He levers himself up from his position by the fire and joins me in peering out at the landscape. We're both silent for a while. In a fold of the hill in the half-distance, a wisp of chimney smoke climbs up into the pale, late-winter sky. The house from which it emerges is hidden. I think again of the bluebell palace and involuntarily glance back at the circular wreath. It remains fixed in place, like a talisman against the plain glass, hinting at the ethereal and the blossoming promise of spring.

Rob strikes a match and lights the fire. He bends and blows a little, waiting a moment for the flame to catch fully, then shuts the stove door and gathers up the newspaper. With his spare hand he picks up his sweeping brush and a plastic bag containing the ashes from the grate.

'Right, job done,' he says. I follow him towards the exit and down the steps. He closes the door behind us and wipes his hands once more on his trousers. 'Time for a cuppa tea, methinks.'

We head across to the caravan house.

*

Layla is in the kitchen putting the last touches to a lemon cake. Meri is lying on the floor beside the sofa. The infant is all smiles. Rob picks her up in his arms, and promptly puts her down again. 'Someone needs a nappy change,' he says. He heads through to the bedroom to collect the wipes and a changing mat.

'Tea? Coffee?' Layla asks.

A coffee would be great, I say. She puts the kettle on the hob and finds a cafetière. I ask how she's doing. Everything is fine, she says. 'Touch wood. Meri is sleeping well. She's got a good appetite. Some of the newborn clothes are already getting too small because she's growing so fast.'

And her girls, have they both taken well to the new arrival? 'Goldie absolutely loves her,' she replies. 'She thinks she's a cuddly toy.' Tilda has taken a little more time to come round, but then she has her own issues to work through right now. 'Nothing serious, just your average eight-year-old going on thirteen.' Rob and she are learning to ride out the tantrums. 'It's all fine,' she reiterates.

From certain people, the insistence on all being well might have the ring of denial to it. Living with three kids in a small space has to be stressful, even if the children are total angels. The baby still wants feeding in the middle of the night. The older girls still need to be coaxed out of bed in the morning, and then dressed, breakfasted and driven to school. The bus still has to be cleaned, the sheets and children's clothes washed, the welcome cake made, the email enquiries answered, the garden kept, the chickens fed before the girls are picked up and fed, bathed and put to bed and the cycle begins again.

Layla, however, is remarkably determined and resourceful, which helps see her through. She also knows her own mind. She doesn't do mums-and-tots groups, just as she kept clear of antenatal classes. There are no parenting books gracing the shelves and no Mumsnet fora open in her internet browser. She has Rob and her own maternal instinct. Together, that's support enough.

More than anything, she is fully cognisant of the choices they have made and the implications these entail. The life they have is no accident. Arguably, it's as curated as the bus. They knew when they moved here that if they ran out of milk or nappies, then the nearest shop would be a twenty-

minute drive away. They were aware that if the diesel gen-
erator were to break down it would mean hand-washing
the sheets or travelling all the way to the laundrette in
town.

By the same token, she and Rob also knew they would
have the independence to do what they wanted, when they
wanted. They aren't shirkers. As with all their other previous ventures, they built up the bus business off their own
backs. And they pay their own way. There are no benefit
cheques arriving in the post when bookings slow up.

The upside is manifest: they control their own agendas
and can shape their own destinies. For that reason, their
girls can be raised in open countryside where the air is clean
and adventures ever-present. As parents, they can both be
on hand to share in their childhoods. The girls need never
hear words like 'boss', 'office', 'commute', 'childcare'. No
minder will ever pick them up from school or cook their
tea. No babysitter will ever tuck them in at night.

It is this willingness to be different and to chart their own
course that I find so refreshing about Rob and Layla. They
could easily be working low-wage jobs, striving to meet
their house repayments, returning home at night to a
cramped city flat. Or, just as easily, I suppose, they could be
high-flyers jetting off around the world on company
business.

Instead, they started by opting for the life they wanted
and worked back from there, devising a way to make it
happen. Emma and I can empathise. Although our vision of
what that ideal life looks like may be slightly different, our
rationale for moving here has much in common.

The Marches, in this sense, is a broad and accommodating
church. Culturally, the area is remarkably non-dogmatic. It

allows you the space and freedom to do your own thing, to explore your own path. Being non-conventional is actively encouraged, in fact. It's a place where every other person seems to be embarking on their own project or running their own venture. One incomer I know has set up a lavender farm deep in the hills. Another runs a Buddhist retreat.

Of course, not everyone is like this. There are plenty of folk living ordinary lives, happily clocking in and clocking out. The point is that there is licence here to do otherwise. In that respect, it reminds me a lot of Argentina, where everyone is always experimenting with the new and reinventing the old.

'Do you take sugar?' Layla asks.

'No, thanks. Just a bit of milk.'

She places the cup on the table in front of me and returns to the kitchen to put the cake in the oven.

The kitchen occupies a small internal alcove at the edge of the twin caravan. Beneath a large window that looks out onto the garden below stands a small plywood unit with flamingo-pink doors. Adjacent to it sits a 1950s kitchen sink that Rob picked up on eBay. The cooker is similarly sourced. Above it, where you might expect an extractor hood, hangs a rack of china mugs. Beside it, boxes of herbal teas rest on a shelf.

On the opposite wall stands a kitchen dresser, its doors painted a milky white and its upper shelves weighed down with saucepans. An overlapping display of old photographs covers its midsection, creating a wallpaper of flash-brightened smiles and red-dotted eyes. The remains of Layla's cake-baking cover the wooden work surface: sieve, mixing bowl, grater, flour. She begins to tidy them up.

Between the cupboard and the oven is an empty doorway that leads into a narrow corridor. A small bathroom lies straight ahead, with the main bedroom off to the left. Goldie's box-shaped bedroom is reached via her parents' room, while Tilda's bedroom is located at the far end of the living room. It doubles as the girls' play area.

That's the house, half a dozen small to middling-sized rooms. A raised decking area outside the front door provides some additional space in the summer. The only stairs in the whole place are the three or four that lead up to the deck from the sloping driveway below.

With Rob still on nappy-changing duties and Layla clearing up the kitchen, I kill time by scanning the decorations on the wall. Children's drawings compose the bulk of what's on show. Observed together, the artwork acts as a sort of childhood retrospective, building up from a toddler's crayon squiggles on a blank page through to well-crafted and clearly discernible depictions of cartoon cats.

Beside the latter is a short story. The square paragraph of text is printed on a white sheet and mounted on yellow card. 'Mad Town', the title reads in bold Helvetica script. The story describes the life of Turbo Tom, who dashes across the city and enjoys eating flying pop. He has one friend, Egg Eater, who works on a farm and whose favourite animals are chickens. This is despite not having any chickens of her own. The tale ends abruptly with the author's name: 'Matilda'.

I reread it, intrigued in particular by the character of Egg Eater. In such a short space, she opens up a Pandora's Box of ethical and psychological dilemmas. How, for example, does her proclaimed passion for chickens fit with an egg-based diet? Is Egg Eater unaware that she's wolfing down her favourite animal's progeny? If so, are we to suppose that a harsh coming-of-age is heading her way?

'Put a log on the fire, could you, Rob?' Layla shouts from around the corner.

'Give us a sec, I'm just finishing up with Meri,' he replies, turning to the infant and asking which of the two Babygros she wants. Pink or white? The girl giggles, all dimples and delight for her father. He opts for white.

'I hope Tilda got a good mark for this,' I say, loud enough for both parents to hear.

'Yeah, top of the class,' Rob and Layla reply in unison.

It's a habit they have, this tendency to say the same thing at the same time. Or a gift, I guess. They complete one another's sentences as well. One will start and then, if they pause or stutter, the other will carry on. It's entirely natural. I doubt very much they even realise that they do it.

Layla continues with the theme, describing in detail how her daughters are doing at school, the subjects they enjoy, the feedback from the teachers at parents' evenings, the friendship dynamics in the classroom, the house rules they have about homework.

Education is clearly important to her. She wants her children to enjoy learning and she's happy that they do. A picture of Tilda and Goldie with their fellow pupils at Gladestry Primary School adorns the front of a storage cupboard beside the main door. Three rows of identically attired little ones line up in the playground in front of a brick classroom. They all sport beaming smiles. Collectively, they would just about squeeze into a single class of a large inner-city primary.

In Layla's case, she left school before her eighth birthday. Her parents were hippies, part of a wave of US-inspired counterculturalism that swept Britain in the late sixties and early seventies. They moved down to the Welsh Marches from London before Layla was born. They weren't the only ones. A hotchpotch of other like-minded folk had begun to take up residence in the hills hereabouts as well. Bohemian, alternative types, all of them long-haired and slightly louche.

Her parents lived in a quasi-commune close to Hay Bluff at first, where commons rights ruled and magic mushrooms sprang. After a while, they separated themselves off, both from collective living and from one another. Her father took up residence in a variety of benders, barns and caravans dotted about the place, while her mother rented a succession of dilapidated cottages in the hills. Both lived on the dole, a habit they have proudly retained most of their non-working lives.

The couple rejected conventional aspirations such as paid employment, house ownership and holidays by the sea as the corrupting artifices and duplicitous deceits of an oppressive economic hegemony. Ruses to keep the Establishment sitting pretty and the proletariat sitting quiet. All while the planet spirals into a nuclear-powered descent towards Armageddon and the next great extinction. More free love is what we need, they maintained. Not more power or ambition, and certainly not more 'stuff'.

Formal schooling, with its bias towards rules and hierarchy, was a piece of this same puzzle. The instrumental piece, the foundation upon which all the system's building blocks would rest. Generation after generation, packed off with their lunch boxes to be trained in conformity, compliance and consent.

Layla recalls her father always having run-ins with the

teachers. After one particular row, he withdrew her and her brother from school completely. She can't remember what the argument was about now. Something about her brother, most probably. He was dyslexic, but the condition went undetected and he was branded a trouble-maker instead. The two siblings never went back. They dropped out of the system and, the way Layla tells it, the system more or less dropped them in turn.

With no one to teach her, Layla read. Books, magazines, comics, whatever she could lay her hands on. She loved reading. Novels, most of all. In the pages of fiction, she discovered a manna that sank as protein shots into her soul, feeding her hopes, nourishing her dreams. In the characters of books, she also found friends. In their plot lines, solace. In their endings, succour. Books offered her escape, a wormhole to distant lands where dragons and princes roamed and cities stretched far into the sky.

What she relished most about books was their ability to fill the loneliness. She may have been free as a bird growing up, but it was a sense of solitude that marked her childhood most. She and her brother didn't go into town much because the local kids would round on them and the shopkeepers would eye them suspiciously. Back in the early 1980s, to be a hippie in these parts was to be tagged a 'druggie' or a 'drop-out'. Such labels applied to the offspring of hippies too. The sins of the fathers, etcetera.

For all its celebration of the alternative, Marcher tolerance for outsiders clearly had its limits. Despite his inclusive spirit, Kilvert was not immune to petty prejudices. He found tourists 'noxious', for example. Yet his real ire was saved for the Nonconformists. He was only too ready to hold Chapel folk responsible for stealing the bells from

Llanigon's parish church. When 'some Barbarian' cut down the beautiful silver birches on Little Mountain, he quickly fingered the probable culprit: 'A dissenter no doubt – probably a Baptist.'

Such feelings are echoes of the Anglican establishment to which Kilvert belonged, and go a long way to explaining why his curacy overlapped with the fabled first voyage of Welsh Nonconformists to the New World. The 162 émigrés set off with three ministers aboard a tea clipper to Argentina, of all places, to the windswept plains of Patagonia, as remote a wilderness as they could ever hope to find.

In general, however, Kilvert's reaction to outsiders was more one of curiosity than distrust or dislike. In rural Victorian society, where everyone had their place and new faces were few and far between, the sight of a stranger was first and foremost a novelty.

One sunny July day, the *Diary* describes Kilvert stumbling upon a man lolling in the long grass on Mouse Castle, a wooded hill on the Hay side of the river. A troupe of children with rosy flushed cheeks are frolicking around him, all of them 'full of fun and larks as wild as hawks'. The man is wearing a velveteen jacket and the diarist struggles desperately to place him. The lithe, lissom youths, he decides, are like young antelope and fawns. So alien is the whole party to him that he concludes with characteristic romanticism that they must have fallen from the sky.

Layla's father and his fellow hippies must have caused similar confusion on their arrival. Not that their social unorthodoxies were all so unusual. I recently spoke with an ex-hippie from the same era, who squatted for several months in a dilapidated mud-floored barn high up in the

Black Mountains. She insisted that the living conditions among the hill farmers exceeded theirs for dirt and squalor.

Back then, electricity and running water had still to reach most outlying farms. The occupants of the neighbouring farmhouse – two bachelor brothers and their spinster sister – she described as living entirely on bread and jam and leaf tea. 'We all smelled,' the one-time hippy recalled. 'That's why they got on with us.'

Mutually dubious hygiene won't be the bonding agent for everyone, but the experience of *convivencia* is impossible without establishing some form of common ground. In its absence, there is nowhere to meet, no way of meaningfully coexisting. Those who by dint of background or temperament are not naturally like-minded have to discover ways to at least get along, if not necessarily to agree. To live between a widow and a plumber, as per Updike, is all well and good, but not if your neighbours spend their days hurling insults over the garden fence.

For Rob and Layla, neighbourly relations aren't a major concern. The farmer next door lives by himself and well out of earshot. Otherwise, they are more or less alone, marooned on the north side of their hill. Not that they're antisocial. They count a wide network of friends across the area. Yet living on an isolated smallholding means being content with your own company. In that respect, they're a tight unit, dependent on one another not only for when the boiler breaks or when the interminable winter cold feels never-ending.

'How long is it you guys been together?' I ask Layla.

The question is sparked by an unframed snap of their wedding that is stuck to the kitchen wall with Blu Tack.

The image shows them on a sun-drenched lawn, the brick-work of a walled garden in the background. Blonde, petite and blushing with joy, Layla looks positively Pre-Raphaelite, a fair Rosamund in a white summer slip, flowers woven into her hair. Standing at her side is Rob, an arm around her waist and a grin from ear to ear.

Layla does some quick mental arithmetic on her fingers. Twenty-one years, she calculates. 'Yeah, blimey, twenty-one years it'll be now.' Where did they meet? Rob was with his 'travelling crew' back then, she explains.

Leaving Meri on the floor, content in her freshly laun-dered white onesie, Rob picks himself up and approaches the table with his second-hand smartphone in his hand. He has just reconnected via Facebook with an old friend he hasn't heard from for years and years, he says, and shows me a photo that his old acquaintance had sent through.

The blurred image reveals about fifteen people standing in front of a battered old bus. They look undernourished and impossibly young, their hair matted and their clothes bedraggled. Several are smoking roll-ups. One has a child on her hip. In the foreground, a dog is smelling another dog's crotch. I remark how few of the men have beards. It was the early nineties then, Rob says, 'not a very beardy time'.

'Where's it taken?' I ask.

Down near Erwood, a village west of here on the banks of the Wye. They had pitched up in a lay-by beside the road for three or four months, he explains. Other than Wol, his new Facebook contact, he hasn't been in touch with most of them since. Rob points to a fresh-faced young man in the front row. 'Done lots of things, Wol has.' Rob doesn't embel-lish on what these might be.

'That's Muchie,' he continues, indicating another face in the crowd. He sighs heavily. 'He's dead. Massive heart attack in Brighton. She's dead too.' He points to the woman third from left. 'Remember her, Layels?'

Layla moves across from the kitchen to see the picture. She does, she says, although she hadn't heard about her having died. Rob is hazy on the details. 'Died in the public bogs in Glasgow, smack overdose.' That's what he heard. Although maybe she broke both her legs. 'Something about her, anyway, something bad.'

Layla was sixteen when she hit the road with Rob. Her parents had no objections to her travelling the country at the height of the rave scene, living on the road with an older guy. In fact, her father helped them negotiate the purchase of their caravan.

A vintage Eccles, sixty-five pounds, bought off a bloke in Hay called Boot. I can see it from where I'm sitting now, parked at the top of the garden under an awning that Rob built especially for it.

'Ah, blast, the lemon cake,' Layla blurts out, suddenly remembering her baking.

Rob jumps up and rushes over to the oven. He removes the cake and inspects it closely. It's a little burned but probably fine, he reckons. Layla gets up to check for herself. Then Meri starts crying and Layla returns to the sofa to feed her.

I mention to Rob that I'd be interested to see the rest of their plot. There's a second bus parked up by the entrance, on a narrow patch of molehilled scrub between the driveway and the stone barn. Could he show me? 'Happy to,' he says, and we head outside.

A curved silver trim runs from the front of the bus to the

back, starting just below the passenger windows before arc-
ing in a graceful wave down toward the tailpipe. The bus is
painted a faded cornflower blue below the trim and a
diluted ox-blood red above. Both colours are flaking badly,
the rust beneath breaking out like fungal spores. Several
windows are broken and the skylights are missing. Just
inside the main door there's a hole in the wooden floor big
enough for a small horse to fall through. The bus looks as
though it's been dredged up from the sea.

It's a Thames Yeoman 1962, Rob tells me as we walk
down from the house. He bought it from a guy in Bromyard.
I ask if Rob had ever ridden in one during his traveller days.
He almost did, he says. He had once tried to cadge a lift in
one from North Yorkshire down towards Bristol. The
owner couldn't get the engine to start though, so Rob missed
the opportunity. 'Ended up hitching instead.'

On reaching the bus, Rob motions for me to ascend the
steps. I enter ahead of him. 'Watch where you tread,' he
shouts up. I quickly see why. Apart from the hole, the floor
is covered with sharp fragments of fallen plaster and broken
ply. Bare nails poke through the woodwork. Any exposed
metal is barbed and brittle with reddish rust. A waft of
mouldy damp carries through from the back, the aroma
brushed forward by a cloud of buzzing houseflies.

Rob coughs apologetically. 'So, as you see, there's quite a
lot of work to do.'

I look about me and agree. But then he's done it before, I
say. 'It shouldn't be too hard to make it ship-shape, right?'
I'm trying to sound upbeat.

He shrugs. 'No, it shouldn't,' he agrees. Although it's a
big job. He starts pointing out the challenges. The relatively
low ceiling, the curved sides, the undecided location. 'It's a

big job,' he repeats. Still, if they could turn it around, then they could potentially double their income. Once he's paid off what they borrowed for the first project, that is.

'How much was that, then?' I ask.

''Bout ten grand,' he says. 'Not including the bus itself. That cost me – what did it cost now? – about seven hundred quid, I got it for.'

The idea of converting the Bedford into accommodation hadn't initially occurred to Rob. He bought it on a whim after taking Tilda for a ride on a vintage locomotive. The smell of the train's worn diesel engine took him back to his hobo fleet of dog-eared vehicles cranking into life, exhaust fumes rising in the cold morning air, leaving him with a hankering to get his hands on an old bus again. He'd use it as a family camper, he thought.

He doesn't have any regrets though? I ask. Oh no, he says. And the rental business is doing okay? Sweet, he replies. 'People seems to get a real kick out of the whole self-sufficient thing.' When their guests come to leave, they frequently say they're planning to put a wood-stove in their bathroom or start growing their own veg in future. This always tickles Rob and Layla, the idea that their way of life might be rubbing off on other people.

Of course, a fair number don't 'get it', he admits. He couches the final phrase in crook-fingered quotation marks, as though he knows the 'it' is nothing more complex than a bus in a field with some minimal comforts. At the same time, he's also aware that selling rustic minimalism to town-ie types requires dressing everything up with back-to-nature branding and vague promises of metaphysical renewal.

They have only ever had one instance of really negative feedback, Rob says, shaking his head in exasperation. 'Bet you can't guess who that was from?' I can't, but I take it to be a rhetorical question so await the answer.

'Other travellers,' he says. He's right: I wouldn't have guessed. A friend had posted about the Majestic Bus in a closed Facebook group called Bus Love. We got ripped to shreds, Rob says. Money-grabbing capitalists, they called him and Layla. Trading off their lifestyle. Ripping people off. 'Proper trolling, it was.' In retrospect, he finds it amusing, although it upset them both at the time.

The picture of Rob and Layla as totems of capitalism almost makes me laugh. The whole idea is totally absurd. Their stone barn lies in disrepair because they don't have a penny to renovate it. Layla's flowerbeds lie untended because she's cancelled most of her gardening work to look after her baby. I love the home they've created for themselves, but, as Rob himself admits, it's still 'a glorified caravan'.

With Layla's upbringing and Rob's traveller experience, it could have been very different. They had an established crew, after all. A ready-made group of accordant companions, all of them carefree wanderers, kindred voyagers, not a stitch of responsibility or a fixed abode among them. Everyone around them 'in their game', as Updike would say.

Strange as it sounds, the vitriol they received from the Bus Love community shows how far they have come, how much they have travelled. The Marches are, in their own way, their Ipswich, MA. Most markedly for Rob, the former traveller from Suffolk. For Layla, it's more complex. She grew up here. Yet the world she inhabited as a child is demonstrably different from the one she has created for herself since.

In the Marches, people place hippies into one of two broad categories: the 'hardcore' ones, who live in the hills and cut themselves off; and the 'chequebook' ones, who dread their hair but have a Mac laptop in their insulated yurt. Neither label fits Layla. She's like one of old Hannah Whitney's fairies, dancing freely to a tune all of her own.

*

We climb down from the bus and take a stroll through the garden. A small digger is parked across the driveway. It's borrowed from a friend in preparation for the earth-removal work required for the new nursery. A shipping container runs along the hedge by the access road, its contents hermetically sealed. Next to it is a trampoline with high netted sides, beside which is a polytunnel that, like the flowerbeds, is showing signs of recent neglect.

Moving back up the bank towards the house, we pass the veg patch. Tilda recently helped plant some spuds, Rob says, pointing to a section of freshly dug earth. He lists the other vegetables he plans to grow: broad beans, French beans, cabbages, courgettes, carrots, garlic. They don't sell anything, he clarifies. 'It's all for us to scoff.'

Our tour is over. Before heading inside, I turn to take in the view one last time. I gaze out over the garden and the derelict barn, over the bramble bushes and hawthorn hedge, and out to the sheep-spotted fields and whale-shaped drumlins beyond. I soak it in, guarding the scene for future savour.

Rob sees me sizing up the vista and second-guesses what's going through my mind: I'd like a piece of it for myself. My own Upper Tumble. We could sell Pottery Cottage, buy ourselves a field, go off-grid, let the children roam. He has seen it before. The dreamy glaze, the wistful longing, the sprinkles of stardust.

Hands thrust into his pockets, T-shirt hanging loose, Rob leans his elbows on the wooden railing that borders the porch deck and joins me looking out into the distance.

'There aren't many people like who live in places like this,' he says, eyes staring fixedly ahead. 'People come here and say it's wonderful and all that, but they wouldn't actually do it. It's too . . .' He breaks off, looking for the right word. '. . . too blooming hard.'

He recounts their first winter with Tilda as a baby, no proper heating, all of them sleeping curled up in a ball by the fire, ice on the windows. It was minus fifteen Celsius outside. He makes a sweeping gesture with his hand. 'There's all sorts of stuff you don't have living here.'

Kicking off his wellies, he opens the door to the house and walks through to the kitchen, where he washes his hands and starts preparing a salad for lunch. I follow him in.

Layla is still on the sofa, Meri asleep in the crook of her arm. Putting down the baby, she wanders over to the kitchen to offer Rob a hand. He passes her some peppers and asks if she could chop them.

Conscious of her mother's sudden absence, Meri stirs, letting out a doleful whine. Rob puts down the lettuce he's holding and goes over to reassure her. The two trade gurgling noises for a while as he tries to coax her back to sleep.

I cross over to the kitchen and enquire if I can help. It's fine, Layla says. She invites me to pour myself a glass of water and I stand by the kitchen unit. Meri has quietened and Rob moves off to check on the fire. He sees the log basket is running low and tells Layla he'll pop across to the barn to get some more wood. Picking up his faithful deer-stalker, he opens the door and steps out.

I mention our conversation about the Bus Love incident to Layla. She rolls her eyes. It was pretty nasty at the time, she admits. She pauses, the chop-chop-chop of her knife on the board momentarily stilled. If I really want to know how she feels about it, she says, looking at me over her shoulder, then she's more irritated by the whole thing than upset.

She resumes her chopping, slicing faster and harder now, her cheeks flushing salmon pink. For a minute or two it seems that's her final word on the subject. The peppers cut, she brushes the thin strips along the board with the flat of the knife and into the salad bowl.

'They are forever talking about loving others and being open to ideas,' she then says, turning round to look at me straight. 'But, honestly, if you were to ask me, I'd say it's quite a negative and close-minded place they're coming from.'

Rob comes back in, his arms laden with logs. He places them as quietly as he can in the basket so as not to wake Meri. I finish my glass of water as Layla moves the salad bowl to the sideboard of the Welsh dresser.

They have a friend coming for lunch, she tells me. Someone she knew when she was growing up. Layla gives me her back story, about how she had moved away for uni-versity, got married, built a life for herself in the West Midlands, and about how she had now decided to move back after her father's death and how she had picked up a dream part-time job with the National Parks.

I reflect on how the area seems to draw people back, and Layla agrees. It's to do with the landscape, she thinks. 'You know, the hills, the tumbledown cottages, just the beauty of the place really – when I moved away, that always stayed with me.'

Rob has sat down at the living-room table and is glancing through the old photo album that Layla brought through from the bedroom. He calls her over. 'Remember her?' He points a finger at the picture of a woman with spiked pink hair. 'Wow,' Layla gasps, turning towards the window to examine the image in the light. 'Punk Annie. Now, that takes me back.'

For a moment they flick through the pages of the album together, Layla standing at Rob's shoulder, both of them sighing and smiling and shouting out an occasional name, lost in their own joint memories.

Layla returns to the sideboard and starts hunting for the ingredients to make a salad dressing. The pictures have put her in mind of another draw to the area. The people around here, she says. 'They're another big reason I came back.'

I ask what she means, conscious that most of her old crowd moved on long ago. The mix of people living here, she says: it's grown much wider. Before, it was basically farmers and hippies. Now, there are all sorts. Rob backs her up, pointing out that further along on their same hill live a photographer, a writer and an IT expert. 'All of them incomers but pleasant enough.'

Their observations give me heart. My experiences at the Rhydspence and among the Young Farmers had exposed me to worlds I'd hitherto not known and ways of being I'd not previously encountered. Meeting Rob and Layla took me out of my bubble of personal experience once more.

Illuminating though these encounters were, they all left me perplexed as to where my place might lie. If I didn't fit into any of these camps, if I wasn't ever to be embedded in the inner sanctum of the 'local', did that mean I'd be left stranded on the edge, my aspirations for an experience of community 'knit' dashed?

Not necessarily, Layla and Rob seemed to be suggesting. The Marches, as with almost anywhere else, is made up of an amalgamation of different subgroups. All have their own norms and nuances. Conforming excessively to one leaves you in danger of closing off avenues into others. It's a form of belonging, but a very narrow one. The Bus Love syndrome, in other words.

I'm aware their lunch guest will be arriving any minute and it's time I took my leave. I've brought my running kit with me and I ask Layla where I might get changed. She looks at me quizzically, just as the farmer's wife did on our first day, and then points me to the bathroom.

A few minutes later, having thanked them profusely and wished them well with the new bus, I am jogging away down their rutted track. Soon their caravan house and majestic buses are behind me. I press on, bound for home, the silvestrian queen singing in my ear.

When I enter Clyro an hour or so later, the village feels like a hubbub of activity compared to the solitude of the hillside home. My run has given me space to think. Kilvert's footsteps have so far taken me to a variety of contiguous, confined worlds. Do they ever meet, though, and what happens when they do?

To answer that, I realised I'd have to go to the miniature melting pot of 'town'. And not just on any day. A Thursday, it would have to be. For the week's fourth day is when the trumpets sound and the clans gather. Thursday is market day in Hay.

5

The Thursday Market

When people were going to market on Thursday mornings they would exhort one another to come back in good time lest they should be led astray by the Goblin Lantern, and boys would wear their hats the wrong way lest they should be enticed into the fairy rings and made to dance.

Kilvert's Diary, 14 October 1870

Both men are dressed in jeans, heavy shirts and hard-wearing construction gloves. Andy, a thickset Londoner with white stubble and a genial smile, has added a striped beanie to the uniform. From underneath the hat, wisps of grey emerge around his ears. He and his assistant look tired. Above their heads, the town's clock tower is creeping towards 6 a.m.

They are midway through constructing a rectangular metallic frame. With brittle poles for legs and four plywood tabletops for a thorax, it resembles a gigantic stick insect. Only flatter, and with yellow rubber non-slip pads for feet.

The invertebrate market stall stands stationary on the junction between Lion Street and Broad Street. Propped up beside it on the tarmac is a red metallic road sign, the frame rusted and chipped. Two lines of white lettering run across the top. 'Ffordd', reads the first. 'Ar Gau', the second. A translated version appears beneath. Somehow the English words feel more perfunctory and considerably less polite: 'Road Closed'.

As yet, there is no one to pay heed to the bilingual injunction but us. The town is still snoring. It's too early for work, too early for morning dog-walking, too early for much other than soft-duvet sleep.

Somewhere in this Marcher Llareggub a friendless alarm clock has probably just begun to bleep or a kettle clicked into life, its steamy hiss waking the cat. The town's dawn murmurings must be behind soundproofed walls, however, because here on the street all is quiet, the only noise an avian canticle from the telephone-wire choir overhead.

Andy takes another wooden tabletop from his stack, stored in a trailer hitched to an SUV. Each measures about five feet by three. Kaley usually sets up the weekly market with him, but he has hurt his back. Kaley's replacement doesn't say much, other than that he needs coffee and wants his bed. Andy, by contrast, is the talkative type. He worked Camden Market for many years, trading woollen Afghan socks, mostly. Now, he runs his own locally based market-garden business as well as overseeing the Thursday market.

I ask how Hay compares to Camden. 'Quiet,' he says, and laughs. It's not just Hay: all rural markets around here are struggling. He blames the supermarkets, especially now they offer home delivery. 'Llandrindod market has, what, five or six stalls maybe, and Brecon and Builth are on their uppers.' So, by comparison, he'd say Hay is in 'pretty good shape considering'.

Andy sucks in his teeth when I ask about the forecast for the day. Rain scheduled, he says: showers early morning, gradually deteriorating. He prods at the heavy waxy covering that stretches tight across the roof of the stall. A good tarp will keep the rain off, he assures me. A cold wind is what market traders really hate. 'It's a right bitch, the wind, no mistake.'

We both look up at the insipid sky. A trickle of watery grey light is just breaking through the cloud cover. A feeling of foreboding pervades. Andy gives the metal frame a final shake to check that it's secure and then claps his gloved hands together to brush off the dust. That's them about done, he says. Then it's back at four o'clock this afternoon to take it all down again. His assistant says his farewells and saunters off down the road. His bed, he reiterates, is calling.

Andy leans into the trailer and rearranges the remaining poles and tabletops. As he's finishing up, he takes me through their setting-up routine. They always start in Memorial Square, he says, just below the castle. A stone cross to the veterans of the two world wars gives the tarmac square its official name, although most of the town's residents refer to it by its everyday function: 'the car park'.

He starts counting off the stallholders on his fingers. There's Craig the Veg, who takes four tables. Chris and Nicky the Cheese, they take three. They've been coming every week for over thirty years. There's the Fish Man too. He's another long-timer. He parks up in his own van and sells directly out of that. So no need for a table. Same with Jason the Sock Man, who brings his own trestles with him. He has the spot right in the middle of the car park. Andy lists his inventory with an expert's appraisal. Multipack work socks, walking socks, sports socks, kids' socks, ladies' socks, tights, stockings.

Then come the one-man bands. They just need a single-table stall each. The numbers fluctuate a little from week to week. Andy can generally bank on half-a-dozen regulars turning up. 'Who would that be, then?' I ask. So the Card Lady, the Florist, the Pot Plant People, the Jewellery Girl, the Bag Lady, Primrose Organic. He ticks them off one by one. Some traders move on. Like the Burger Van Man who used to come here but found more trade in Hereford. Others chirp up and try their hand. Russ the Knife, for example. He's new. He calls himself Russ the Knife, Andy explains, but he sells saucepans as well.

The only other mainstay in the car park is Tom's Junk Van. They don't set up for him because he comes in his own removals lorry. He parks up behind Chris the Veg, over in the far corner. His speciality is auction salvage, the assorted fruits of which spill out directly onto the tarmac: rickety chairs, wooden bedsteads, mirrors, picture frames, second-hand books, rusty gardening tools, metal stepladders, china vases, lamps and shades, bins and baskets, watering cans, book-ends, bicycle racks. A marvellous medley of miscellanea.

Afterwards, Andy moves across to the Cheese and Butter Markets. The two structures are distinctive for being covered, permanent and close to 200 years old. The first abuts the car park, just behind the fishmonger's van. Constructed on the site of the ancient Guildhall, it's recently undergone a comprehensive restoration. A tableau of black-and-white photographic images along with accompanying text describes the market's 800-year history, from the town's beginnings as a fortified settlement to the steam-driven excitements of the Victorian era.

A private door to the side of the twin-arched entrance leads to a steep set of stairs and an old meeting room above. Once a manorial court, where farmers and market traders paid their taxes and fines, the Cheese Market has seen life as a theatre, a Masonic lodge and, in more recent times, a Catholic place of worship. The building's revamp has led to its latest guise as a holiday flat, equipped with a king-size bed and matching turrets directly outside the window.

Alongside is the Butter Market, a stubby flat-roofed building whose stone-plinth support columns and open sides give it a Romanesque feel. The effect is enhanced by its semi-elevated setting, the consequence of one side being three or four feet lower than the other. A wide walkway lined with a small gallery of shops runs along the upper side. Beneath is a truncated road down the middle of which the townspeople wander at will, the bullying motorcar for once compelled to wait.

Andy tackles the Cheese Market first. It's the smaller of the two, accommodating just four stallholders. Tree the Coffee Roaster and Tim the Jam occupy the left-hand side and request just one table each. Stretching along the rear arch, immediately opposite the entrance, is Joe of 100% Hay, an organic veg producer. He requires two tables. Then next to him, on the right-hand side, is Bernie the Baker, who takes two as well.

In the Butter Market, which is probably double the size of its neighbour, a food theme also predominates. Among the regulars are Kate the Bread, who does a popular line in Danish pastries and raisin whirls, and Chris George, a butcher whose family has been in the meat business since Kilvert's day. Some of the other habitual stallholders include the French Patisserie Man (who is genuinely French), the Wool Woman, Lewis the Woodworker, the Parkinson People with their preserves and, last but not least, the lovely ladies of the Women's Institute. Most require just one table, except for the butcher, who takes three.

The third and last section of the market runs up from where we're standing beneath the clock tower at the opening of Lion Street's wide estuary mouth. From here, the road curves up past Golesworthy's outdoor store, then

narrows as it heads upstream past Richard Booth's bookshop and Bartrum's stationers, Hay Deli and the newsagent's, before splitting off at Murder and Mayhem
bookshop into divergent tributaries, all of them narrower
still. The stalls run for only fifty yards or so before banking
off up a steep alleyway towards the Cheese Market.

Occupying the largest pitch is the stick insect, whose
tabular body is divvied up between Alex Gooch, Artisan
Breadmaker, with his prize-winning sourdoughs, and two
meat specialists, one selling 'Hungarian Smoked Delicacies',
the other hogget and mutton. The remaining stalls line
either side of the pavement. Russ the Knife, Avril the
Flowers, Andrew CD, Julie the Soaps, Malcolm the Carpets
and the Falafel Fellow, who, unlike the now-departed
Burger Van Man, does a roaring lunchtime trade.

With all the stalls now ready, I ask Andy when the
traders will start arriving. Not for at least an hour or more,
he tells me. I'll find Chris the Cheese setting up already,
although Andy warns me off disturbing him. 'He likes
everything so-so, you know.' Try the Butter Market, he suggests. 'Chris George gets here plenty early.'

He taps the back of the trailer and climbs into his 4x4.
'Rain,' he repeats, peering up at the sky once more and sniffing the air. 'Definitely, rain.'

*

Chris George is making toast. As the bread browns, he runs
his eye over a sheet of paper on the tabletop with a list of
customer orders. He calls this 'multitasking' and seems
pleased at his capacity for time-management.

Every week Hannah and Sal, who manage the stall during the day, arrive at 5.30 a.m. Chris meets them there, having driven over from Talgarth with the butcher's van. The three unload the bulky produce onto the tables opposite their stall, then transfer each item across to its allotted place. The trestles split roughly into thirds: fruit and root vegetables on the right, meat in the centre, and greens on the left. Three supermarket aisles compressed into one.

When the customers start filing through, Chris heads back to Talgarth where his father, Bryan, is currently at the helm of W. J. George Butchers, the family firm. Bryan is seventy-six years old and in no rush to give up his day job. Chris's father took over from his own father, who retired at seventy-five, but only so he could throw himself into a second career breeding racehorses. 'We don't retire early, us lot,' says Chris.

The ten employees at W. J. George know their meat. When Grandfather George took on the business from an uncle, Talgarth could count five butchers, three of whom had their own slaughterhouses. W. J. George is the only one to have kept with the tradition. It's also the only one still in business. Whether it's tunnel-boned lamb you're after or pork shanks or thick-cut chops or slow-cooking chuck steak, then Talgarth's old-school butcher's is widely recognised as the place to go.

Dylan Jones, editor of *GQ* magazine, is a big fan of the meatery. The media sophisticate, who has a holiday house nearby, tells a funny tale about being eyeballed by men with meat cleavers after asking for 'salt marsh lamb'. 'What's wrong with our grass-fed lamb?' came the stony response. His newspaper piece about the incident appeared under the title, 'Don't mess with the man in the apron.'

Chris has ditched his butcher's apron today in favour of a brown woollen jumper and red ski jacket. He's cheerful and chatty despite the early hour. He started at the market aged eighteen, he tells me. He's now fifty-one. There was a long wait to get a pitch back in those days. The town was crammed, he says, pointing out through the Butter Market pillars to the surrounding streets.

The last time he actually manned the stall was during Hannah's wedding. He forgets how long ago that was exactly, and shouts over to Hannah to ask. Almost a year, the younger woman responds from behind the stall where she's stacking a pile of cucumbers into a precarious triangle. 'Better than my first effort, then,' he shoots back. He chuckles, as does she.

Rosy-cheeked and energetic, Hannah has a full-time job at the local estate agent, although she takes Thursdays off to work the market. I'm intrigued why she keeps up with it. Aren't the early starts a killer? They are, she admits. Her feet ache by the end of the day, but working the market is something she has always enjoyed doing. It's nice to get out of the office, she admits. 'It's really sociable, as well. That's what I like the most.'

The toast pops up.

Chris extracts the two slices from the toaster, which he has rigged up to an extension cable underneath the table. The bread is hot and he juggles it from hand to hand until it's cool enough to butter. This is the team breakfast, he informs me, reaching for a knife and a pot of jam. Hannah wanders over to tell him that the stall is more or less finished. A couple of pre-orders to make up and then they'll be done.

As they're talking, a tall gentleman in a pink woollen hat walks in off the street. Chris strolls over and greets the man warmly. 'Come for Mrs Griffiths' order?' he asks. 'Aye,' says the man. Chris reaches behind the stall for the food parcel, which is neatly arranged in a flat cardboard box, the kind with small holes for handles that apples and oranges come in. He passes it to the man, who exchanges it for two banknotes from his wallet. 'Keeping busy?' the gentleman asks. 'Always busy, John,' replies the butcher, ever chirpy. He hands him his change. 'Got to keep busy,' the man says, 'that's the way it is.'

Regulars like John account for a good proportion of their trade, Chris tells me. He points to the vacuum-packed cuts of topside beef and pork tenderloin when I ask him what sells well. I look over to the severed animal parts wrapped in see-through tourniquets, the striated veins bulging against the polythene sheeting. It should be a hellish, morgue-like scene and yet it's not, overfamiliarity having inured us to the sight of so much raw, eviscerated flesh. 'People around here like a joint on a Sunday,' Chris observes. I nod, wondering if the same would be true if we had to butcher it ourselves.

Most folk usually pick up a few rashers of bacon too, he adds, his outstretched finger hovering over several deep rows of pinkish packets. Sausages, as well. All of them home-made. Pork and leek is today's special, according to a small blackboard sign on top of a glass-fronted cabinet in the centre of the table. Beside it is a second board giving details of the day's pie selection: steak and ale, steak and kidney, pork with jelly. The pies are mounted three high in tinfoil dishes along the cabinet's bottom shelf. On a narrower shelf above are eight Zeppelin-like black-pudding rinds, cinched at either end.

Tucked into the bottom corner of the cabinet, beside the pies, is a metal tray of faggots. '50p Each. 4 for £1.80' says the hand-written sign fixed to the glass front. 'OWN MADE', it adds. I have never knowingly eaten a faggot, a regional foodstuff made from pig's heart, belly fat and offal, all rolled into a ball and then coated in breadcrumbs. Pressed together in their tray, they could pass for scotch eggs. American tourists will frequently buy a faggot, Chris says. He's not sure why, although he suspects it's because the name amuses them.

Talk of faggots reminds me of a story that I'd heard second-hand about the Falafel Fellow. Week in, week out, an old farmer gent used to go to his stall for his market day lunch. 'Marvellous faggots, these,' the elderly Welshman remarks one time, a mistake that the stallholder feels honour bound to correct, explaining that falafels are made from chickpeas and spices. The old farmer never came back. I repeat the story to Chris, who chuckles. He can well imagine it, he says.

The three breakfasters turn out not to be the Butter Market's only early arrival. At the other end of the building, I see that Lucretia the Octogenarian's stall is also laid out. I wish the three luck for their day's sales and head over to introduce myself.

Lucretia is a petite woman with a sharp wit and a pencil-thin smile. Green highlights streak through her white bobbed hair. She could be Kilvert's friend old Hannah Whitney, I ponder.

I find her sitting patiently in a wheelchair, her legs tucked under the table and a thick blanket resting on her lap. She is accessorised entirely in green: so knitted green gloves, green brooch, green earrings, green neckerchief. Even her eye-brows are painted leek-green. Saving her from total meadowy monochrome is a collarless grey jacket with brocade strips around the buttons. She looks a card.

The sprightly stallholder is flanked by two men; her husband Woody, sitting on her left, and Simeon, her eldest son, standing to her right. 'Don't mind him,' Lucretia tells me, nudging her left elbow towards her spouse. 'Dad's got a bit forgetful,' she says.

Woody smiles out from beneath a black woolly hat. His kindly, narrow face is obscured from below by the zipped collar of a thick overcoat. This is also black. As are his over-sized gloves. His absence of colour contrasts so strongly with his wife's flamboyance that I wonder if it's not deliber-ate. A final, public gesture of his adoration for the woman who lightens his life.

Dad has had one or two previous 'incidences' on the drive over here, Simeon explains, a half-nod in the direction of his seated father. 'So I've said enough is enough, and I drive Mother in now.' In his mid-fifties, Simeon is a large, amic-able man and evidently an obliging son. He dresses up on a Thursday, exchanging his usual farm clobber for a shirt and jacket.

'He's all right,' Lucretia says, looking over lovingly to her partner of six decades. 'But he's not all right, if you know what I mean.'

Woody's dementia is not so advanced as to make him blind to the attention directed towards him. 'I've got a story to tell you,' he suddenly declares, his voice frail but perfectly clear. 'When I qualified to represent Great Britain in the World Ploughing Competition in Austria . . .' He peters out.

I feel awkward, partly on account of Woody's evident confusion, but mostly because of Lucretia, who is watching the man of her life and father of her four children slowly fade away in front of her.

Turning to Woody, I ask how he fared at the competi-tion. Did he win? 'No, no,' says Lucretia, replying on his behalf. 'Seventh, you were.' He doesn't respond. Instead, he leans back a little further in his chair, folds his hands in his

lap and stares out in front of him, a look of quiet content-
ment covering his face.

I glance down at Lucretia's array of produce. A cloth of
pink and purple petals covers the tabletop, which bows
under the weight of three days' worth of baking. The result
of her industry spills over the edges of shallow paper trays,
from greengage fruit pies and jam tarts to gingerbreads and
barra apple cakes.

A sticker with 'Lucretia' written on the top and the image
of a chocolate box cottage gives the name of the product and
its basic ingredients. Self-raising flour, sugar, butter, eggs and
water provide the base layer for almost everything. Treacle,
mixed spices, fruits and milk provide a second, differentiating tier. The Welsh cakes, I note, contain 'Sweet Snow'.

The price also appears on the label, written in pen. A puff
of smoke rises from the cottage chimney, suggesting cosiness
and simple domesticity. A separate green rectangular sticker
makes clear that 'Own Free Range Eggs Are Used' in the
cakes. The eggs that survived the cake mix are sold by the
half-dozen in cardboard egg boxes, row upon row of them.

The market's oldest vendor keeps a small semicircle of
space free in front of her. This way everything she needs is
within reach from her wheelchair. Her purple handbag,
cash box, glasses case and spiral-bound notebook with customers' orders. A list of names appears under the heading
'eggs'. One is already crossed off. There are separate orders
for a lemon and blackcurrant cake, and a sponge. 'Dial-a-
Ride' is scribbled into the margin. Last week, she made fifteen fruit cakes for a customer who was arranging a charity
event. She gave him a good price.

'You stay up all night on Wednesday, don't you, Mother?'
says Simeon, glancing at his mother with filial affection.

Lucretia doesn't drive, so it falls to 'Sim', as she calls him, to pick her up and drop her off. He leaves his home in Ross-on-Wye at around 4 a.m. and drives the twenty-five miles to the old family farm at Ty-Caradog in Michaelchurch Escley, where Rob pitched up with his traveller crew all those years ago. One of Simeon's younger brothers farms there now.

They are usually on the road again by half past five, the boot packed tight. Each and every Thursday, he says. Then, at nine o'clock on the dot, he takes his father to the Granary café for a full English breakfast. They set their clock by their arrival, the waitresses like to tell him. Father and son always leave just before the hour so as to avoid the traffic warden.

I ask Lucretia how long she has been coming to the market. Her hearing is poor and she cranes forward in her wheelchair. Simeon repeats the question, louder this time. She can't remember exactly, she replies. Too long, mocks her son. He's pleased that she comes, really. It keeps her active. She used to be with the Women's Institute, but for reasons undisclosed there was a falling out and she struck out on her own. She has a 'system', she explains to me. There's a Rayburn and two other cookers in the kitchen, all of which are fired up when she's in full flow.

'I had a write-up in a book,' she tells me. She grows suddenly coy. 'Best Places to Go in . . .' She pauses. '. . . in the World, it was.' Her chapel-going instincts against immodesty jump in. 'They've got to write about somebody, haven't they?' she says, almost by way of apology. She didn't know anything about it until someone brought her the book. '"You must visit Lucretia's stall. She's an octogenarian" . . .' Her voice trails off. She is not-so-secretly chuffed.

Simeon fills the gap, explaining how for years his mother used to cook evening meals at home for paying guests. The family found her collapsed on the kitchen floor one morning, so they've made her go more slowly since then. The enterprise began with cream teas, which she announced via a sign at the farm gate.

'Father's comment at the time was, "You won't make enough to pay for the sign, woman,"' Simeon recalls. Lucretia smiles. Woody doesn't react. Busloads used to come, says her son. Father would play the fiddle, and Mother the organ, 'for a bit of entertainment'.

The spirit of hospitality is deeply engrained in the hillside communities of the Marches. On his long walks and pastoral visits, Kilvert would often find himself waylaid by a generous farmer or friendly cottager. 'I believe I might wander about these hills all my life,' he reflected, 'and never want a kindly welcome, a meal, or a seat by the fireside.'

Together, mother and son recollect their more notable visitors. 'Do you remember the three cathedral organists?' he asks his mother. 'What about that party from France?' she responds. He raises her one, citing the visit from the Bulmer family, the cider-making dynasty from Brilley. 'It's the only time we've had three Rolls-Royces in the yard,' he says with a child's fascination. He even remembers the number plate on the lead car: C1DER.

Adaš Dworski, the potter of Pottery Cottage, used to be a regular visitor as well. One night, he came with the Chief Cashier of the Bank of England, Lucretia recalls, the man whose signature appeared on every banknote, from ten shillings upwards. 'Of course, you won't remember the ten-shilling note.' I sadly don't, I tell her, but I do know his son, Jasper Fforde, a best-selling novelist who lives just outside Clyro and who's part of my small hiking group. 'What a small world,' Lucretia remarks, evidently pleased with the new footnote to their family lore.

I imagine all the strangers who have sat in the front room of Ty-Caradog and can picture Kilvert among them, pleasantly ensconced as though it were the homely kitchen of Whitty's Mill, with little Carrie on her jingling old harpsichord, the smell of Mrs Gore's freshly baked bread wafting through the room, 'so irregular and full of odd holes and corners, so cosy and comfy with its low ceiling, horse-hair couch [and] easy chair by the fire'.

Not one to be outdone, Lucretia trumps her son with mention of Sir John and Lady Betjeman. The elderly farmer's wife seems more taken with the Poet Laureate's wife than the great man himself, leaping straight into a lengthy discussion about her death and how her ashes were thrown over the Himalayas from an aeroplane. '"Him-aaarh-ly-ers", that's how she pronounced it,' says Lucretia, in mimicry of Lady Betjeman's Raj-era diction. Her father used to be a Governor of India or something high up, she clarifies.

Sir John Betjeman had a lady on the side, Simeon chips in. And another little child. Lucretia shushes him. She finds talk of other people's moral shortcomings sullying and unedifying. Kilvert was of a similar mind. Although references to children born out of wedlock and even suicides pepper the *Diary*, they generally appear as part of a wider narrative and without judgement. Lucretia's moral sensibilities are unfortunate for her eldest son, whose sense of humour is what the Victorian curate would have probably termed 'colourful'.

Later, out of earshot of his mother, Simeon tells me about the swingers' scene in Ross. Everyone is playing with everyone down there, he assures me. 'The cleaner walked in on them all.' He pauses. 'You know. At it.' 'At what?' Lucretia wants to know, her hearing evidently sharper than she lets on. 'Oh, nothing, Mother. You wouldn't understand,' he says, giving me a knowing wink.

'They came to stay with us, and then they bought a cottage just near us. Right by the forestry land,' Lucretia says, picking up the Betjeman story. The cottage didn't have a bathroom at first, she adds, so the ennobled pair would come down to Ty-Caradog once a week for a hot bath.

I enquire what caused the Betjemans to visit the area in the first place. As well as dinners, Lucretia used to offer bed and breakfast at home, she explains. Lady Betjeman spotted their advert in the *Farm Holiday Book* and wrote asking to make a reservation. They lived in Wantage in Oxfordshire, Lucretia recalls, impressed enough to have committed the fact to memory all these years. When Lucretia wrote back explaining that their farm was very humble, she received a letter saying 'the humbler the better'.

Simeon interrupts, reminding his mother how he had once made their famous guests a set of toasting forks. Does she remember? Shaped like a deck of cards, they were. She gives him an indulgent look.

The subject then turns to Ian Fleming's daughter, who lived near by, and to the tragic drowning of her husband and daughter. 'Was it them who was buried on the farm?' Simeon asks his mother after she finishes with the full tale. 'No,' she replies. 'That was the next lot.' Over the years, they have seen many people come and go, she reflects. 'It's difficult to keep track.'

The remark provides the launch pad for mother and son to embark on a wider discussion about incomers. My ears prick up. Always moaning about something or other, Simeon says. About the boys having a 'bit of a rip' on their motorbikes or shooting cans with their air rifles. Or about the state of the footpaths. He views recreational walking as an imported, urbanite hobby. Footpaths originated as a means of travelling from A to B, he says. Not for rambling here and there.

He has a point. Kilvert once meets a 'humble cavalcade' making their way up through the windy passes of the Black Mountains. The footsore group is led by an old basket maker, who has the reins to a mangy bay pony in one hand and the hand of his 'stout rosy cheeked' daughter in the other. An older, thinner daughter is bringing up the rear, holding a third chubby child on a donkey. Kilvert speaks with the basket maker and learns that he has another eight children at home and that he has walked all the way from Gloucestershire to ply his trade in Talgarth.

On another occasion, the curate is out walking when he becomes mesmerised by a bank of heavy rain clouds that rolls across the valley and hides the mountaintops in a misty fog, before suddenly disappearing in a pillar of golden dark smoke. He watches as a single dazzling cloud lingers in the clear blue heavenly skies and the snowy peaks emerge, glittering so much that 'no fuller on earth can white them'.

Witnessing this wondrous spectacle unfold before him, he desperately wishes for someone to share it with but the only person around is a man on his carthorse, who appears entirely oblivious to the primrose light streaming in from the west and the cold grey tint creeping up in its wake, 'quenching the rosy warmth which lingers still a few minutes on the summits'.

Kilvert thinks to stop the man but suspects that he will think him mad, just as the basket man must have thought the sight of an adult man walking the mountain footpaths to no obvious end most bizarre. Not for the first time, I think back to the curious look of Tony's wife when I turned up on her doorstep in my jogging gear.

The oddity of rambling is the least of his worries, Simeon says, continuing with the theme of incomers. They try and 'rule the place', don't they? That's the main problem as he sees it. Well, go stir the fat somewhere else, is what he thinks. He has a good mind to buy a tank. 'Then they'll have to worry about keeping their cups of tea on the table.' This time his mother doesn't join in with his laughter.

Lucretia is more moderate and empathetic in her sentiments. She doesn't want to criticise and isn't against people coming into the area. Some incomers contribute a great deal, she concedes. Why do they have to knock something down as soon as they arrive, though? This is something she simply can't compute. Having modern 'conveniences' must be very important to them, she reasons. Of course, they think they are changing everything for the better. 'Perhaps they are,' she admits. 'Still, the outcome is complete change.'

Unsettled by the conclusion, she falls silent for a moment. When she finds her voice again, her tone is more placating. So many newcomers can be disorientating, she observes. People stop and ask where So-and-So lives, and half the time she doesn't know.

I assure her that all the locals I've met seem very friendly. The answer seems to satisfy her. Lucretia is a hill person, her whole life spent in the shadows of the Black Mountains. 'We always say, the closer people are to the mountains, the friendlier they are.' She amply proves her own point.

In the hope of winning over a few credits for my incomer tribe, I cast my eye over the table for something to buy. I settle on some sugary cupcakes. 'Six in a Bed', the label reads. The name derives from a nursery rhyme Lucretia used to sing to her children when they were little, she explains.

Simeon thinks it's all very funny. He is grinning lewdly. So, for once, is Woody.

*

My attempts to locate Mr Bird at Hay's livestock market are proving unsuccessful.

None of the half-dozen old men sitting drinking tea around the plastic cafeteria table has heard of him. The two white-haired ladies serving hot drinks and bacon butties at the static hot-food stall can, they regret, offer no assistance either.

The refectory area is positioned beside a semicircular pen which I take to be the show area for cattle sales. Access is via a narrow ginnel that runs off the high street, just beside Jones's hardware store. The cramped passageway is easy to miss.

I press on into the guts of Hay's beleaguered livestock market, which is the shape of a large barn. Grey-tinged sunlight floods through the far end, which is open and which leads down to a yard. Two staggered rows of vertical steel girders run the length of the building, propping up the sloping tin roof. I imagined a sweet agricultural smell would pervade the place but it doesn't. Instead it carries a clean, slightly caustic odour.

Lining both sides of the enclosed market area are rows of twin-set pens. Only twelve are full this morning, putting the total number of ewes at no more than a hundred. The sheep occupy the bottom left-hand section, about eight or so to a pen.

Out of the huddled mass of curly wool, the bald head of a ewe will occasionally poke up, her front hoofs perched on the back of a neighbour, swivelling her head a couple of times to get a lay of the land, the panic in her eyes increasing. Bleating, she then slips back into the throng, knowing her number is up, knowing all their numbers are up.

A man in a flat cap and muddy overalls is standing by one of the pens, his foot on the lower rail, elbows resting on the top one as he leans in and sizes up the sheep with an expert eye. I ask if he knows Mr Bird. He doesn't. I'd be best speaking with the auctioneer, he suggests. I enquire where I'd find him and he points to the exit where the light is streaming through. 'Down the ramp there.' I follow his directions.

I find Rob Meadmore in a square wooden shed reminiscent of a cricket scorer's hut. The shed has a large glassless window at the front, behind which Rob is seated on an office chair next to another man. The cricket analogy is apt, given how similar the auctioneer looks to an umpire, with his white lab coat and diagonal-striped tie. The only major anomaly is his wellington boots.

'What can I help you with, young man?' he asks, his manner breezy and personable, two qualities of all successful salespeople.

'I'm looking for Mr Bird,' I say.

His forehead scrunches. 'Mr Bird,' I repeat, explaining that he's the father of a friend of mine. Farmed around Clyro for a long time? I hint. Often comes along on a Thursday?

'Mr Bird,' the bemused auctioneer says quizzically. 'Now, are you sure you've got the right name?'

Then it dawns on me. My friend Mary is a Bird by marriage. I rack my brains for her maiden name. 'Price, sorry, not Bird. Mr Price,' I say, correcting myself. Prices proliferate in the Marches, much like Williamses and Davises,

Nichollses and Lloyds. Regrettably, I can't recall his first name.

'Clyro, you say?' The auctioneer looks pensive. 'Well, that'd have to be Mervyn Price, then. Used to farm up at Penlan?' That's the one, I tell him, thinking of Mary's white-washed farmhouse above the village. 'He's got a place over on the Cradoc side of Brecon now,' Rob tells me. 'Not sure if he has any land that way or not. His son David farms out Presteigne way.' But, no, sorry, he hasn't seen him yet today.

A middle-aged farmer strides over from the parking area below the shed. 'Hello, Rob,' says the auctioneer, addressing his namesake. 'You doing all right?' The man, who is dressed in a green hoodie with the words 'Erwood YFC' printed on the back, shrugs his shoulders. 'You tell me,' he says. 'How am I set to do today?' The auctioneer assures him he'll get the best price he can for him.

'He farms between Hay and Builth, does Rob. One of them that took over from his dad, see,' the auctioneer explains, as the farmer makes his way up to the pens. 'He sells a bit in Builth, but I see him most weeks this time of year.'

Another farmer approaches the shed door and com-mences a hushed discussion with Rob about a private mat-ter. I turn to the second man in the shed, whose long face is matted with a grey and white peppery beard. He is wearing what look like fishing waders.

He's the grader, he tells me in a strong North Wales accent. I ask what a grader is and he patiently explains that it falls to him to assess the quality of the sheep and weigh them before they enter the market. Then he asks how much I weigh. I tell him that my fighting weight is seventy-three kilos. 'A welterweight then,' he replies, smiling.

It turns out that the flat iron sheet that I took to be the

floor is actually the grader's scales. He presses a button in the shed and an electronic figure flashes up on a monitor above him. Seventy-eight kilos. My bag is heavy, I tell him. He laughs a deep, chortling laugh.

'How many sheep do you typically get in?' I ask, wondering if today's showing up in the pens is typical.

More than this, usually, he says. 'We're very quiet because the trade has gone down.' He provides a string of reasons for the dip. A strong pound against the euro. Low consumer confidence post-recession. Trade restrictions against Russia. Greece. It's simple economics, he notes. 'Supply and demand.'

Rob finishes his conversation and turns back to us. I ask what he expects the sheep to fetch today. Somewhere between seventy and seventy-five pounds for the best lambs, he says without hesitation. It was a tenner higher last week. 'But this week, unfortunately, they've gone to where they've gone to.'

He looks gloomy. Realistically, he needs about three times as much stock just to break even. Besides that, there's only one buyer, he tells me, nodding towards a balding thickset man in a sleeveless black fleece top who is kicking his heels next to the nearby holding pens.

Rob isn't about to give in to despondency. Hay has two high-street butchers, he informs me, both of which take five or ten lambs a week off him. They always want the very best, so in his market report he's able to say that he sold 'such and such number of lambs at top dollar'.

I take the opportunity to ask him what I'd planned to ask Mr Price, about the old days of the livestock market. Traditionally, the stalls that Andy spends his pre-dawn hours erecting would have played second fiddle to the real business of selling cows and sheep, geese and pigs.

Rob takes a deep breath. 'Way back, the farmers would

have driven their sheep and cattle off the hills and sold them in Broad Street. Mind, that was a long time ago, decades back now.'

I'd heard that everyone used to congregate in the town's pubs after the business of the market was over and I enquire if the custom still persists. The auctioneer gives me a wistful look. I'd have to go back to the 1970s for that. Three or four times a year the farmers might get together to 'have a bean', as he puts it, but today most of the socialising is done in the market itself. 'It's more work running a farm these days,' he reasons.

Trade was certainly busier when he started out. Three thousand six hundred ewes they had one Thursday, he recalls. Many hill farmers have 'gone out of sheep', he adds, opting to rent out their land or turn it to the plough.

'You remember Garlands, where the Owenses are now,' he says, turning his head to the grader. 'There would be two or three hundred lambs a week from there at one stage . . .' He doesn't continue the sentence.

I take out my notebook and ask what other factors he feels influence the fluctuations in the market's success. Seeing as I'm going to be writing it down, he says, he best give it some thought. He rubs his chin.

Competition between markets is probably the biggest factor, he reckons. In Hay, they deal exclusively in 'fat lambs', while Hereford trades across the whole spectrum. 'You can sell old cull ewes, ewes that are worn out, you can sell store lambs, you can buy user lambs – "couples" they call them – you can sell fat lambs and all that,' Rob says. Not that the prices are any higher, he insists, but he recognises that Hereford has become increasingly popular and that a 'crowd draws a crowd'.

Reminded of my conversation with Woko, I ask about selling direct to the slaughterhouse. Rob winces, his red complexion darkening a fraction. Hateful places, he spits. They offer a set price, so he understands why farmers go. To his mind, however, slaughterhouses strip the trade of its aesthetic and relational underpinnings. Farmers become mere 'producers'. Livestock, 'red meat'.

Of course, the livestock market is ultimately about business too. People come to buy and sell, Rob concedes. Yet the social ambit in which these transactions occur is, in his opinion, almost as important as the transactions themselves. 'I think it does farmers good to come out and talk about what's going on,' he says, and points up to the pens above where the old men from the cafeteria have now begun to congregate. 'Even if all some of them do is grumble.'

The auctioneer's words strike a sudden chord with me. Ever since arriving in the Marches, I've been looking for a magic formula, a recipe for levering my way into the community and helping me feel as though I belong. What if the answer is easier than I thought? What if it has nothing to do with social networking or assimilation strategies, behavioural patterns or character types? What if it's as straightforward as Rob suggests: the simple act of spending time in other people's company, of talking and listening, of showing interest in one another's lives?

Rob casts an eye down to my notebook and recommends that I include the auctioneer's enthusiasm among my reasons for the market's ups and downs. When the auctioneer is young, he's busy phoning everybody up and trade is consequently good. When he gets old and knackered, it all goes down and he gets a hundred sheep instead of a thousand.

The example comes out sounding closer to the bone than

he had perhaps intended. 'We're not knackered, are we?' he half-jokes, looking to his colleague. The Welshman beside him merely grunts.

Well, it's been nice chatting, Rob says. But I'll have to excuse him now. There's some sheep need auctioning. He opens the shed door and walks towards the pens, his wellington boots padding silently on the concrete ramp.

*

Leaving the livestock market, I head up the narrow alleyway and emerge back onto the high street. It's the mid-morning-coffee hour, and I find the three ladies jabbering away at their usual table. Through the partition doorway, first on the left. Their mugs of watery coffee are still hot.

Ann is sitting at the far end, presiding. She has twisted the chair side-on to the table. Spanning the wall opposite her is a syrupy lakeside scene painted entirely in shades of purple. The picture is dominated by the image of a wooden pontoon, which stretches out across lilac waters towards a damson sunset.

Against the wall is a set of stairs that heads down to a basement lavatory. The projection of the staircase matches that of the pontoon, only angling down rather than up. Their mirror imaging seems as though it might hold a meaning, although it beats me what it is.

Ann's repositioning of the chair sets her square-on to Pat and thus directly in line with her better ear. Next to Pat, at the other end of the table from Ann, sits Cynthia.

Ann and Pat live on Castle Estate in Clyro, a hundred yards or so up from my house. Ann has a bungalow, and Pat a small flat. Both properties are owned by the council. Ann is on at them to come and clear a patch of overgrown scrub by the road, but so far to no avail.

Cynthia is their friend from Llowes. She has maintenance worries too. Her lawn is in danger of falling into the brook at the end of her garden. Because she owns her house, it is her husband who is being badgered to sort it out. From the way she tells it, her petitions are falling on equally deaf ears.

They welcome me as I come in, lifting up their coffee mugs as if they were tankards of beer. Pat makes room for me on the corner and I pull up a chair between her and Cynthia. My back, fortunately, is to the arresting melange of purple that is the dusk-lit lake.

'You all right then, pet?' Pat asks. She usually calls me 'pet'.

Then Ann insists on introducing me to Cynthia although we must have met half a dozen times already. Not only on market day for coffee: our paths crossed when Ann invited me to the indoor bowls night at Clyro village hall. We've also run into each other at the gates of school, where Cynthia's grandson and my boys are classmates.

Still, Ann likes to introduce me whenever she can. It gives her proprietary rights over me. I don't mind this. In fact, she's developed a set patter for her introduction. It starts with my name and the fact that we're neighbours, which gives her the opportunity to say I live in Pottery Cottage.

Because the house is on the Hay road, most people know it. Then she'll say, 'Ah, I can remember some good times we had in there,' referring back to when her friends Ken and Eileen Hughes used to own the cottage thirty-something years ago. But she won't go into details, she'll say, for the sake of propriety. Her whole manner, however, invites the opposite.

'Oh, yes, of course you've met,' Ann says. 'And how are we today?' she then asks. 'And those little boys of yours?'

I assure both Pat and Ann that all is well on every front, and double check that I'm not interrupting them. I never am. At least, they never imply as much.

The three are women of habit. Monday is bowls night ('Seven-thirty, immediately after *Emmerdale*'). Tuesday, bingo. Wednesday, a day trip to Hereford. And Thursday is market day in Hay. Pat remembers it as a child. Cynthia too. Ann, in contrast, grew up going to the market in Builth. She's a latecomer to Hay in that respect.

The ladies meet at the back of Isis every week, between ten thirty and ten forty-five. 'If I wasn't there, they'd wonder where I am,' says Ann. It's one of her favourite phrases. Nor is it exclusive to the market. She trots it out before every bowls match, for example, and in the run-up to every farming-related funeral for ten square miles.

The expression also crops up in reference to the local summer fairs, especially Erwood and Builth, although here the phrase is extended to 'If I wasn't there *with my Welsh cakes*, they'd wonder . . .'

Isis is half shop, half café. It enjoys a prime spot along the main high street, located between an outdoor store and the old electricity board office (now a homeware shop). The retail part of Isis occupies the front section of the building and has two large windows looking out onto the pavement.

Its shelves are sparsely stocked with quartz-like minerals, crystals, wood carvings, conches, beads and other paraphernalia of a loosely Eastern origin. Greetings cards, umbrellas and plastic helter-skelter tubes called 'spiral spinners' are also for sale. Two large, randomly situated sofas cover much of the floor space on one side of the shop. I presume these are an overflow from the café at the back, although they could just as easily be for sale.

Ever since Islamic militants started wreaking havoc around the world, people have speculated if the café's owners will change the name from Isis. So far, they haven't. Perhaps they figure they were here first. Whatever, their determination pleases me, for it keeps alive a fantasy I entertain of the three retirees meeting every week to plot a caliphate in the Marches.

Saying that, the café name's murderous associations appear entirely lost on the ladies. When I first asked Pat about her Thursday coffee date, she couldn't recall what the place was called. 'Whatchamacallit,' she'd said. The truth is, none of them have ever really paid much notice to the name above the door.

'Barry Gibbons' place, is what we all know it as,' Pat had said.

'Right,' I'd replied hesitantly. 'And, sorry, but who is Barry Gibbons?'

She looked at me quizzically for a moment, then said, 'Well, you know Chrissy Gibbons?' The inference was that I should. I didn't. 'Well, he's Chrissy's nephew.'

This piece of information didn't really help me progress any further. Pat guessed my confusion. 'Chrissy . . . you know, from the butcher's on the high street,' she pressed. I knew the butcher's, but thought it was run by Geraldine. I told Pat as much. It is *now*, she'd said, clarifying that Chrissy used to run it for years beforehand. Geraldine is Chrissy's daughter. She took over from him.

'Him?' I ask. 'Yes, Chrissy, Chris, you know,' she said.

'So Chrissy is retired?' I'm confused.

'Yes,' Pat answered.

'So he doesn't work at the butcher's?' I asked.

'No, not any more. He passed away not so long ago, in fact.'

At that point, I gave up.

We eventually nailed the café's location by another route. 'The place that sells them lovely stones,' she explained. 'You know, the one opposite the new greengrocer's.'

The greengrocer is called Stuart, a splendid English gent who dresses in lustrously coloured corduroy trousers and wears the handlebar moustache of a duke. After a decade or more trading in Hay, 'new' isn't exactly a word I'd identify with him. Yet the elasticity of time is something I'm slowly learning from the ladies.

I put myself in Pat's shoes. She grew up buying her vegetables from Tony Pugh the Grocer, who also doubled as a fishmonger, collecting his daily produce from the morning train and storing it in his own ice house. Over the last half-century, she's probably seen half a dozen shops come and go in what is now the greengrocer's. On that timeline, Stuart quite reasonably qualifies as 'new'.

As for the café, the stones rather than the greengrocer's proved the real giveaway. Even in a market town as independent and eclectic as Hay, the high street has space for only one charm seller.

Chrissy's nephew Barry is a thin, affable man with a ponytail. As often as not, he's out smoking on the street rather than serving behind the counter. The ladies are fond of him and, as Thursday morning regulars, he gives them a client reduction. Whenever I join them, I qualify for the 'ladies' rate' too.

Of the three women, I know Ann best. Most weeks she'll pop round for a cup of tea and a catch-up. She wears thick fleece garments and has a fondness for pink lipstick on special occasions.

Born just before the outbreak of World War II, Ann grew up in the hills above Erwood. She moved down into the village itself aged ten when her father died and her mother had to give up the farm. Born 'Wilkins' ('"Wilks", some folk still call me'), she married a Jones. His first name was Derek.

There's another Derek Jones who lives just outside Clyro, as it happens. Ann and her husband used to rent some grazing land off him. 'No relation, mind,' she clarifies, pre-empting the question asked of every Jones across Wales.

Ann and her husband spent most of their married life on a farm in Cwmbach, a small hamlet above Glasbury-on-Wye. With the holding came another name, 'Ann the Cwm'. They rented the land from the council at an affordable rate and kept a mix of beef cows and sheep. Belgian Blues were always her favourite breed of heifer. 'A beautiful animal is a Belgian Blue.' As for ewes, they used to rear Texel crosses and Suffolk crosses, although she never took to sheep as she did to cows.

She moved to Clyro twelve years ago. Her husband didn't retire so much as slow down. They sold twenty-seven cows at auction, each of which went for about £700. 'That wasn't a bad price back then,' she assures me. I do the maths. It strikes me as precious little from a life's labours but, along with her state pension, it sees her through.

None of her four children – three boys and a girl – has opted to follow her into farming. One of her boys is a scientist, researching cures for cancer. He lives near London.

Another runs a pub in Carmarthen. The third is a builder in nearby Kington. Her daughter works for the outdoor store Mountain Warehouse, doing what exactly Ann isn't sure. Marketing, she thinks. Anyway, her daughter gave her some rubber-soled shoes for Mothers' Day. They match her lipstick. Ann is overjoyed with them.

Alongside farming, Ann worked for the Milk Marketing Board for many years. She would visit dairy farms up and down the Wye valley, taking milk samples for quality-control and billing purposes. She'd always tarry a while, meaning few people had a better handle on everyday goings-on than Ann. Who was looking to sell some ground; whose kids were playing truant; whose marriage was on the rocks; who had a problem with the bottle and was knocking his wife about. She knew it all.

Ann's grapevine today is less salacious. Now, all the flings and fistfights are a generation or two removed. It's So-and-So's daughter who's run off with Such-and-Such, or Someone's grandson who's taken up with You Know Who. For the ladies, the talk of the town now concentrates mostly on mutual ailments and pending funerals.

Pat's block of flats is immediately opposite Ann's bungalow. She has one of the two bottom-floor apartments, which she shares with several dozen cats, one real, the others porcelain. The feline miniatures crowd the mantelpiece and sideboards in her living room. Pat lost her only son, Gareth, to alcoholism when he was in his thirties. He used to work 'at the Rover' in Solihull. Her husband found him dead on the bed, the TV remote in his hand.

She has an enlarged passport photo of Gareth hanging on the wall in her front room. His ex-work colleagues sent it to her. The tragedy still takes a huge toll on her emotionally.

Pat suffers from hip and back problems too, which cause her to waddle and stoop simultaneously. Lately, she's taken to using a stick to keep her balance.

Of the three, Pat is the only one who actually grew up in Hay. She moved here in 1948 when she was six years old. She was a war baby, she tells me with pride. She lived in her nan's house, a two-bedroom terrace along Chancery Lane, close to where the town library now stands. Her mother, who divorced soon after Pat's third birthday and was one of ten children, had grown up in the same house. The house was knocked down in the late sixties to make way for the library, the zinc roof of its outdoor privy still visible in the wall of the adjoining car park.

Just after her nineteenth birthday, Pat went out for a night on the town with her mum. The pair went to the Mason's Arms along the high street as they always did. It was there, on the front step, that she first clocked eyes on her Barry (not Barry Gibbons, a different Barry). He was down from Birmingham, visiting family. The two hit it off and married shortly afterwards.

Her mum had chided her that she might meet the man of her dreams before they left the house that night. Pat puts great stock by the comment, as though 'our Barry' was pre-destined and her subsequent move to his home city was written in the stars. Over the years, her soft Marcher accent gave way to an unmistakable Brummie drawl. She calls me 'bab' as well as 'pet' and asks for 'elbow of pork' at the butcher's rather than 'belly of pork'.

Pat worked as a cleaner in a factory for twenty-seven years. The company manufactured paraffin lamps, mostly, plus a few other household objects. They made her redundant at the age of sixty-one, the day after her summer holiday break. She was upset at the time, but it gave her an excuse to move back to Hay. She persuaded Barry that the country air would be better for them in retirement. So when Barry's pension kicked in and the flat came up in Clyro, they took it. Things didn't work out as Pat had hoped. Four years later, after a short illness, Barry died.

The Mason's Arms is long gone (it's now a Spar), although the step is still there. I once happened on Pat standing right on the spot. She was leaning on her stick, looking blankly out at the street. Loaf of bread in hand, she seemed in no rush to move on. An expression of profound distance clouded her face, whether inspired by pleasure or pain I couldn't tell. Both, very probably.

A little before Barry passed away, Ann's Derek died too. The two drew on each other in their grief. Together with Dot, a mutual friend from the village whose husband also died around the same time, they jokingly refer to themselves as the 'Merry Widows of Clyro'. They attend the same social events, go on outings together and generally look out for one another.

Pat doesn't drive, so Ann ferries them both around. On market day, Ann will pick up Pat in her palatinate blue Toyota SUV and they'll head into town together. They park in the main car park, where Ann nabs a disabled spot nearest the exit. Heart condition, she tells me when she sees me looking at her blue badge.

From the car park, the two then make their way down to Isis to meet Cynthia. Sometimes Gwyneth, who used to run the petrol station in Clyro, joins them as well. She's not here today, which leads to a minute or two's speculation about where she is and how she's faring.

In her late sixties, Cynthia is noticeably younger than Pat

and Ann. She's the sparkiest too, quick to joke and poke
fun, and even quicker to laugh. Ann and Cynthia used to
work together at a nearby Outward Bound centre. Like Pat,
they were both employed as cleaners. 'Seventeen years and
never a cross word between us,' Ann likes to say. To which
Cynthia always raises her eyebrows and smiles wanly.

This morning, all the talk is of education. Powys Council
has announced that it is to close the nearby secondary school
in Three Cocks and move all the pupils to a new combined
campus in Brecon. Cynthia thinks it's a disgrace. They did
the same with all the small village primary schools, she
notes. The council puts them on warning, so the parents
take their children out, then there aren't enough children to
keep the schools open.

Pat used to go to Gwernyfed, the secondary school in
question, she interjects. She went back just the other week
for a car boot sale. In her day she remembers there being
gardening and country dancing and pageants and all manner of sports on offer. 'I said to Lizzy's daughter. Do you do
this? Do you do that? And she said no,' Pat recounts.
Gwernyfed used to have a farm when she was growing up,
Cynthia recalls. And Clyro school had a milking parlour,
Pat adds.

The conversation oscillates back and forth over the next
thirty minutes, flitting between affairs present and memories past, always localising the national, always personalis-
ing the local.

Having exhausted the topic of education ('P. G. Davis
was the headmaster,' says Ann. '"Pig" we used to call him'),
it moves onto the council's plans to build a new community
centre (Pat will believe it when she sees it), then to other
new housing developments in the area and thence to the

problems of affordable housing, pensions and the upcoming Budget, then to Ann overpaying the electricity people and getting a refund, followed by the price of petrol, Pat's hospital trip and that poor boy from Brecon who died skiing, and to Tom Edwards's funeral, until finally someone notes the time and Ann says they'd best be off and Barry Gibbons comes over to collect the empty mugs.

We traipse out. The portended rain has arrived as a nasty, gusty drizzle. The ladies lift the hoods of their jackets. Cynthia says her farewells and scampers off, keen to complete her chores and get back home. Ann and Pat dawdle longer, discussing what they plan to do next and arranging when they'll meet back at the car. Twelve thirty is the agreed time.

Ann is heading in the direction of Memorial Square. I'm hungry and anxious to get to Bernie's in the Cheese Market before she sells out, so I suggest strolling down with her.

'Ta-ra then, pet,' says Pat, who also has some jobs to do. I say goodbye and she steps gingerly off the pavement and waddles across the street, her stick tap-tap tapping in time with the rain on our jacket hoods.

Walking with Ann turns out to be a sociable experience. Within the first seventy yards, she has already exchanged greetings with three elderly acquaintances. Each time, she says hello, asks after their health, mentions the weather and then moves on. I'm also introduced. By the time we reach the market stalls in Memorial Square, we're up to ten. At least twenty-five minutes have passed.

I'm taken aback by how many people she knows and, after each interaction, I pester her to tell me more about them. She obliges my curiosity only too happily. So I learn, for example, that Trevor Price is also known as 'Trevor the

Lorries', 'because he used to drive all the stock lorries'. And that Peggy Smith used to run the post office in Glasbury. And that the mother of Ted Williams, who drives the Highway Maintenance truck parked by the bank, lives out by her childhood home in Erwood. And that Mrs Venables, who farmed up in the hills for years and years, has now moved to one of the almshouses in town, 'and, oh, she loves it there'. And that Judith from Llanigon 'parted company' with her husband and that her ex-mother-in-law has a place in Clyro.

A few are even related to her. So Annie, the blind lady sitting in a car whom Ann salutes by banging on the passenger door window, turns out to be her sister-in-law. The man beside Annie is Mervyn, her husband, whom people always used to mistake for Ann's brother because they grew up on neighbouring farms. 'Not as far as I know, he's not,' she tells me. And then there's Jill, who has a shop in town and whose granddaughter, as she informs us at length, seems worryingly lackadaisical about her GCSE revision. Jill is Ann's niece, the daughter of her now deceased sister, Barbara.

Not all her encounters are so serendipitous. We pop into PSM, the outdoor store, for example, to say hello to the daughter-in-law of Hilda, who lives near to Ann on Castle Estate. Then we make a detour into St Michael's Hospice charity shop to meet Lynn, who lives up on the Begwyns. Lynn always puts aside a small selection of beads and glass and other bits of broken jewellery for Ann's Thursday afternoon art-and-craft group. Later, after we part, she'll stop by at the Red Cross outlet as well, where Monica, an ex-neighbour when they were both recently married, occasionally volunteers.

When we reach Memorial Square itself, Ann makes a

beeline for Craig the Veg. She buys what she always buys, one pound's worth of grapes and three bananas. 'The usual, darling?' the stallholder says as her turn in the queue comes round. He says the same every week and it tickles Ann enormously.

Other than fruit, I ask what she purchases. Nothing, she tells me. Not even a little fish? I suggest. She's 'not a fish person', she informs me, and then embarks on a long story about once being given a salmon by an angler and not having the least idea how to cook it.

Cheese? Meat? Veg? I go through the other options available at the market. No, she says to each in turn. She does her weekly food shop at the Co-op. Why would she need to purchase anything at the market?

It is then that it dawns on me. The contents of the market stalls are almost incidental to Ann's Thursday trips. Traders could put what they liked on Andy's tables and she'd still come. Japanese kimonos or children's slippers, it wouldn't matter.

As Rob the Auctioneer rightly observed, a crowd draws a crowd. Well, Ann is that crowd. She's a constituent member, a loyal affiliate. Hidden amid all the bustle, there are shoulders to bump against and conversations to be had. This refreshing of acquaintances, this catching up with friends, this is what keeps her coming back.

For two hours on a Thursday morning, it's not her alone in her bungalow. She's part of something bigger, something to which she feels a connection, something that will wonder where she is if she doesn't show.

Ann's list isn't entirely empty. She has to go to the news-agent's to pick up the *Hereford Times* for Sibyl and Dennis, who live in the next door bungalow to her. They're too

infirm to get about these days. And Angie, another neighbour, has asked her to pick up a pound of sausages and a
pound of bacon from the butcher's. Ann raises her eyebrows
at the mention of this second request. Angie is a stick of a
woman, she tells me. 'Where's she going to put it all?'

Not everyone is like Ann. There's plenty of buying done
on market day too. Later on, I hang around the Cheese
Market for the best part of an hour, chatting to Bernie after
wolfing down the last of her moreish steak pasties.

Despite the bad weather, which has grown progressively
worse during the morning, trade is relatively brisk. By
noon, all Bernie's muffins and chorizo pizza slices and
Caerphilly pies are sold out. In her hot pot, which bubbles
on a camping stove, only a ladle or two of stew remains.
Once that has gone, her lunchtime customers will be down
to choosing from the last few salmon quiches, sausage rolls
and goat's cheese tarts.

The pace at 100% Hay is slower. Joe absents himself at
one stage, leaving Tree the Coffee Roaster to cover for him.
But sales still tick along and, just before packing up, his day
is salvaged by a young woman carrying a Bag for Life who
clears him out of asparagus, beans and tomatoes. For good
measure, she buys some spuds, onions, lemon grass and
sweet peppers too. He'll leave happy.

Shopping and socialising are not mutually exclusive.
Despite the weather, almost every customer stops to talk.
One moment Bernie is advising a middle-aged lady about
switching gas providers, the next she's sharing cough rem-
edies with an elderly gentleman.

Joe, meanwhile, talks chilli types with the new chef at
Kilvert's Inn, a pub in the centre of town, then earnestly
explains to a young mum why his sweetcorns won't be ready

for another month ('We try not to buy anything in,' he explains. 'It's all about seasonality, you see').

Below the Cheese Market, in Shepherd's ice-cream parlour, the tables are full with groups of coffee drinkers. Several of his regulars place their orders first, Joe explains, then come back later once their coffee dates are done. Bernie is the same, advising one of her customers to text her if he's busy and she'll put a muffin aside for him.

Ann never goes in the Cheese Market, so we go our separate ways at the entrance. Before we do, however, my eye catches a box of old LPs at the end of a table. The table is pushed up against the building's outer wall, just beside the door to the upstairs holiday flat. It's full of Tom's spillover bric-a-brac and small-scale junk.

I start flicking through the box, asking Ann if she recognises the artists. Connie Francis, Frankie Vaughan, Tammy Wynette, Max Bygraves, Jimmy Young, Eddie Arnold. She very much does, she says, and moves next to my shoulder to see the album covers for herself.

I turn over the next record sleeve and a young Tom Jones stares back. She places a hand on her chest and pretends to swoon. It's a compilation of the Welsh heart-throb's greatest hits. She's got every single one of them, she tells me. 'Thunderball'. 'Delilah'. 'Love Me Tonight'. On vinyl, and on CD.

Five times she's gone to see him live in concert. Five times! She holds up her palm, each finger purposefully outstretched. Five times! I ask what her favourite track is. Her answer zings back without a second thought. 'Why, "Green, Green Grass of Home", of course.'

6

The Festival Crowds

Hay Flower Show, the first they have had, a very successful one. A nice large tent, the poles prettily wreathed with hop vine, and the flowers fruit and vegetables prettily arranged. There was an excursion train from Builth to Hay for the occasion. The town was hung with flags. The whole country was there.

Kilvert's Diary, 30 August 1870

At the guide's direction, our tour group skirts around the base of Hay Castle along a muddy path towards the ancient keep. Open to the air, the ruined tower stands four storeys high and is sprouting with Virginia creepers. Below the foliage, a spectral cloak of lichen green spreads across the structure's mottled stone skin.

Two old ladies are edging along in front of me. Both grasp the metal grille fencing that runs beside the narrow walkway as though fearful of being buffeted off the castle bank. They are wearing slip-on shoes with flat soles that gather a coating of wet butternut mud around the trim as they shuffle along. Ahead is a young couple with a child of seven or eight. Dressed in rain macs and sensible outdoor clothing, they stand in the drizzle as the old ladies approach. The father pulls a smartphone from his pocket and, with determined holiday cheer, says, 'Smile'. His wife obliges.

His daughter, on the other hand, scrunches her face into a ferret-like moue.

A menacing bank of cloud appears on the horizon. It rumbles in from the west, tracking the course of the Wye, bearing down on the chimney-pot hats of Hay. The young father looks over his daughter's shoulder, staring forlornly at the middle distance and the long afternoon ahead.

Once we're all assembled, the guide draws our attention to the arched gateway at the bottom of the keep. Two ancient timber doors guard the entrance, above which is a sluiced groove for the portcullis. As the guide begins a long explanation about dendrological tests and renovation plans, I turn to look at the town below. The stormy weather has lasted two days now. Ahead of this latest front, however, a speck of glacial blue has broken through, a lone and lovely tarn amid a mountain of cloud. I watch as a rare shaft of sunlight burnishes the sopping town, bouncing off the puddles and painting the rooftops with a joyous sheen.

The tour group moves off around the corner and I decide it's time to slip away. The morning visit is almost up and my need for coffee is stronger than my desire to learn any more about carbon dating or battlement design.

Below the castle, next to the car park where the Thursday market is held, is a walled lawn. The furthest side runs along the main high street and has a small doorway opening out onto the pavement. On the castle-facing side of the wall are three or four open shelves cluttered with titles that the town's second-hand booksellers can't shift. Tatty textbooks predominate; redundant monographs such as *Using Windows 98* and *An Introduction to the Yugoslav Economy*. Payment is via a rusty, red deposit box embedded in the wall. Today, however, the honesty bookshop is largely hidden by the colourful awnings of food stands and their chalked-up menu boards. The temporary fair looks inwards to a huddle of trestle tables and benches in the centre of the lawn.

It is late May and the annual Hay Festival of Literature and Arts is now in full flow. For weeks the town's shop-keepers have been perfecting their window displays and dusting down their stock. Busy hands have been scrubbing floors and making calls. Suppliers delivering double orders. Shop assistants clocking overtime.

Well over 100,000 visitors will flood to the town over the ten days of the event. Pop-up bars pop up. The restaurants and pubs fill to overflowing. Even the Groucho Club gets in on the act, taking up residency in the castle's Jacobean wing.

As the festival progresses, I'm slowly working my way through my envelope of event tickets. For weeks they have sat on my desk, brimming with advent promise. I opted for a mix of writers; some well known, some less so. With each torn stub I find the world looks a smidgen different, its possibilities a fraction broader than before.

As well as the 'real business' of talks and panel discussions, the festival is marked by dinners and after-parties, book launches and lunches. Night One, we'd been out at an exhibition opening. Night Two was a soirée hosted by a magazine editor. Last night, the Globe put on a live set.

Day Four and my energies are beginning to flag. My city self has grown sluggish, its ability to work hard and play hard dimmed. This surprises me slightly. As does my reaction to Hay's sudden transformation, which oscillates between irrepressible excitement one minute and frustration the next.

Part of me is elated that the outside world has landed on our doorstep. For a brief window in late spring, everywhere I turn there are urbanites like me. People I sense

I've seen before, folk I feel I might know.

Simultaneously, part of me recoils. Like Woko, I feel invaded. Some traitorous wretch has spilled word of our rural haven and now legions of out-of-towners have arrived, overrunning the place with their unmuddied cars and city manners.

Of the two emotions, I secretly relish the second more. It makes me feel as though I've crossed an invisible line, that I'm now vested enough in this place to get possessive about it, to become jealous about sharing it, even. It gives me a frisson of pleasure, this sense of 'us' and 'them', locals and outsiders. I have never felt it before.

Yet, at the same time, I realise these sentiments are neither pleasant nor uncomplicated. I was a visitor once, after all, content to treat the town as a mere backdrop to my own pleasure, a place that – for a weekend at least – wasn't the city. Some will think me a visitor still, my invisible line an act of mistaken presumption.

I can't ignore the pull I feel towards this invading army too. I may have tried to split off from them, to put myself at a distance, but they remain my tribe. The Rhydspence crowd simply avoid Hay for a fortnight, turn their backs on the whole rigmarole. I wish I could too. But I feel drawn in, a moth to a flame.

Emma suffers none of this angst. She simply throws herself into whatever social circle she finds. Local, outsider, humanoid, Martian, she doesn't care, doesn't even think about it. She can't understand my interest in the question of belonging and not belonging. To her mind, it's immaterial, inconsequential.

I wonder if Kilvert would agree. Intimately attached as he was to the Marches, his life encompassed a host of people and places beyond it too. He seemed to straddle this division without problem. So, as in 1875, during a May week like this one, he could spend time with his parents in Wiltshire, take in a show at London's Haymarket Theatre, wander around the Belgian gallery at the International Exhibition and still be back in Clyro to celebrate Mrs Venables's birthday with his parishioners and to check whether the bog beans below Gwernfydden were yet in flower.

It helped that Kilvert had a job specific to the locality. This gave him a very particular purpose for being here, not to mention a clear mandate for involving himself in community life. He also brought with him to the countryside an idealised pastoral aesthetic, his own private Wordsworthian wonderland. And naturally, as with all of us, he saw what he wanted to see. Sweet damp air. Cool fresh lanes. Mellow afternoon sunlight. Everything so 'sweet and still and pure', especially when compared to the 'dust and crowd and racket of the town'.

Our expectations of a place inextricably impact our experience of it. The same is true of 'community', the physical appearance of which is coloured and ultimately captured by what we preconceive it to be. We try to build the communities of our imaginations and, once built, whether soundly or shoddily, we strive to see them as we first imagined them. Yet what if people come with different concepts of where they are and what they expect of it? I had come looking for the 'knit' of which Updike spoke. What binds people to one another and to this place? How do they weave together? What are their individual stitches and what is mine? These are the issues that interest me and thus the lens through which I see.

Others bring with them alternative motivations and therefore divergent viewpoints. For Emma, moving here is all about embracing the new: the making of discoveries, the kick-starting of projects, the striking up of friendships. Kilvert's inclinations lay elsewhere again. The pages of his diary – indeed, the very idea of keeping one – reveal a deep thirst for beauty, and in beauty a quest for love, and, perhaps, in love a pursuit of the divine.

I ponder these thoughts as I make my way down a flight of flagstone steps towards the food stalls in search of coffee. If true in any measure, the need for fellow citizens to talk and listen to one another is more imperative than ever. How else can consensus emerge about what and whether community might be?

A wooden handrail accompanies the stairs. It's damp and clammy to the touch. Simon and Garfunkel greet me as I descend. Fat Charlie the Archangel wants no part of this crazy love. A mini sound-system on the counter on the PommePomme Foods van lays bare his lyrical secret. Inside, a man with a pitch-black beard that matches his pitch-black spectacles is busy grating cheese.

Across at Parsnipship, beneath the chalkboard advert for bulgur wheat salad and beetroot bomblets, an irritable conversation is taking place. At issue is an empty gas cylinder. 'I closed the valve, honest,' says a man on the defensive. 'You couldn't have,' a hostile, supervisory voice responds. The argument bats back and forth. 'Ah, bugger,' says one. 'Just forget it,' says the other. The stove won't light. The vegan pakoras and chickpea burgers remain uncooked.

The sight of a stainless-steel coffee machine, its silver cylinders steaming, sets me on a beeline to Love Patisseries. I pass the seasonally inspired flavours on offer at the Cothi Valley Ice-Cream stall without breaking stride. Welsh honey, stem ginger, vanilla and saffron flavours, all made with '100% goats' milk'.

I make a fast choice from the options on the billboard menu. Americano, extra shot. No messing, straight hit. But the man behind the counter has his back to me. I cough politely but he's blind to my presence.

Hunched over, the apron-clad proprietor is bludgeoning the rim of a wooden bin with a black-handled filter holder. Wads of wet coffee granules disappear into the bin, plummeting into the composted darkness, swallowed whole like fresh earth in an open grave. I watch him work, my impatience briefly quelled by the intensely deliberate approach he is taking to his labours. Eventually, he pulls a damp cloth from a rail and wipes away the few rogue grains that remain before returning the filter to the machine's twist-grip care. He's a man of method. Not one to be rushed. I respect this. He'll attend to me at his own pace.

Love Patisseries' coffee-making arm seems to occupy only a peripheral part of the business. Cramped on a table in one corner of the bunting-laced stall, the Fracino machine is dwarfed by rows of fluffy fruit-laden cakes and cream-topped pastries. Each sugary creation is dolled up as if in preparation for a beauty pageant. Apple and cinnamon strudel vying with the meringue for the Casual Wear crown. Chocolate, orange and cardamom cake pitted against her toffee, pear and hazelnut twin.

I weigh up buying a chocolate brownie, judging it to be just about within legitimate bounds for breakfast. Before I make my mind up, though, the man swivels round and looks in my direction. 'Oh, hello there. What can I get you? Latte? Cappuccino?'

It's Johnny, a cheerful Hay resident whom I've met at several social events around town. I feel embarrassed at not having recognised him. Thrown temporarily off balance, I ask for a latte with an extra shot. 'No, no, sorry. Make it an Americano, please.' He turns again and starts spooning the coffee into the recently cleaned filter holder.

'I hadn't realised you'd gone into the coffee business,' I say.

Johnny and his wife, Catherine, own a successful bed and breakfast down by the main bridge into Hay. Both are popular townspeople: kind-hearted, community-spirited, quick to wave in the street. Johnny used to sit on the Town Council, while Catherine conducts the local community choir.

'Yup, thought I'd give it a go,' he replies, tapping his new machine with affection. 'What've I got to lose?'

'Too right. No, good on you,' I say, admiring his sense of enterprise. 'Did you just teach yourself or did you get someone to show you?'

He did a half-day course at Bournville College, he tells me. And then another half-day with Peter James, in Ross-on-Wye. 'A hands-on thing, you know.' He picks up a bag of roasted coffee beans, the word 'James' printed across the front.

For a confessed novice, he is exhibiting remarkable confidence at the Fracino's helm. Even so, the new machine sports a confusing array of gleaming buttons, knobs and gauges. 'It must be a bit complicated, no?'

He shrugs and assures me it's actually relatively straightforward. It's all about getting the right grade of coffee, he says, pointing to a sleek electronic measuring device on the sideboard. 'Sixty millilitres in a double shot, expressed for twenty-five seconds.' He presses a button and sets the coffee machine spluttering.

As he prepares my order, a woman in an expensive waterproof and spotted Joules wellies saunters up to the counter. She has a poodle on a lead. It, too, looks expensive.

'Do you do decaf cappuccino?' she asks in a cut-glass, Home Counties accent. He does. 'Then I'll have one, please.'

Her tone is prickly. It punctures all the goodwill from her 'please' and turns the entreaty into a demand. 'With soya milk.' The friendly B&B owner smiles and invites her to take a seat in the courtyard. 'I'll bring it over to you.' She moves off with her dainty dog in the direction of a bench, no word of recognition or thanks.

He raises his eyes as she saunters off. City ways, the expression says. 'I had a woman in yesterday. She asked if we had anything gluten-free. "We've got brownies," I told her. And d'you know what she said? "Everyone's got brownies," and she stomped off.' He chuckles.

A former city-dweller himself, Johnny knows the drill. He recognises that stress, that incessant rushing, that too-busy-to-talk glaze in the eyes. That's partly why he moved here. For the change of pace, for the extra time. Time with his wife and two children, time for his hobbies, time to build friendships and construct a happy home. Time, the infinite gift so temporarily bestowed, to be snatched while you can.

He was based in the Birmingham area previously, in a job he liked but didn't love. Catherine, too. Midway through middle age, they now wanted out. Each hankered for a life free of line managers and client meetings; a life in which phrases like 'end-of-year appraisal' and 'company protocol' held no sway.

So they bought a second-hand camper van. Every week-end for the best part of a year, they trundled down the M5 and made the winding crossing into Wales, where they reckoned their money would go further and their dreams might prosper. Up and down the Marches they drove in search of that perfect place. The derelict farmhouse on the south-facing slope. The dilapidated barn ripe for renovation. The gable-ended longhouse with its own wood and well.

Ahead of the van, bouncing along the road, ran their imaginations. They saw their kids playing in the blackthorn thickets behind the house, a pair of untoggled scouts with permanently sun-freckled noses. Catherine would have a dapple-grey horse that would trot in contented circles around her purpose-built paddock. Johnny would be tending the veg patches, packing their larder shelves with home-grown produce that would nourish their souls.

Never did it rain in these vivid imaginings. Only sun or snow, a condensed climatic couplet. Nor did the bills for the bottled gas or veterinary visits ever put in an appearance. There were no pot-holed roads, no snowed-in driveways, no dial-up internet, no mice in the bedroom, no foxes at the chickens, no power cuts, no broken fences. Only cloudless skies and empty days.

Then, a three-storey, end-of-terrace town house in Hay popped up on the estate agent's website. 'Charmingly restored, views of the river, centrally located.' It was exactly what they *weren't* looking for, Johnny happily confesses. But it burst their bubble. The affordable price, the extra bedroom, the proximity of the school and the shops: it all made eminently more sense.

I think of Rob and Layla up on their smallholding, living out Johnny's fantasy. Does he regret not doing it? He laughs. No, not once. Deep down, he's a 'people-person', he now realises. The isolation of the hills would have sent him around the bend. When he had his fiftieth birthday a few years back, almost 200 people turned up. Everyone dancing, drinking, mixing among themselves. In truth, that's more his scene.

He is still chuckling when a second customer approaches.

She is younger and fresher-faced than the first, a small boy at her side. The child is clasping his mother's hand. She'd like a latte, please. It's her second already today, she tells him. 'But who's counting, hey?' A glow of holidaymaker happiness infuses her manner. She's pleased to be away. Away from where, Johnny asks. They're from Hatfield, in Hertfordshire. Just off the A1.

She must be finding it quiet, Johnny says, his soft sarcasm hidden behind a good-humoured grin. Yes, she says. She thought it would be busier. She supposes it's the rain. I smile at Johnny, who doesn't disabuse her of the idea by telling her how much more sedate the town usually is. Instead he asks her if she's enjoying the festival. It's not the first time he's asked the question, nor will it be the last. As with all successful local retailers, Johnny genuinely appears to enjoy small talk. He listens for her reply, twisting his head over his shoulder as he prepares my drink.

The coffee is black and hot when it comes. I take a sip and feel my spirits lift immediately. For a brief moment, my senses register nothing but its velvety warmth. When I re-enter the world, the woman from Hatfield is saying how she went to four talks on her first day and three yesterday. She's two more planned for this afternoon. 'I'm more into the artsy, happy side of things,' she's saying. 'Less economics and politics and what not.' There's something for all tastes, Johnny responds, liberal and likeable as always.

Her boy starts tugging at her arm, lured by the next door ice-cream van. 'Okay, okay, Freddy,' she says. The ice-cream man isn't about to go anywhere. Johnny tells her not to worry. He'll bring her drink over once it's ready. She thanks him and walks off, the little boy pulling at her coat sleeve.

Johnny looks towards his first customer. She is sitting

stiffly on the bench in the centre of the garden courtyard. Next year, he'd like to get some kind of awning for the seating area. 'Give it a more Mediterranean feel, you know.' He turns and twists the filter holder from its socket. A fine steam rises up from the damp pocket of freshly pressed beans as he holds it above the bin.

I move to go, holding my cup aloft in gratitude and wishing him well for his new venture. I'm not sure if he hears. The courtyard is already reverberating to the sound of hammering.

*

Turning left along Castle Street, I set off towards the tented festival site on the western edge of town, where I have a date with a newly published author.

Pedestrians fill the narrow pavement, persuading the more impatient to chance walking in the road. Parked outside the Swan hotel is a young man on a cucumber green bicycle rickshaw. It's the best part of half a mile to the festival entrance and trade is busy. Payment is on a donation basis. 'A foreigner, every time,' he tells me, when I ask who his ideal customer is. 'Brits are such misers.' I continue walking.

Further down the street, just after the left turn heading up to Hay Bluff, where Castle Street merges into Brecon Road, Richard couldn't disagree more. Sporting jeans and a grubby black T-shirt, he is standing behind a makeshift bar on the front lawn of the Masonic Lodge. His beard and hair are remarkable for achieving precisely the same degree of dishevelment.

'Can't complain,' the young brewer from Whitby tells me when I enquire how business is going. Books and booze, he sees them as a natural fit. I ask where he's staying and he points to the floor behind the bar. 'Someone has to watch the barrels,' he says. Not that he sleeps much anyway. Last night, his final customers didn't leave until about 3 a.m.

I'd been lured into his beer tent by his colleague, who is stationed on the pavement with a tray of taster cups. 'American hops,' he'd told me in a thick Yorkshire accent, inviting me to try the black IPA. Dry, peppery and caramel sweet, it tastes good. Inside, I find a clutch of others have come to the same conclusion, all of them with a lunchtime pint in their hands and the sheepish look of absentee husbands on their faces.

One of them, Martin, who has two days of stubble on his chin and a six-year-old son at his side, isn't wasting any time. He tried the Platform 3 first ('Sort of nutty taste, but goes down smoothly enough') and is now nearing the bottom of a pint of Jet Black. We fall into conversation. His wife is currently at an event starring the actor Benedict Cumberbatch. Last night they had both gone to see the comedian Marcus Brigstocke. Very funny. Have I been? He suggests I get tickets for one of the evening stand-up routines. They've been coming down to the festival for six years. 'We always try and catch at least one comedian.'

He asks where I live and I explain that I've recently moved to the area. He looks momentarily wistful. 'We love it here,' he says. They stay in the same bed and breakfast every year. 'Hay feels just like a village, don't you think?' I nod. He'd like to get into the hills or go canoeing next time. They've still not done anything like that.

He checks his watch. Fifteen minutes. He necks the remainder of the Jet Black and catches Richard's eye. He'll have another, 'for the road'. The young brewer gladly takes his glass. 'Saltwick Nab?' Richard touches the respective tap handle with the flat of his hand. 'It's a best bitter. Four point . . .' he twists the tap to read the label. 'Yup, four point two per cent. Good malty kick to it.'

Martin evidently enjoys the ritual accompanying his beer: the choosing, the pouring, the admiring. He listens intently to the descriptions of the brewer-barman. The Saltwick Nab sounds like a fine idea, he says, and reaches into his pocket for cash. 'Shame not to try them all, eh?' His mood is jocular, the alcohol in the first two pints already sceping into his bloodstream.

I order a half for myself.

They've just been round the second-hand bookshops, Martin tells me. 'Haven't we, Nath?' The boy is sitting on the floor, cross-legged, his nose in a comic-strip version of 'Three Billy Goats Gruff'. He loves that story, his father says. Found it in the first shop they went into. He didn't see much point going into the others. 'We can do that tomorrow, right, Nath?'

We drink in silence for a while. He looks down at his boy. They went to see the toll bridge yesterday, over the Wye, in Whitney. There's a book about Walter, the friendly blue troll who lives under the bridge. His son loves that one too. The boy looks up at his father and grins.

'You got kids?' he asks me. Two, I tell him. Must be a wonderful place to bring them up, he says. It is, I tell him. 'Yeah, it's kind of old world, isn't it? Hay, I mean,' he replies. He looks momentarily pensive. It strikes him every time they come down: how tucked away it is, how much it feels like stepping back in time.

He loves the fact that the nearest big supermarket is twenty miles away, for instance. They're from the Wirral.

He has an ASDA, Sainsbury's and LIDL more or less within walking distance of his house. 'And the beer in all of them is terrible,' he says, slapping his thigh and roaring with laughter.

It's my turn to check my watch now. I hadn't meant to stop so long. Wishing Martin and his bibliophilic offspring the best, I head back out onto the pavement.

Almost as soon as I step out of the beer tent, I bump into a couple from Clyro Primary School, their limbs laden with small offspring. They've just been to the 'Make and Take' tent. Had I been? Jimmy just loved it. The older boy gets his hair ruffled, an action that sends a swatting hand upwards. 'Maa-umm.' I explain that we've rented out part of the house for the week and that Seth and Bo are with their grandparents. 'Where? How?' the mother asks. There is envy in her voice. Or is it disapproval? I am a childless parent; fancy-free, beer on my breath, denying my kids a unique cultural experience.

She's right, of course. The breadth of talent that finds its way to the Marches every May is truly remarkable. This year's itinerary runs to nearly 500 events, with iconic US writer Toni Morrison topping the bill. Last year's headliner was the Peruvian author and one-time presidential candidate Mario Vargas Llosa, fresh from winning the Nobel Prize for Literature.

Behind them come the breakthrough first-time novelists, the rising star of Africa's 'new wave' or an entrant in Granta's latest 'Best of . . .' list: all of them dripping with talent and bravado, the literary world at their feet. Then there are the jobbing authors, churning out solid material year after year, working the festival circuit as they go with dogged charm and well-worked witticisms.

Finally, the crowd-pullers who make the economics of it all work: Martin's comedians, for one. Plus the food writers, the children's authors, the historians, the scientists, the biographers, the campaigning provocateurs, the sports stars, the sci-fi wonks, the columnists. A potpourri of publishing output, in short.

'They're back at the end of the week,' I blurt out to the mother, in reference to Seth and Bo, and excuse myself speedily.

On the left of the road is an old churchyard, Hay's fire station and the town's sports fields, where the boys have tennis lessons and Saturday morning football club. Beyond are open fields, converted momentarily into overspill car parks. On the opposite side of the street, beyond Richard's beer tent, are some almshouses and a home for the elderly, then a long row of semi-detached 1930s properties. Every other resident of Oakland Villas seems to be out on their front lawn, either rattling a charity tin or flogging cold drinks and foodstuffs.

Outside No. 4, a lady in a plastic poncho is standing under a temporary gazebo armed with a two-way radio. Her free hand is resting on a table laid out with jams, jigsaws, craft items, second-hand clothes and other charity knick-knacks. She's raising money for Parkinson's UK, a banner declares. Tea and cake are advertised as well. She too invites me to step in off the pavement.

'What sort of cakes do you have?' I ask, yet to commit but feeling my resolve weaken. Oh, all sorts, she says. 'Come on through, now, why don't you.'

I like the fact that the residents of No. 4 see the festival crowds as an opportunity to raise money for charity rather than to line their own pockets. Kilvert, who used to dispense blankets among Clyro's poor, would have approved. So too would Updike, I imagine. What is charity if not a clear expression of loving your neighbour in the old sense?

Persuading people to donate is obviously the primary purpose of charity fund-raising, but philanthropic endeavours have a core secondary function too. They bring citizens together. Rarely does a week pass without an invitation to attend a concert or coffee morning for a good cause.

Such occasions strengthen communities. Not just because their focus is often local: a refit of the playground where the kids play and the young mums congregate, say, or a new minibus to help the elderly group get out and about. More fundamentally, they reinforce the ethos of communal living, reminding us that we are collective beings, born not to live behind high fences but in relationship with one another.

With such thoughts in mind (plus the promise of something sweet), I follow her outstretched arm down a narrow path towards the back of the house. The crackle of a radio sounds from around the corner. 'Young man . . . cake . . . yes, right now.'

Waiting for me in the back garden are David and Val, a friendly retired couple decked out in matching aprons. Thick slices of coffee cake, banana bread and Victoria sponge look out invitingly from behind a glass casing. Lining up beside them are plates of bara brith and millionaire marble, homemade biscuits and the obligatory Welsh cakes. Lucretia has found her match.

I ask for a flapjack and then spot the price, a bargain at fifty pence each. 'Make that two.' He picks up the flapjacks with a pair of tongs and drops them into a paper bag. I hand him a pound coin.

The couple are pros. It is the cake stall's tenth anniversary. Over the years, they've bought an urn, invested in some tables and chairs, developed a team of volunteer cakebakers. A few years back, David even landscaped the garden and extended the patio. I admire his handiwork, particularly the gurgling water feature.

A former accountant at the builders' merchant in Hay, David is Hay born and bred, he tells me. So are Val and her sister out front, both of whom grew up in No. 7 Oakland Villas. 'So she's not travelled far,' he says, repeating what must be an oft-repeated gag but one that lands a smile from his wife all the same.

We talk briefly about the festival. Does he go to many events? They're busy on the stall much of the time, he says, although he tries to get along to at least a couple of things. The day before last, in fact, he went to a talk about the formation of the solar system. Despite falling briefly asleep in the middle, he enjoyed it thoroughly.

I'm fifteen minutes late for my meeting when I finally reach the festival site, which looks far bigger up close than it did from the Llanigon community hall. It feels like a university campus, only entirely under canvas. The entrance area, which is as large as a sports hall, gives way to a maze of walkways. Populating these carpeted corridors are restaurants, market stalls and pop-up shops, all of them full of festival-goers killing time and spending money.

I find Jim Saunders in the entrance corridor of the Green Room. He is sitting in a partitioned cubicle containing five or six chairs, next to a corpulent man at a desk. The man has a speakerphone strapped to his head and an extensive checklist with names and times in front of him. As well as writing, Jim works as a driver during the festival. The man with the phone is his boss, whose job it is to co-ordinate lifts to and from Hereford railway station.

On a good run, the cathedral city can be reached in half an hour. The local 39a bus, which avoids the main roads in favour of the pretty Lilliput hamlets of backcountry Herefordshire, through fields so green they look spray-painted, can easily take double that. It stops periodically to pick up a sixth-form college student or day-tripping pensioner, catching its breath for a moment before its wheezing engine carries it on its bumpy, bumbling way.

In Clyro, the Hereford bus passes just once a week. It leaves on a Wednesday, at 11 a.m. The Marches' best defence against marauding Englishmen these days is not its castle mottes or ancient battlements. It's the lousy public transport network.

I apologise to Jim for arriving late and he brushes away my tardiness. 'Us drivers are used to waiting,' he says, and suggests we go through to the lounge area of the Green Room. We pass a temporary office space, where the festival's administrators tap away at keyboards. Among them I spot Peter Florence, the event's charismatic director, sitting behind a desk. He is leafing through a newly published novel, a bulbous set of headphones strapped to his ears. He looks absorbed.

We enter a large, brightly lit room, with four or five sofas against two walls and a bank of round desks along a third. The far end is made from glass or perhaps a polymer equivalent. It has a door that opens into a small square section of field which is masquerading as a garden. The wall beside the desks has a doorway that leads to a private seating area, presumably for writers with immobilising stage-fright or novelists with enormous egos.

Jim's book contains a collection of photographs and accompanying text along the theme of its title, *Hay: Landscape, Literature and the Town of Books*. The blurb on the back explains that he used to work as a field officer for the Offa's Dyke Path. His wind-blasted complexion and slim physique suggest that he hasn't hung up his walking boots.

As a boy, I'd done short sections of Offa's Dyke with my father. Based on an eighth-century linear earthwork, the route runs from Prestatyn in north Denbighshire to Chepstow in south Monmouthshire. It constantly slips back and forth between England and Wales along its 177-mile journey, embodying the Marches' own ambivalence towards national borders, a reflection of its wandering spirit that welcomes the lost and embraces the found. Remnants of the dyke are still visible today. Grass-capped and hunchbacked, they worm their way across hilltop ridges and clutch hold of valley slopes. It's as if an ancient army of giant moles had once trundled past this way, whipped on by a crackpot cast of blind generals in a hapless quest for the sea.

We find a seat and Jim immediately excuses himself to get a coffee. He's had a tiring morning, he says. It kicked off with an interview with BBC One Wales, then a local radio station had wanted to speak to him. The whole festival experience, it's a 'bit out of his comfort zone', he tells me. The Women's Institute, that's his usual stage.

In his absence, I briskly survey the room. There are two types of writer: those who have not long finished their events, and those who are about to go on. The first are easily identifiable, looking relaxed and grasping white roses, the literary equivalent of a marathon runner's medal. The second type is distinctly more fretful, either flustering over speech cards in a corner or sitting hunched around a table with their event chair.

Proud spouses, bored kids, event sponsors and other hangers-on also dot the room. Some are sitting on the table next to me. A suntanned young Californian with blond curly hair and a fitted leather jacket is holding court, recounting to three young women about how 'way-out' the city of Austin is. 'Like, if you're white in the hood at night, you can walk around no problem.' It's a good bet for real estate investment, he reckons. 'Ripe for gentrification.'

On the other adjoining table, a grey-haired lady is telling her elderly companion about the recent trip she and her husband Howard took to Turkey. They went on a marvellous tour of the markets. The whole experience was, apparently, 'a ball'.

Festival representatives make up the Green Room's remaining cohort. Some are staffers, their status given away by their clothes. Floral shirts, casual jackets and skinny Chinos for the men. Patterned skirts, oversized lambswool jumpers and linen scarfs for the women. It's the unofficial uniform of all reputable book festivals.

The remainder are interns, elvish models recruited direct from a fashion shoot with their translucent skin and languid limbs. I picture them as literature-loving undergraduates dreaming of a beatific life in a Bloomsbury garret, reading Yeats and penning verse. One is standing in the middle of the room holding a hardback book. She is slowly scanning the sofas and desks in the hope of identifying her assigned speaker from their back-cover photo. She stops beside my table. 'Are you Henry Nicholls?' Her tone, a mix of doubt and desperation. I'm not, I inform her with regret.

Jim returns with a frothy coffee and, at my request, offers

a potted description of his book: the town's history; brief biographies of some well-known residents; notable buildings; the surrounding landscape. If I'm interested, I should come to his presentation on Saturday morning. He has been assigned the 400-seat Oxford Moot tent. He'd welcome the support.

I say I'll do my best and we move on to why he originally moved to the area. He was born and brought up in Slough, he begins. Not a propitious start. His parents were from rural Buckinghamshire, however, so tales of scrumping and unpasteurised milk had peppered his childhood. 'I've always had this feeling that that was what real life was about.' Which is why he eventually tired of waiting for Betjeman's friendly bombs to fall and fled Slough's bright canteens for the countryside.

He liked the idea of the Chilterns. As a boy, they would visit an uncle who used to manage a farm there, near Henley. Now, the whole area is awash with stockbrokers and City types, he says. Even if it weren't prohibitively expensive, he wouldn't fancy living there. With its security gates and pristine Range Rovers, it's not what he'd call 'real countryside' any more. The horny-handed sons of toil have long fled.

'This is the real stuff,' he says, waving a hand at a print of the Wye valley wrapped in sunshine that covers the wall behind us. Jim lives in the border town of Knighton, where he has found his own version of rural bliss, replete with apple orchards and spring water, peaty sod and hillside paths. 'Plus I can afford it,' he adds. 'Just about.'

Returning to the book, I ask about his intended audience. He has clearly given the question some thought, and rattles off three categories of potential reader: local people, tourists to Hay and the festival crowd. He's banking on the last lot, really. If he had a mission with the book – which he doesn't, but if he did – it would be to encourage people to look beyond just the festival and the town. He snorts when I ask why he thinks this is necessary. From what he gleans from conversations with his passengers, most folk leave with a highly distorted view. Half don't even know if the place is in England or Wales. The other half think it's full of literary sophisticates all year round. It's not Hay and its environs they see; instead, it's the town's abstract offspring, 'Hay, the brand', with its global franchise of affiliated festivals from Beirut and Dhaka to Cartagena and Xalapa.

His advice for them would be to spend a little more time here. Hire a cottage. Go for some walks. Potter about the place. 'You probably have to be here when the festival isn't on to see what it's really like.' I agree, but his counsel causes me a degree of trepidation: they might just stay.

I am thinking of Johnny's customers and Martin in the beer tent. The area is gradually filling with people like them, folk who came here first because of the festival and then end up moving down on a full-time or semi-permanent basis. Does he ever worry that such an influx could change the character of the area?

'It could, I suppose,' Jim concedes. 'You hear about the internet changing everything, with people able to live any-where. If a lot of people from the south-east or Birmingham or wherever decide to move here, then it'll inevitably change. You'll see the house prices going up and a lot of the old buildings being renovated.'

'Is that a bad thing?' I ask, echoing the concerns Le Quesne first voiced about Clyro nearly half a century ago.

Jim is unsure. If they bring urban values into the coun-tryside, then, no, that's not good. A local friend who lives up in the Radnorshire hills recently told him how he no longer liked Hay 'because it was full of *Guardian* readers'. And he wasn't meaning the weekly *Farmers' Guardian*, Jim clarifies. I take his point.

Still, he doesn't think the Marches are about to go the way of the Chilterns. It's too far to realistically commute to London or other major cities. Indeed, its rural disconnectedness is what appeals to many newcomers. Nor do most want a Starbucks on the corner or a choice of department stores. These are what they're fleeing, more often than not.

In his view, there is probably an ideal number of incomers. Too many and they begin to swamp the place. Hay, he thinks, is at a tipping point. I'd probably agree.

Saturday morning, bright and early, I'm back at the festival site sitting in the Oxford Moot. Jim is a confident public speaker, the experience of all those village-hall lectures to the Women's Institute paying dividends. After an hour he closes his final slide, thanks the audience and is shepherded off towards the bookshop by an amicable intern.

Amid tables stacked high with books, their pristine pages untouched and inviting, a queue of fifteen has already formed. Jim is shown to one of the four signing desks, which are lined up like exam tables side by side. His sister and niece have come down from Huddersfield to lend their support. The latter snaps photos of him on her iPhone.

'Could you sign it for Dorothy, please?' the first lady in the queue asks, handing Jim a copy of his own book. He takes it from her and opens it to the title page. 'She lives in America now. It'll remind my nieces and nephews where they are from.' Similar requests follow. One man's family are all in Australia; another has a brother in South Africa.

The final couple in the queue present themselves as recent arrivals to the area. They live in Brilley. His presentation was inspiring, they tell him, and explain how they recognised only a few of the places in his slideshow but their appetite is now whetted to discover more. He asks their names and writes his signature with a flourish. A photographer from the *Western Mail* passes just as Jim's pen leaves the paper. 'Just hold it there a second.' Jim fixes a smile, his pen static. The camera clicks. 'Rogues' gallery', his sister jibes with affection.

*

I arrive at Eighteen Rabbit's new store as the white-haired painter-decorator is leaving. It's forecast to rain tomorrow, he is telling Andrew, the shop's co-owner. Brightening up the day after. He thinks it's best they start inside. 'Great stuff, man,' Andrew says. 'Seven thirty it is, then.'

The man slopes off, his footsteps falling silently down the empty street. It is Sunday evening and the other shops along Lion Street are shut except for the Chinese takeaway across the road. The bare strip lights of the oriental outlet emit an insipid yellowish light. A bored-looking staff member stands alone, drumming his fingers on the service counter, waiting for the phone to ring.

It's a month or so since the festival finished and the flood of visitors began to recede. Over the final weekend, the sun emerged from the shadows and crowned everything in triumphant, life-giving light. The busyness of the streets already feels like a lifetime ago, however. Hay's metamorphosis is short-lived. Almost as soon as the unsold books are bundled up and marked 'returns', the town brushes itself down and reverts to its habitual self.

As the painter had opened the door to step out, the high-pitched tinkle of a bronze bell attached to the hinge had reverberated through the unfurnished room.

'We're going to have to get rid of that, I think, Andrew,' Louise says to her husband, pointing a firm finger at the source of the noise.

The pair picked up the keys to the new premises about half an hour ago. A lease document rests on the sill of one of the two bay windows that face onto the street. 'HM Land Registry' the top of the page reads. Other than two vacuum cleaners, a stepladder and a pile of dust sheets thrown into the corner, the shop is more or less empty. Only a few odds and ends remain on the built-in shelving along one wall: a roll of duct tape, a fixed-line telephone, the Yellow Pages, a container for business cards and a small plastic sign saying RE-OPENING AT 2 P.M.

Andrew has a job list that the couple are working through feverishly, anxious to have the place prepped for painting in the morning. The first two tasks are ticked off already: remove picture-rail, extract protruding nails. Andrew is now turning his attention to the third entry, the removal of the convex security mirror hanging from the ceiling. He scales the stepladder and starts poking a screwdriver at the bolted metal bracket holding it in place.

Louise, meanwhile, has disappeared into a side room armed with a decorating knife and a pot of plaster filler. An open doorway on the right of the main retail space gives access to the moderately sized annexe. Off it runs a cramped storeroom, with a cubicle toilet at the far end. They are still deciding their customer lavatory policy. Louise is keen to keep it off-limits.

'What was it like, signing on the dotted line?' I ask Andrew, who is standing crouched under the mirror, struggling to get traction on any of the screws.

'Yeah, it's exciting, man,' he says. And then adds as a qualifier, 'But daunting at the same time.'

Since setting up Hay's first-ever fair trade store two years ago, they have been trading on the castle's cobbled bailey. The space is cheap, although it doesn't get the same footfall as the high street. This new shop on Lion Street will see them located right in the heart of the town.

It should be better for business, Andrew reckons. The downside is that it leaves them with nowhere to hide. Before, if they had a quiet day trading, they could blame it on the location. 'If it doesn't work, then it's down to us.'

They work well as a pair. Andrew is from Edinburgh, although he sounds almost cockney. Posh cockney, really. So few expletives, but liberal use of the word 'man' and the filler 'yeah, yeah', which quite often coalesce into 'yeah, man, yeah' or 'yeah yeah, man'. He is outgoing, smart and personable, three qualities that saw Hay's Chamber of Commerce come knocking at his door when the chairmanship recently became vacant.

Dorset-born Louise is quieter, a little shy perhaps. She's by no means a pushover, though. If her 'I think' about the bell seems to suggest ambivalence, then forget it. The ringer is coming down.

Mid-career professionals, Andrew and Louise are symptomatic of the new wave of incomers to Hay. Entrepreneurial, independent, community-minded, dynamic. They moved down a couple of years ago from London, where they used to run their own agency managing sustainable events. They first met in an indie music club in Brighton that Louise ran. She was a student. He was working at the record store HMV. They both still DJ regularly.

Looking to move out of the capital and start afresh, they

tossed up between relocating to Brighton or heading down to Hay. Louise knew Hay from helping organise events for one of the literary festival's sponsors. Of the two, Hay struck them as the most 'extreme'. If they were going to leave London, they figured they might as well 'go the whole hog and do it properly', as Louise puts it.

The ring of the bell sounds again. Derek and Joanna walk in with Bertie, their Border terrier, on a lead. Tall and bearded, Derek is from Scotland. He owns the town's Wholefoods and Deli store, which is located next to the takeaway directly opposite Eighteen Rabbit's new store. He trained as a landscape architect and worked for a number of years for a specialist firm in Kington, twenty miles to the north. Deciding the job involved too much travel and too much stress, he opted for a career change. He now works from dawn until dusk six days a week, but he does so on his own account and seems infinitely happier for it.

Joanna, a smiley brunette, is from Cork on the south coast of Ireland. She too changed jobs recently, dropping a full-time position with a food hygiene auditor to work on a freelance basis. The switch gives her more control over her diary and travel commitments, which makes living in a remote location such as Hay more manageable.

The two play to national stereotypes; he a little on the taciturn side; she all bubbles and cheer.

'Hell-oooo,' Joanna calls out as she steps through the door.

'Hey guys,' says Andrew, laying down his screwdriver and climbing down the stepladder. Louise drops her tools too and greets them cheerfully. It feels like a housewarming visit by neighbours, which it is of sorts. Just no cake.

'Wow-ee,' Joanna exclaims, clapping her hands and

moving into the middle of the room. 'This is so much bigger than I thought. It's huge. This is amazing, guys.'

'Thanks, man. Yeah, it's all good. All good,' says Andrew.

Louise offers to show them round, which doesn't take long, given that there are only two main rooms and both are empty. They walk across the click-clack laminate floor into the side room, Joanna peppering her with questions. What layout do they have in mind? What colour scheme are they going for? When do they hope to open? Will there be an opening party? It's giddy-making, but Louise takes it all in her stride.

The two women are good friends. In fact, they spent the whole day together yesterday as part of Hay's delegation to the International Fair Trade Towns Conference in Bristol. As well as trumpeting the cause of ethical commerce, Louise works part-time for the Wales Green Party. She also volunteers with a local charity that supports people in Hay's twin town of Timbuktu. She is, to use the political jargon, an 'engaged' citizen.

Andrew is no less so. Before the last national elections, he organised hustings events at the Globe for the parliamentary hopefuls. He is also the driving force behind the town's nascent Totally Locally initiative, a national 'shop local movement' that encourages independent retailers to work together. The idea is gaining traction, but it's slow, he admits. The problem is Hay's shopkeepers: they are all too independent.

The women's conversation moves from the shop on to the events of yesterday. They discuss the highlights: the charismatic mayor of Bristol, the coffee farmer from Nicaragua, the interfaith groups from Lebanon. 'I actually cried, telling Derek about it, I was so emotional,' Joanna admits.

I move back into the main room, where Andrew and Derek are talking lights. At present, three lighting tracks run the width of the ceiling. Eight shadeless pendant light fittings dangle above the bay windows at the front. Two bulbs are missing. Another doesn't appear to be working. It's a good idea to flood the back wall as much as possible, Derek thinks. 'Draws people in.' Andrew nods.

And rabbits, Derek want to know: will there be rabbits? Andrew laughs. There may be some 'rabbit elements', he admits. They have someone working on the sign for outside right now. 'Painted or vinyl?' Derek asks. Vinyl, Andrew says. His fellow shopkeeper approves. 'Good choice.'

'So, guys, it's all going to be great,' says Joanna, bouncing back into the room. 'It's so exc-iii-ting.'

Derek wishes them well, assures them everything is going to be a huge success and says to call by if they need anything. Louise jokes that the proximity of the Deli isn't going to help Andrew with his sausage-roll habit. I suggest they establish a barter system. Andrew likes the idea and proposes two sausage rolls in exchange for a pair of origami birds. Derek says he'll give it some thought. The couple leave, Bertie trotting after them.

Andrew and Louise return to their respective workstations. A minute later, Louise comes back into the main room. 'Look what I've found,' she says, brandishing a mini electric drill. The metal bell is summarily dislodged. With a look of satisfaction, she places it on a shelf.

I follow her back through to the other room. As she sets back to work scraping the wall, I ask her how they came up with the name for the business. Eighteen Rabbit was a Mayan king, she informs me. 'A real supporter of the arts and creativity.' Andrew and Louise lived in Mexico for a while and had learned about his story there. When they came up with the idea for a fair-trade store, it struck them as an apt name, although continually having to explain its derivation can become a touch tiresome. 'I wonder if we shouldn't just have called ourselves, Hay's Fair Trade Shop,' she admits.

The store focuses mostly on craft and clothing from fair-trade designers and co-operatives in the global South, she continues. T-shirts, dresses, hats, gloves, bags, wallets, candles, toys, bowls, jewellery, skincare, homeware. 'Traditional techniques, with a modern twist' is their general goal. Which is why she can't stand the bell. It reminds her of all 'jingly jangly things' you find in ethnic shops. They are keen to avoid a 'hippy' vibe.

'We don't want people buying our stuff out of sympathy,' she adds, looking up briefly as she prises the lid off the Multi Purpose Polyfilla. 'We want to be selling products that people genuinely want to buy because they're cool and stylish. We like popular culture, I guess, although neither of us are, like, massively fashionable . . .'

'Speak for yourself,' says Andrew, who, having succeeded in unscrewing the mirror, has wandered across to help.

'Okay, you're quite fashionable,' she replies, a patient smile on her face.

She looks across to her husband who is wearing Adidas Original Superstar trainers, a pair of dark skinny Nudie jeans and a short-sleeve, cobalt-blue summer shirt. The jeans are made from organic cotton. 'Swedish,' he tells me. Above it, he has a casual, slim-fit blazer.

Louise, whose blonde hair and fair skin contrast strikingly with Andrew's darker, almost Latino appearance, has a similar pared-down metro aesthetic. She eschews dresses and skirts in favour of branded jeans, Ethletic Fairtrade pumps and stylish cotton T-shirts or blouses.

They make an attractive pair. And while they may not be über-fashionistas by London standards, they are considerably more hip than the average Hay resident. That said, the local fashion bar is not a high one. Well-worn jeans and an unironed shirt is the basic look around town. In winter, a fleece jacket or oversized jumper is added.

'And how's it going?' I enquire. 'The business, I mean.'

Some of the older crowd find it all a bit disorientating, Louise says. They come in looking for Fairtrade-certified tea and greetings cards made from recycled materials. Instead, they find repurposed leather bags and hand-knitted alpaca beanies. 'It's not like Traidcraft, is it?' marks a refrain the London couple has had to get used to. They bite their tongues.

By and large, however, most folk who come into the shop seem to 'get' what they are trying to achieve, according to Louise. They've enjoyed some press coverage too. A national newspaper gave them a short write-up a little while back, which helped drive traffic to their website. And *Conde Nast* recently described them as 'the coolest fair-trade shop ever'.

As part of their marketing strategy, they both Tweet and Facebook extensively, which is building them up a steady following on social media. 'So, yeah, I think there's a buzz beginning to grow around the brand,' she says.

Andrew and Louise have arrived just as Hay's iconic second-hand book trade is beginning to totter. The instinct of modern book-buyers is first to look online if they want an old title, not to search through the disorderly shelves of a physical store. There's a last-ditch effort to stem the tide. Addyman Books has a banner outside its Castle Street store declaring Hay to be a 'Kindle Free Town'. Yet you sense the writing is on the wall. All the town's booksellers are busy cataloguing their inventory for AbeBooks and Amazon, Addyman included.

None is modernising faster than Booth's Bookshop, the most iconic of Hay's second-hand bookstores. Ownership of the once rambling, musty book emporium recently passed into the hands of Elizabeth Haycox, a wealthy American incomer whose initial connection to the town also came via the festival.

Bolstered by a background in high-street retail (she used to work in San Francisco for The Limited, a US women's clothing chain) and a husband with deep pockets, she is dragging the store into the twenty-first century.

So new books have appeared on the shelves and oak varnish on the floors. A calendar of regular events now runs week-to-week, ranging from book launches and concerts to kids' trails and evening talks. Soft-cushioned sofas grace a sunlit corner on the first floor. Next to them, an artfully decorated space is given over to ornate hardback editions of literary classics published by the Folio Society. Downstairs, there is an airy restaurant with sliding glass doors and a sun-trap patio. Built on to the back, meanwhile, is a swanky forty-seven-seat cinema, the first in town for half a century. Booth's Bookshop is also available for weddings.

A few recalcitrants regret the sprucing up of the iconic store, but it's either that or see it disappear. Incomer retailers all have to innovate to survive. Unlike local shopkeepers, the majority of new arrivals don't have the privilege of selling what people actually *need*. So the butchers, the hardware store, the post office, the newsagent's, the pharmacy, the mobile phone shop, the farming supplies outlet, the hairdresser's, the beautician's – all were snaffled up by long-term residents years ago.

Hence, the town's new breed of retailers tend to concentrate on the sale of what marketeers refer to as 'non-essentials'. For decades, that basically meant used books. With demand for second-hand titles now in abeyance, incomers like Andrew and Louise are having to look elsewhere. The result is a sudden flurry of pop-ups, vintage clothes stores and niche gift shops on the high street. Hay's most recent addition is a lingerie boutique, called UnderWhere?

Although some locals patronise such outlets, many deride their wares as 'expensive tat'. Eighteen Rabbit is unlikely to win much custom from the Merry Widows of Clyro, for example. Try as they do to appeal to all-comers, Andrew and Louise's business model lends towards the tastes – and wallets – of premium-paying outsiders, be they day-visitors, holiday-homers or residents 'from off'. So too with the Beer Revolution off-licence, which mostly sells individually packaged bottled ales from award-winning brewers. Likewise Derek's Deli, with its selection of 'biodynamic' sparkling wines and black puddings from the Outer Hebrides.

The truth of this came home to me when I once asked Pat if they'd ever consider meeting in Booth's café for their weekly coffee rather than Isis. 'It's not our kind of place,' she told me, and pushed her nose up with her forefinger to ensure I knew what she meant.

Her perspective saddened me because it seemed less a financial or aesthetic decision than a social one. The fact that social divisions should exist in any community is nothing new, I suppose. The human condition seems eternally bent on differentiating itself. History is, to a certain way of reading, just a catalogue of our schisms, squabbles and splits. A tortured tale of 'them' and 'us', 'me' and the 'other', 'my group' and 'their group'. Sometimes the fault lines are visible, sometimes not.

For me, the actual cause of division seems less important than our innate compulsion to divide. To desegregate, to stand apart, to cleave, to define ourselves one against the other: such is the essential impulse of mankind, it seems. We are social beings, but only to a point, only within our circle.

In modern Britain, the tenor of the times is shifting. The circle, we're told, is widening. Discrimination is most definitely *not* okay these days. Today, thankfully, we legalise against divisions of race and ethnicity, gender and religion. Our political elite, meanwhile, strives for an everyman kind of equality. It's all first-names and selfies now for the ruling classes. Helping them along is the widespread habit of toff-teasing, seemingly the last permissible prejudice.

The impression this gives is that ours is a permanent dress-down Friday society, in which everyone is 'mate' and no one's background counts. Of course, this is a bold-faced misinterpretation. Ephemera such as wealth and class matter. They shouldn't, yet they do, even in an out-of-the-way place like the Marches.

Society needs its divisions to function, political theorists and economists will argue. At a macro level, it would be impossible to expect seven billion people to organise themselves as one. Historically, the nation-state has stepped into the breach, divvying us up by geography and ethnicity into broadly manageable chunks. Rules are set, national myths created and cross-border trade negotiated.

The same rationale sees us split into ever smaller units: provinces, districts, municipalities, parishes, villages, right down to individual neighbourhoods. It's all about accountability these days. Everyone getting their voice heard. Which works just fine until certain voices begin to dominate and demand that the dividing lines are redrawn.

Divisions exist at an interpersonal level too. The much-fêted British anthropologist Robin Dunbar has suggested that we have capacity for an optimally sized friendship network. He puts the figure at around 150, now known as 'Dunbar's number'. More than that and our brains can't cope with the cognitive demands that genuine friendship requires.

The theory is often trumpeted as an antidote to the social media compulsion to count our 'friends' in the thousands. Twitter gives its users regular 'engagement' updates, proposing figures for an individual's 'possible reach' or 'share of voice' that run into four, five, even six figures. Beyond the little endorphin rush this offers, such numbers make sense only if you're marketing a product (or marketing yourself). From a relational standpoint, they are devoid of any material consequence.

If, as human beings, we're limited by the number of meaningful social interactions we can sustain, then this presupposes that divisions must begin to occur in communities of more than seven score and ten. Interestingly, Dunbar maintains that the average village size at the time of the Domesday Book was 150, give or take a few. Today, Hay is ten times that figure. Clyro, five.

So the critical question for social harmony becomes the grounds upon which these divisions occur. If the criteria are broad and benign, such as having children the same age or attending the same spinning class or, ideally, living on the same block, then the possibility of social circles intersecting and overlapping is ripe. In such communities, individuals find themselves at the epicentre of a mutually reinforcing Venn diagram of diverse relationships.

Where communities begin to malfunction is when entry to people's circles is over-prescriptive or precluded by prejudice. The outcome then inevitably tends towards exclusion. So only whites, or only those with a public school education, or only farmers, and so on. It is the trap of like-mindedness writ large.

Again, the requirements for entry are less important than the very existence of requirements at all. The word 'only' contains the crux of the problem. In it lie segregation, mistrust and all the attending baggage on which lonely, atomised communities are built. A society of circles spinning by themselves, insular and apart, always orbiting, never merging, every interaction containing the threat of a collision.

This corner of the Marches that we plucked from the map finds itself – praise God and Uncle Francis – in the non-prescriptive category. There are no 'gated communities' here, either physical or figurative. Since arriving in the Welsh borders, I have poked my nose into more pockets of the community than most. Some have embraced me, some have not, but none has closed the door.

Saying that, I know what Pat means by not being 'their kind of place'. Not about Booth's, which is *exactly* my kind of place, what with its paperbacked nooks and hardcover crannies. But about the Catholic Church, for instance, I guess I might say the same. Or the town's Conservative Club, with its painting of Mrs Thatcher in the hall.

If my short time in the Marches has taught me anything, it's that a warm welcome generally awaits across such thresholds. Maybe there's a future friend to be found or, if nothing else, a shared experience to be had. This is how I see communities growing, as well as our own individual lives becoming enriched. I remind myself to ask Pat to join me for a coffee at Booth's next time I meet her. Perhaps I'll garner an invite to Tuesday night bingo in return?

Inclusivity requires work, however. Oftentimes, we're all tempted to retreat into our private comfort zones. From a community perspective, there's nothing wrong with that, just as long as 'oftentimes' doesn't become 'all the time'.

The door swings open again, this time silently.

It's Trish, co-owner of the tapas bar a few doors down. She's hand-in-hand with Alex, her Uruguayan boyfriend, who's down visiting from London. They're heading over to the pub, she says. 'Just thought we'd call in and wish you well.' Andrew ushers her inside. It's his turn for the tour this time. The visitors 'ooh' and 'aah' in all the right places, and, as with Derek and Joanna, they predict great success ahead. '*Mucha suerte*,' Alex says as they leave five minutes later. Andrew waves them off. 'Cheers, man.'

A confab follows over the dampness and flatness of the Polyfilla. Andrew would like to sand it down tonight, ideally. Louise reads the instructions on the pot. 'One to two hours, surface dry.' They opt to leave it until the morning. Andrew worries it'll be too bumpy. Louise thinks it'll be fine. 'We'll just call it a Mediterranean cottage look,' she suggests.

Barely have the last visitors left when Val walks in. Another relatively new arrival in town, Val recently bought the narrow three-storey building between Booth's Bookshop and the Chinese takeaway. The bottom floor is currently a gift shop. She points to it through the bay window. Andrew and Louise's Prius hybrid is parked in front, with its 'HAY' and 'I Love Chilaquiles' stickers in the back window.

A boxy facade covers the front of Val's shop. Her plan is

to pull it down as soon as the current tenant's lease is up. Val has a designer's eye. In a previous life, she used to own an art gallery in Surrey. She now runs occasional sound therapy sessions with gongs. Beneath the facade are some beautiful original tiles, she says.

Val takes a seat on the sill of one of the deep bay windows. She asks questions similar to Joanna's and Louise patiently offers a similar set of replies. Val knows a good sign-maker if they need one. They thank her sincerely but say they've already commissioned someone. What will they do for internet? Val can recommend Mi-Fi. They were thinking of standard Wi-Fi, but thank her again for the suggestion.

The discussion then turns to the colour for the frontage. Andrew describes their preference for a 'sedate' look. To add some spice, they're thinking of painting the door orange. The idea seems to please Val, who says she's in conversation with Elizabeth at Booth's Bookshop regarding the Chinese takeaway. It looks a little shabby, she thinks. She hopes her wealthy American neighbour might have a word with the owner about redecorating.

Noting the time and guessing that the new tenants are keen to get on, Val levers herself off the sill and moves towards the door. 'Well, I'll love you and leave you, then. Good luck.'

Andrew thanks her for popping in and says he's looking forward to being 'neighbourinhos'. They will be moving their stock across in the coming days, so he apologises ahead of time for any disturbance. 'Give us a week or so and we'll be up and running.' Val smiles and waves goodnight.

Louise turns to her husband. First thing in the morning, they are blacking out the windows. Andrew agrees. He's 'on it'.

7

The Snail Chase

I knelt and prayed for charity, unity, and brotherly love, and
the union of Christendom. Surely a Protestant may pray in
a Catholic Church and be none the worse.

Kilvert's Diary, 7 September 1875

Hay has a king. His name is Richard. Richard III.

Dressed in a threadbare woollen jumper with flecks of
brilliant pink, his white hair ruffled as usual, he is sat with a
merry band of courtiers in the back room of the Swan hotel.
His red and white polka-dot walking-stick is lying flat
across the table in front of him, an unconventional sceptre
for a most unconventional king.

It is early evening and the drink is flowing in the Heorot
of Hay. Richard III sips from his pint of beer. He has himself an audience around him and is, as a direct consequence,
in ebullient mood.

As I enter, he is recounting his days as the official tourist
attraction of Wales in the mid-1970s. 'Now where was I? Yes,
the American ambassador . . .' An extended anecdote then
follows about an afternoon tea party he put on with the Welsh
Tourist Board. At the time, the king was living in Hay Castle
and was still in favour with the authorities in Cardiff (he'd
later denounce the Tourist Board in an excoriating pamphlet
as a bunch of corrupt and lily-livered nitwits).

In honour of the US ambassador and his wife, the party's star guests, they flew flags at full mast, piled pyramids of Ferrero Rocher on side-tables and left the cellar door off the latch. In no time, the king's retinue was royally inebriated.

'You remember, don't you, Jerry?' he says, looking over to a balding, mild-looking gentleman on the opposite side of the table. The king breaks off from his tale to explain that Jerry is his head of secret intelligence, an announcement that earns a fierce scowl from the Director of C.I.Hay.

Anyway, the ambassador's wife was dressed in a fabulous red dress, the king continues, oblivious to his security breach. And Jerry here was tottering across the room with some tea for her. 'Weren't you, Jerry?' The not-so-covert operative raises his eyebrows in grimaced assent.

'At that time I had Marianne Faithfull staying with me,' the septuagenarian sovereign adds, a reference to one of the more famous Swinging Londoners who fraternised his court during the heyday of his reign. 'Some apparatchik from Welsh Tourist Board tried to steer off Jerry from approaching the ambassador and his wife. But Marianne told the little sod in no uncertain terms to bugger off . . .'

The room breaks into giggles.

The king continues in this vein, ambling from oft-repeated anecdotes and slanderous asides, to his familiar hobby horses of mass media domination and his desire to relocate the capital of Wales to the riverine hamlet of Erwood (a move rationalised by its location on a 'strategic line of communication' beside the Wye and the A470, which, in the king's opinion, comprise the country's most important river and road respectively).

Born Richard George William Pitt Booth to a military family on 12 September 1938 in Hay, the town's monarch reputedly pronounced himself regent in the pub. The proclamation, it is said, was inspired by the presence of two journalists and the prospect of some cheap publicity. The story may or may not be true, but it's the version that local people like best and thus the one that has stuck.

The ruse worked. After appointing his horse as prime minister and issuing his own passports, the eccentric new sovereign won his fifteen minutes of fame, with accounts of his coronation appearing everywhere from *The New York Times* to *El País* and the Kingdom of Hay duly finding its place on the map.

In the tradition of all good self-appointed rulers, the king got busy establishing his own fighting force. A friend with a biplane became head of the Royal Hay Air Force, another friend with a rowing boat became Admiral of the Fleet, while all able-bodied townsmen were put on standby in the event that the realm ever needed defending.

The idea of turning Hay into a town of books all began with King Richard too. He set up his first second-hand bookshop on Castle Street as a young man and soon established several more. He likes to say he was born with one fortune, made two and lost four. The crippling running costs of the castle eventually obliged him to move back to his family home ('the Royal Palace', as he calls it) in Cusop Dingle, a leafy hamlet attached to Hay.

The Royal University of Cusop Dingle is Richard III's latest harebrained venture. I heard about it first when an invitation to the inaugural lecture fell through my door a few months ago. Accompanying the note was a request to choose our own professorship. For inspiration, the 'Uri Gagarin Chair of Space Poetics' was cited as an example.

Tim the Gardener, a self-taught classicist who lives in a

caravan up on Boatside, entertained us with his unique interpretation of the Iliad. 'Was Homer taking the piss?' his chosen lecture title ran.

Next up came Eugene, a much-loved local artist and ex-member of a Catholic order, who is now in his eighties and who, in the spirit of Jenny Joseph's poem 'Warning' (about dressing in purple and a red hat), enjoys wearing patterned neckerchiefs and bright coloured trousers.

Eugene spoke passionately on the 'Creative Life', lamenting society's subjugation to the utilitarian and urging us to re-embrace the imaginative wonder of our childhood selves. The lecture attracted a wide gathering from Hay's substantial bohemian crowd, as well as sparking a brief monologue from the king about the acclaimed artist Sidney Nolan, who lived nearby in Presteigne and who sold him a couple of paintings for a song. The event ended with the promise of a royal exhibition at the Palace in honour of the king's 'old pal, Sidney'.

This evening is the third in the university's lecture series, with none other than Richard III himself presiding. His subject is typically non-specific: 'You Cannot Make a Silk Purse from a Sow's Ear.' I sit waiting for the event to officially begin as His Majesty continues with his episodic warm-up routine.

After a short yet fervent digression about the Dark Lords of the Welsh Assembly, he brandishes a copy of today's *Western Mail* and begins a fresh assailment against media collusion with the establishment. The newspaper has a full-page spread concerning Hay, all of which is complete poppycock, according to the king. One whole hour he spent talking to the journalist on the phone and the cretin has got everything 'arse over tit'. He spies a conspiracy at play.

I catch the eye of the gentleman sitting next to the maddened monarch, whom I've arbitrarily decided must be the dean on account of his august set of eyebrows. I indicate that I'd be interested to see the newspaper and he pushes it across the table towards me. The offending piece runs over thirty short paragraphs and is dominated by a large image of Hay's sovereign. He is pictured dressed in a crushed-velvet cloak and copper crown, sunlight bathing his regal frame as he looks pensively out of his study window. Shelves thick with books fill the foreground. He looks resplendent.

I skim through the article and spot little to justify the king's annoyance. The journalist dutifully recalls his 1977 coronation as well as his early benevolence (the Kingdom's new subjects, it's reported, received free money in the form of edible rice-paper banknotes). There's even a plug for the king's website, where dukedoms (priced £55), earldoms (£50), baronetcies (£40), and knighthoods (£30) are available for purchase.

A second, closer reading reveals what a thin-skinned soul might see as sideswipes or slights. All are comparatively minor, the most obvious being the use of the common-law 'Mr Booth' rather than the king's royal honorific. At one point, the adjective 'eccentric' is used to describe his royal personage, although I suspect that it might be the one word in the whole piece of which the king thoroughly approves.

It then dawns on me that the king's displeasure lies not in *how* he is portrayed but how *much* he is portrayed. For although his royal visage adorns the page, his name does not appear in the title and the paragraphs are only tangentially about him. The real star of the piece is a Mr Derek Addyman of Hay, aged 59, whom the journalist describes as 'Prince',

'Royal' and, most presumptuously of all, 'King Richard's spiritual heir'.

A fellow bookseller in town, this upstart rival is described as the driving force behind a referendum on Hay's ongoing independence. The ballot aims to discover if residents believe the town should remain a sovereign state. An ancillary question bundled up within the popular vote asks whether Hay-on-Wye's official postcode should be switched to the more dramatic 'HOW1'.

'The first bookshop opened in Hay in 1962,' Mr Addyman (59), is quoted in the article as saying. 'Since then, because of the work that our king Richard Booth did throughout the world promoting the international book economy, there are now somewhere in the region of 100 booktowns worldwide.'

Although this sounds flattering, I wonder if it may be another reason for the king's ire. The concept of the 'booktown' is one that he holds very dear. It's also one that he doesn't want to lose his grip on. The International Organisation of Booktowns, of which he is both founder and president, recognises a mere seventeen bona fide booktowns. This privileged elite stretches from Sysmä in Finland to Paju in South Korea. Their number might drop, however. Wigtown in Scotland has entered an alliance with the regional tourist authority. The king does not approve.

I clock back into the king's conversation. He is still on the theme of collusion, pointing out that public officials depend on journalists, just as journalists depend on public officials. Hay has ridden to power on this kind of mutual back-scratching, he insists. 'And as for how they have treated the official attraction of the Welsh Tourist Board of the last thirty years . . .'

'Sorry, Richard, but if I might interrupt ever so quickly,'

says a feisty, dark-haired woman at the far end of the table.

The king splutters to a stop, a look of bemusement crossing his face.

'In your own time, of course, Richard, but we would like you to announce the results of the referendum,' the woman adds.

A young man beside her, who has been writing furiously throughout the king's talk, puts down his Moleskine notebook and picks up a camera. He is a new recruit, a fresher chronicler perhaps. He gets up from his chair and walks around the room, stationing himself directly opposite the king. He trains his lens and waits. A sense of suspense arises.

The lady reaches into her pocket and pulls out a folded scrap of paper. She passes it to the person beside her, who passes it on to the next person and so on until it reaches the middle of the table where the king is seated. Richard III unfolds it, squints and then hands it to the dean on his right. The light is too bad, the ageing monarch declares. He can't make out what it says.

Clasping the paper between thumb and forefinger, the dean holds it with outstretched arms as though it were a parchment scroll. Pushing his glasses down his nose, he clears his throat and begins to read.

'Total votes cast, five hundred and thirty.'

'Can you speak up?' someone at the back asks.

'Total votes cast, five hundred and thirty,' he repeats, no louder the second time but considerably gruffer. '"No" votes, forty-three.' Enthusiastic applause. '"Yes" votes, four hundred and eighty-three.' A spate of frenzied cheering and clapping of hands breaks out. 'Spoiled, . . .' he barks, but the number is lost to the din of celebrations. The young chronicler snaps his camera furiously.

Once the hubbub has calmed down a fraction, Pat, the king's faithful secretary, a lady whose physical and moral qualities are in delightfully generous proportion, coughs loudly and recommends that the king be given the space to resume his lecture. The Sow's Ear, it would seem, is already mid-manufacture.

After his successful performance at the polls, the king returns to where he left off, re-energised. Characteristically, however, it's not exactly where he left off. 'As I was saying,' he starts, 'I would like to see a return to burning certain books.' He recommends starting with Trevor Fishlock's *Wales and the Welsh*. 'A typical Murdoch hack, creeping up to the Welsh Tourist Board.'

He'd also like to use this evening's platform to discuss another subject that vexes him: Hay's twinning with the town of Timbuktu in Mali. He has recently been reading Doris Lessing. 'Now, Lessing, of course, is the originator of Rhodesian communism, which is very interesting because . . .'

A chair scrapes back noisily along the floor, causing everyone to look round. The king stops again. Then a man in jeans and a long-sleeved shirt stands up and, in an apologetic voice, excuses himself. 'I must take my leave, My Liege. Thank you for a most amusing evening. It's reminded me of working for you all those years ago. Just like the old days.' He offers a blanket wave to the rest of us. 'Adieu all.'

As he heads for the door, he passes the dark-haired woman, who reaches out her hand and touches him gently on the arm. In a soft voice, barely above a whisper, she bids him goodbye. 'Adieu, sweet Prince.'

After the departure of Mr Addyman, the king appears to feel a need to reassert his authority. His mind turns to global matters. He has an introduction to the Polish foreign minister, we should know. He is also working on his links with the 'UN person' for the United States. The thing is, to get into the international world, one must first go through the international cocktail of America and then London, he asserts. 'So I'm going to London.'

What exactly he plans to do there we never learn, however, because mention of the UK capital leads him off on a discussion about Persian bread. A large community of Iranians have settled near his flat in west London. 'Who's your bread person friend, Jon?' The question is directed to a tall man with an angular face. 'Phoebe?' the man responds hesitantly. 'Good, well, ask Phoebe what she feels about Persian bread,' the king commands. Personally, the king thinks it's wonderful.

Time is moving on. The evening is nearing an end and the dean would like to say a few words. 'If I may.' It is not a question.

Unlike the king, for whom evidence and argument are never more than unwittingly related, the dean builds up to a clear point. The university remains in its infancy. It has a crest in the form of a cartoon snail with a cinnamon-whirl shell. It also boasts its own motto, a saying lifted from *Irish Fairy Tales* (1920), which runs: *We get wise by asking questions, and even if these are not answered, we get wise, for a well-packed question carries its answer on its back as a snail carries its shell.*

Yet the institution's purpose and future course still remain very much open for debate. In the dean's humble opinion, we would do well to avoid the grand theories spouted by the Orthodox Academy. These are mere chimeras anyway, efforts by professional scholars to shoehorn the world into neat categorisations.

What really interests him is the fate of those who don't fit into these overarching schematics. What place do the likes of Ruth St Denis, the maverick dancer inspired by an advert for Egyptian Deities cigarettes, have in such restrictive, linear constructs? None, none whatsoever. Instead they're forgotten, tossed aside, lost down what the dean calls the 'rabbit-holes of history'. These misfits in the official canon, these cast-offs of academia, rescuing them would be a noble pursuit for a royal university, he thinks.

The room warms to the idea. Faculty members start nodding their assent. The idea of digging up historical mavericks from rabbit-holes appeals. The king is especially taken, no doubt picturing himself marching at the head of an expeditionary force, excavating dead eccentrics from the dustbins of academic research, the university's very own White Rabbit.

The king, who suddenly looks very tired, salutes the dean and thanks him for his contribution. He heartily endorses his belief in nonsense and gives his blessing to the dean's suggestion. 'And sod everyone else, I say.' He draws a triumphant breath and leans back in his chair.

'Terrific,' says Pat the Secretary. 'So is that all agreed?' The question is met with the sound of laughter and clinking glasses. Pat scribbles in her notebook. The motion, I'm supposing, is passed.

'Now, shall we thank Richard for his talk?' Pat suggests, putting her hands together first. We all join her in clapping. Demurely, Richard III downs the remainder of his pint.

The mood among the Faculty is happy and replete, as though we've worked our way through a gargantuan four-course meal, which in a way we have. We shall all leave knowing more than before about Welsh politics and Persian bread, modern dance and the price of a title. Yet the source of people's satisfaction lies elsewhere. As now formally agreed, the university meets not to search out knowledge, but in the hope of meeting mock turtles and Cheshire cats, of hearing riddles about ravens and writing desks, of poking fun at the powerful and exalting the absurd.

And this we have done. We have feasted on folly. We have chased the snail. It is now time for bed and sleep. Hay's wise old king retrieves his walking stick from the table, tightens his scarf around his neck and, with Pat on his arm, heads home to his Palace up the Dingle.

*

If Richard III is committed to establishing his own ivory tower in the heart of the Welsh Marches, then Rodney is focused on an even more revolutionary task: the drawing up of a Community Plan.

For all my talk of consensus-building and the search for common ground, communities are not manufactured from thin air. Of course, they are informed and nurtured by our constant interactions, by new arrivals and fresh ideas. Equally certainly, however, they build on what came before, on the bricks of the past that are carried forth into the present.

The problem is that the transfer of these pasts is imperfect. Some bricks are recut or replaced, while others are obscured by new facades. For those who moved here in the booktown boom years, the spirit of Boothian nonconformity remains their cornerstone. With every swanky new shop or unimaginative housing development, they lament its passing. For them, the university is a possible bastion, a last throw of the dice.

More recent incomers see things differently. Amused as they are by so much quirkiness, they stand one step removed.

The sight of the town crier in his frilly ruff and knee-length stockings. The sound of the night-time wassailing in nearby apple orchards. These are the witty flourishes that adorn their move-to-the-Marches story, raising a smile when retold to others. It falls to them not to repeat what came before, but to reinvent and reinterpret for today. Hence a tapas bar in rural Wales, for instance. Or a fair-trade shop in an unfair world.

Older residents look on bemused, meanwhile. Their world has changed, but their mental maps of it very often have not. They knew Hay before its bookish craze. They can still see their family's two-up, two-down where the library now stands. They'll still slip a lucky coin to whoever buys their lambs or calves in the livestock market, even as the abattoir lorries rattle past in the street outside. In such a social cauldron, conflicts of opinion almost inevitably stir and stew. Putting to paper what the community stands for and where it's heading requires some diplomacy, therefore, especially for an old Communist Party member like Rodney.

We meet in his house in a converted farm complex just outside Hay. Retired, yet still full of energy, Rodney sports a splendid white goatee-beard and an impish grin. He's always pottering about the streets of Hay, invariably with a friendly word on his lips and a black beret on his head. Today, I find him in a woollen cardigan and moccasins. He serves me coffee from a cafetière and invites me through to the living room.

Creating a Community Plan is not a radical idea at all, he starts by telling me, his voice soft and deliberate. Towns and villages are doing it across the UK. To get theirs started, he has corralled various friends and acquaintances into a working group. Among them is Johnny from the coffee stall. Another is a retired business executive called Nick, who made it his business to get the town's haphazard traffic system straightened out. The man has form, Rodney notes. In a spirit of unity, they have named themselves 'Hay Together'. To get the ball rolling, they held some public meetings in an effort to canvass local viewpoints. It's important that the town as a whole 'owns' the process from the outset, he explains.

Organisationally, the group is slowly taking shape. Rodney and his colleagues have managed to arrange use of a small space up at the castle for a peppercorn rent. The Chamber of Commerce, which has a small fund for community projects, has offered to cover payment. Powys County Council, on the other hand, has stepped in with the offer of a part-time community support co-ordinator.

Now, one year in, they've held plenty of meetings and drawn up plenty of action plans. The space by the castle is no longer the murky storage dump it once was, but a presentable office and meeting room. Across the cobbled passageway outside is a covered area with a pub-garden table and a huge map of Hay along a wall. But there's still no sign of a Community Plan.

I ask Rodney what the hold-up is.

He takes a sip of his coffee and leans back in his armchair. He looks over my head, casting a wistful gaze above the wall of bookshelves to a narrow mezzanine floor. A railing stretches across the edge. Attached to its outside hangs a classic Claud Butler road bike. It is painted bright yellow. Diana, his partner, bought it as a present with the idea of him cycling into Hay. From the bike's current position, I'm imagining that this hasn't come to pass.

Exhaling deeply, he launches into a protracted explanation. It's complicated, he starts. Part of it is the independent nature of the town. People are wary of collective undertakings. They want to be free, unencumbered, self-governing. The local citizenry is also bloody-minded, he adds. So those community groups that do get off the ground frequently end up splitting. 'Why have one group when you can have two?' goes a running joke about Hay's voluntary sector organisations. Rodney has his own version of the same: 'Too many chiefs and not enough Indians.'

There are other impediments besides. One in particular: town politics. Rodney takes another deep breath. To fully appreciate the difficulties of moving forward with the Community Plan, I need to understand its background. He offers me a timeline, charting it out with the edge of his hand along the arm of his chair.

It all started a few years back, when rumours began circulating about a supermarket moving into the town centre. People were aghast. It would rip the heart out of the high street, they warned. Local shops would close, traffic would increase and Hay would become another identikit town: monochrome, clone-like and dead.

Then the Town Council came out and confirmed not only that the rumours were true but that the supermarket plan had their full backing. Swaying their view was the developer's promise to build a brand-new primary school and community centre. A proportion of the town saw this as a reasonable trade-off. Rodney viewed it as blackmail.

He elaborates at length, about how the deal contravened Powys Council's own procurement deals, how it lacked any kind of audit trail and how conflicts of interest abounded. What irked him most of all was the way the whole idea had been cooked up without regard for the community's opinion. 'The whole thing stank.'

A vociferous opposition group quickly formed and

Rodney threw himself into the fray. The anti-supermarket campaigners called themselves Plan B – a canny counterpoint to a public comment by a harassed County Council executive that there was 'no plan B'. The package, as it was presented, was school-plus-supermarket or no school at all. So Plan B set about devising an alternative financing scheme. In the meantime, it set up a subcommittee called Hearts and Minds with the mission of raising awareness about the perils of opening the door to Big Retail.

It didn't take long before the affair turned 'rancorous', Rodney admits. Within a fortnight, Plan B had to close its community Facebook page under a barrage of abuse. On the flip side, town councillors found themselves subject to a widespread whispering campaign about backhanders and 'ransom strips'.

Soon, it was all-out combat. A protest group held a silent vigil at County Hall in Llandrindod. Another took its concerns to the Welsh Assembly. At the height of the conflict, a full-page article appeared in *The Times*. The newspaper's readers were informed that Hay was 'gearing up for civil war'.

Rodney grows vivacious at the retelling. A full-on Marxist, politics is his life's passion. Not the pontificating, dinner-party kind, but banner-waving and picketing. Powerfully influenced by the social democratic ideals of post-war Britain, he joined the Communist Party in the 1960s and remained loyal until the fall of the Berlin Wall.

A fierce anti-Thatcherite even before Thatcher, he worked intermittently as a university teacher for much of his career. His specialist interests are the built environment and the history of commodities. For a while, he became heavily involved in documentary-making for television as

well. Inspired by the idea of 'history from below', he con-
tributed to films on the everyday lives of British workers.
Involvement in a communal housing project in
Herefordshire kept him busy too, as did a sideline in political street theatre.

Looking back, he charts his career not by promotions but
by protest movements: the anti-Vietnam War marches, the
Women's Lib struggle, the miners' strike, the nascent Green
movement.

'I wrote a position paper about all the actors involved in
the supermarket deal,' he explains, returning to the subject
at hand. 'The baddies always have chinks, you see – that's
what my experience in grassroots campaigns has taught me.
You can get people on your side, but first you have to understand who they are.'

At the start of the campaign, he called some old contacts
for advice. One of his former students, now a leading light
in civic mobilisation, laid out various campaign strategies
that the supermarket's opponents might consider. The
counsel of a solicitor friend, meanwhile, was to threaten the
County Council with judicial review. In the end, Plan B
opted for a little of everything and eventually the whole deal
was dropped.

Rodney emerged bruised but defiant. An anonymous
post on a community blog had singled him out for criticism,
claiming that daily deliveries from Waitrose were arriving
at his house. 'They said that's why I was against the project.'
He laughs. He has hardly ever been into Waitrose, he insists.
'I've been a member of the Co-op for forty years.'

The experience left him, and other incomers, with a pro-
foundly dim view of the local council. 'They are entirely
policy-less,' he says. Compared with his subsequent com-

ments, the criticism sounds close to a compliment. Sexist, nepotistic, secretive, unaccountable: these are just some of the barbs he throws at them. 'Even when I was battling with Lambeth in the 1970s against Tory cuts, the councillors were never that bad.'

The council is made up of a small clique of locals, in his view. They all know each other from old. Half are in business together or connected by marriage. Elections are largely uncontested. They co-opt their friends to join. They never think to explain their decisions to the public. '"Oh, well, it's like that everywhere," they argue. I say, "It's like that in North Korea, mate."'

To his credit, one of the councillors called a public meeting in the wake of the supermarket scrap. The idea, according to Rodney, was to heal some of the wounds caused by the conflict. This was back when the Conservatives were talking up their 'Big Society' policy. It was out of that meeting that the proposal for a Community Plan was born.

Rodney levers himself up out of his seat and walks across to a bookshelf by the fireplace. 'You know who came up with the whole Big Society thing?' he asks, and reaches for a slim volume from the shelf with the same title. I don't. Jesse Norman, he tells me. The MP for Hereford and South Herefordshire. He passes me the book and recommends I read it. *An Anatomy of the New Politics*, reads the subheading.

While he's up, he searches for another book. He bought it the first time he visited Hay, back when the book festival was just starting out and long before he moved here permanently. 'Now where is it?' He can't put a finger on it. Later that day, he sends me an email with the title and some blurb. It's a four-volume set on the life of General Sir Charles Napier, who fought against Napoleon in the Peninsular War and whose statue stands in Trafalgar Square. In the mid-1970s Rodney wrote a book about this popular London tourist spot. *Emblem of Empire*, it was subtitled. It sold well in the USSR.

As he returns to his seat, he passes me a copy of the Hay Together Constitution. It's a ten-page document, printed on A4 paper with a rainbow-coloured swish on the front page. I scan the 'Objectives', which are bulleted on page 1 and which note the aforementioned Community Plan. Also appearing on the list are the goals of promoting the town 'as a centre of books', encouraging pride in our community, and working with local government agencies, including the Town Council.

Preceding the bullet points is a single paragraph entitled 'Aims'. It reads as follows:

> To safeguard Hay-on-Wye and its environs (the area of benefit) by gaining local and national support for Hay Together's intention to create an influential community voice in the planning and development of the area of bene-fit's social and environmental future.

The word 'safeguard' leaps out at me.

The supermarket fracas, which was unfolding just as we arrived in the area, is undoubtedly the most convulsive brouhaha to have hit the local area in recent years. Yet it is by no means the only one. Barely a month goes by without someone launching a campaign about something.

So recently there was a fight to keep the public toilets open. Before that there was the to-do about a phone mast above Hay Primary School. Then came the struggle against a proposed wind turbine on Clyro Hill. Next, the fight over a potential chicken broiler complex in Dorstone. The latest skirmish is over the possible closure of Gwernyfed High School.

All, in some way or other, represent exercises in safeguarding. It may be homeowners wanting to protect their view, or 'landscape character' as planning-speak would have it. It could be parents worried about their children's health or residents fretting over noise levels or a village concerned about traffic. Anything, basically. All it needs is for people to feel that something they care about passionately is under threat.

Looked at from outside, such community squabbles can seem terribly parochial. A strong element of self-interest undergirds much of what motivates people to get off the couch and complain, for sure. The classic 'Not In My Backyard' syndrome. As one anti-turbine advocate put it to me, 'If I'm not going to look after my backyard, who is?' She had a point.

Despite its pejorative contemporary associations, however, 'parochialism' as a concept has its merits. The term literally means 'of the parish'. In its purest sense, it speaks of 'the small and the particular and the specific', to quote the writer Paul Kingsnorth, author of *Real England: The Battle Against the Bland*.

As global brands engulf the globe, his argument goes, more and more of us find ourselves living in the shadows of McDonald's Golden Arches or a Best Western hotel. In such circumstances, the particularities of individual place become ever more important. When they disappear, part of us disappears with them. It is hard to persuade yourself that your community is distinctive and different when it looks so similar to everywhere else. The same is true for our own selves.

Viewed as such, the obverse to parochialism isn't open-mindedness. It's placelessness. The doctrine of the 'global

citizen', at liberty to globetrot through life, never putting
down roots, always floating through. It sounds attractive.
It's probably quite fun. But really, deep down? Never having anywhere to call 'home'. Never having anywhere specific to go back to or think back on. We belong to the world,
such people say of themselves. This is true. Equally, they
belong to nowhere. They are ships without a flag, adrift on
the waves. Floating. Anchorless.

Kilvert could never have imagined an era in which such
dislocation was possible. How much more prescient then
his passion to record the singularities of parish life in the
Marches. The villagers' tradition of begging for milk from
the farms so they could bake cakes for Michaelmas, for
example. Or the fact that ground ivy is known alternatively as Robin-in-the-hedge in Radnorshire and Hay
Maids in Herefordshire. Kilvert sensed that such quirks
and customs could perish with the wind, as indeed so
many have.

There's more to it than this for Rodney, though. The lifelong agitator in him sees a point of political principle at
stake. The democratic process, no less, is under threat. It all
sounds rather alarmist, so I ask him for proof. Plan B put up
a dozen or more candidates for the Town Council elections,
he tells me, five of whom won seats. Yet within six months,
all had acrimoniously resigned. Pushed out, one by one,
Rodney would have me believe.

I look back down to the stated 'Aims' in Hay Together's
constitution. Rereading it more carefully, I'm struck by
another phrase: 'To create an influential community voice.'
How high does he rate his chances of achieving such an outcome? He strokes his goatee for a second or two. His thick
spectacles have slipped down his nose and he pushes them

back up with his forefinger. People clearly wish to speak up, he says, his own voice more measured than ever. The issue is whether the 'old guard' are prepared to listen.

'And are they?' I ask.

He scrunches his shoulders and offers a broad grin. He couldn't possibly comment. I should go along to a Town Council meeting, he suggests. 'Judge for yourself.'

*

Much of what Hay Together stands for rings true with me. The importance of all voices being heard. The idea of safe-guarding what makes the town unique. The hope of moving forward together. I struggle to see where the problem lies. Yet it may well be that my incomer blinkers are blinding me. For the sake of balance, I feel compelled to take Rodney up on his idea.

And so it is that, on a Monday evening a few weeks later, I find myself sitting in the upper room of Hay's centrally located council building. The walls are covered with wood panelling and adorned with various plaques. 'War Savings Campaign, 1944' reads one. Another thanks the town's citizens for their refuge and hospitality during World War II, signed 'London's children and teachers'. Among the other wall-hangings are a print of Hay Castle and an aerial photograph of the town.

Outside the room's only window, the clock tower looms large. Nine councillors plus the clerk are seated round a boardroom table watching the minute hand. They are all 'born and bred'. Two of the nine are women. The clerk is the only one in a suit. Five members of the public, all of them women of pensionable age, are sitting on a row of chairs against the far wall. The evening is close and the unventilated room already stuffy.

The clock strikes seven and the meeting commences.

From an accountability perspective, the proceedings start well as chairman Robert Golesworthy, a tall imposing man with a thin face and large, basketball player's hands, invites the councillors to declare any conflicts of interest. An elderly gentleman puts his hand up and lets it be known that he is a Friend of Hay Castle. Another reveals himself to be a member of the Royal British Legion.

The next half hour proves promising as well, with the floor given over to issues raised by the public. First up is the interim director of Two Towns, One World, a two-year government-funded project to support Timbuktu. The programme is wrapping up and the director is here to present a concluding report. When she finishes, a councillor asks her if she's happy with the document, to which she responds that she ought to be, given that it was she who wrote it. There are no further questions.

Next up is a retired gentleman from Rail for Herefordshire, a local action group. He is concerned that the Sunday bus from Hay to the train station in Hereford is due to be axed. Weekend tourism will be affected, he fears. Again, the councillors listen attentively. A short discussion follows, although the Town Council resolves that it can do little to help. Public transport falls outside its remit.

A report from the local police then follows. In total, 138 calls were registered last month, a constable informs them. Most relate to speeding drivers, uncontrolled dogs and petty theft. A nineteen-year-old was detained for abusive behaviour while drunk. A thirty-nine-year-old was found with cannabis in Clyro. Otherwise, all quiet as usual.

With the constable's departure, the Town Council moves on to the main business of the evening and very quickly its true colours begin to show. It is suggested, for instance, that the toilet subcommittee 'needs a man'. No reason is given. Urinal experience, presumably. One of the male councillors thinks a role should be found for the younger of the two women. 'That would scare the lot of them.' The men all laugh. The woman in question does not.

Rodney's allegations about democratic process gain more weight when the subject of new officers crops up. There are currently two vacancies. A call for replacements went into the community's monthly magazine, although as yet with no response. An announcement in the *Brecon & Radnor* would gain wider reach, but it's deemed 'too expensive'. Instead, councillors are encouraged to sound out their contacts to see whom they might co-opt. 'I've already frightened two off,' says one of the longest-standing representatives. Another genuinely asks, 'What's Facebook?'

A little later, the agenda moves on to the renewal of the town's grass-cutting contract. The tender was awarded to the lowest bidder, the chairman announces. 'But how do you know they will do a good job?' one of the female councillors asks. Someone else enquires about the identity of the other bidders. The chairman shuffles in his seat. He looks ruffled. It's not appropriate to discuss the matter, he eventually says. Not with members of the public present. 'We can always leave if that makes it easier,' one of the elderly observers says. Astonishingly, all four of the women then pick up their things and troop out of the room.

I'm flabbergasted. My instinctive reaction is to get up and follow them. I resolve against doing so, partly out of truculence, but mostly on principle. We're there to bear witness.

It's ridiculous if onlookers absent themselves the moment controversy arises. So there I remain, fixed in my seat, looking down at my notes, pretending to be ignorant of what has just unfolded around me.

A palpable discomfort descends. For a moment, everyone fidgets awkwardly. All eyes eventually turn towards the chairman. He coughs. 'So, to the next item,' he says, his voice halting. And there the grass-cutting contract remains, unexplained. 'Ah yes, the Community Plan.' He audibly groans. I feel vindicated.

The National Park Authority, the body responsible for Brecon Beacons National Park, has asked whether the Town Council would be interested in developing a forward-looking strategy for the town. The brief is more or less identical to that of Hay Together. A logical step would therefore be to pass it on to Rodney's group, which is already out canvassing residents for their opinions.

The consensus among the councillors is that the buck stops with them. This seems legitimate. They are the town's elected representatives, after all. So a subcommittee is duly established and a date set for an initial meeting in three weeks' time.

One of the replacements for the ousted Plan B councillors pipes up. He thinks it's important to involve 'other important people in town'. The suggestion earns him some disapproving stares. 'That's at a later date,' a veteran councillor says. The new recruit persists nonetheless. People will expect to have input, he suggests, his tone apologetic. The key step is for the subcommittee to get going with it, he's told.

He tries one last time. 'So, at what stage do you think we need to identify – "partners" is perhaps the wrong word – "other participants", let's say?' Later on, the general verdict runs. The veteran councillor is more emphatic. 'I don't think we want to get too close to anyone else yet, thank you.'

A dozen or so other items remain on the agenda. Doggedly, the board of the Town Council works through them. Residents' parking, dog-fouling, the playground, the Cheese Market. I watch the clock. There's at least an hour more to go, I'm guessing. I am tempted to leave, although, having shown such determination not to do so earlier, I feel honour-bound to stay.

The final item on the agenda is 'Reports from Representatives'. Each councillor is assigned to liaise with a community group. Two or three brief updates are offered. At the end, it's noted that the Town Council currently has no designated point of contact for Hay Together. 'Do we need one?' The question comes with a sneer. No one is appointed.

It is past ten o'clock when the councillors finally leave. I trudge home. Rodney is right. The Town Council is hardly a beacon of representative democracy. At the same time, it is no North Korea. The public is given a hearing, anyone can observe (even if they volunteer to leave) and full minutes are published afterwards.

Nor, I sense, are the councillors venal power-grabbers. Some may well harbour private ambitions. Some certainly entertain illusory notions of aggrandisement. Yet the Town Council operates in a tiny, and shrinking, pond. Its budget is small and getting smaller. Footpath maintenance, sign-posting, anti-littering: these are the kinds of powers within its purview. Not multimillion-pound supermarket invest-ments. Indeed, control of the public lavatories only came its way because of County Council cutbacks.

Yet the councillors' antipathy towards Hay Together is

undeniable. It seems demonstrative of a wider dislike of opinionated incomers. At one stage in the meeting, mention was made of 'Making Hay', a proposed web-based database to promote all the events happening across the town. It's the idea of an entrepreneur 'from off'. A councillor mistook the initiative for 'Hay Makers', a co-operative of designers that rents an outlet in town. The confusion pushed the chairman over the edge. 'Hay Together, Making Hay, Hay Makers!' His head sunk into his hands. 'These paracetamol aren't working,' he declared.

I wonder what lies behind such hostility. Rodney would waste no time in telling me. It's because the town is run by a feudal-minded cabal that feels threatened by the prospect of participative democracy, he'd say.

I decide to ask the chairman for his views, and a few days later I pop into the country outfitters that he owns in town. The business has been in his family for five generations, their surname imprinted in the pavement outside in swirling, gold-coloured script. He is not there, so I leave my number. A few hours later, my phone rings. He'd be happy to meet, he says. I ask when would suit. 'How about now?' he suggests. Twenty minutes later, I'm climbing back up the stairs to the Town Council's second-floor meeting room. I prise the door open. Without all the councillors, the room feels distinctly less cramped.

Robert Golesworthy is sat with his legs stretched out in front of him, his feet resting on the boardroom table. He invites me to sit opposite him. The soles of his enormous shoes are pointing directly in my face. I'm close enough to read the logo on the rubber tread. 'Brasher', it says.

I resolve to be as cordial as possible. From his performance as chairman, he strikes me as a man who doesn't take kindly to being crossed. His views about incomers also seem clear enough. I fear my card may already be marked.

My concerns prove unfounded. The chairman is in a breezy mood. 'So, tell me,' he says. 'What would you like to know?' He rocks back in his seat and opens his large hands to indicate his candidness.

I start with a softball question. What was the town like when he was growing up? He answers without hesitation, depicting an idyllic childhood swimming in the river, playing sports and being chased by farmers for trespassing. His parents had a car and they would travel down to the Pembrokeshire coast as a family. Everyone knew everyone back then, he says, echoing Tony's remark in the Rhydspence.

It was also a time of considerable social change, he reflects. 'A flexible time, you could call it.' The fifty-nine-year-old chairman grew up during the tail-end of the Swinging Sixties. He remembers a Vietnam draft-dodger rocking up in Hay. Wealthy dropout types started arriving as well. That's when drugs started appearing in the town for the first time, he maintains. It was also around then that Richard Booth started 'building up his empire'.

Now I'm not to get him wrong. Mr Booth has done much for the town, the chairman concedes. Raised its profile, generated employment. But he also brought a number of . . . how to put this? The councillor pauses a moment. 'Unpleasant people.'

I ask him to elucidate. He'd rather not. 'Let's just say, they brought city ways round here that were not normal.' I think back to the recent royal lecture and the drunken reception for the US Ambassador. I'm sure it was just the tip of a rather debauched iceberg. Mr Golesworthy, meanwhile, is pressing his long fingers together in an act of apparent contemplation. 'In the cities, maybe,' he snaps, the skin around his fingernails glowing a bloodless white. 'But not for a small market town in Wales.'

Changing the topic, I mention that I'm new to the area, a point that is self-evident to us both but which helps me tee up my next question. The arrival of incomers, how does he feel it affects the town?

He crosses his feet over. I watch them pass in front of my nose.

The hike in house prices, he says. That's the most immediate impact. 'The chances of a young couple buying a house in town these days is virtually zero.' Richard Booth started it, snapping up properties all over the place. 'It is perceived as cheap for them.' Now, it's 'Lady Elizabeth' doing the same.

He waves a finger towards the window, the gesture intentionally vague. The new American owner of Booth's Bookshop has several other retail outlets and houses around town, he informs me. The golf course belongs to her, for example, now converted into her private residence. She is involved in the renovation of the castle too.

Her investment in the town is undoubtedly helping to spruce things up, but some find the size and speed of her buying spree unsettling. His tenor is terse. The chairman is not alone in noticing. Even *The Times* has picked up on news of Hay's new benefactor, dedicating an entire feature to her. 'The new Queen of Hay,' the literary editor wrote, ennobling her even further. Up in Cusop Dingle, I imagine the king's blood must have boiled.

Newcomers are leaving their imprint on the town's culture as well, the chairman adds. When he was growing up, Hay was a local market-based town. 'Quite insular in some ways,' he admits. Over the years, it's become more cosmopolitan.

'How would you call it?' He clicks his fingers, looking for the right word. 'A mixing-bowl.' The image evidently pleases him and he turns it over in his mind. A long breath whistles through his teeth. 'Sometimes it works. Sometimes, it doesn't.'

The supermarket affair looms large in the background. I skirt around it for a moment, keen to learn more about the examples of success. 'Who are the incomers that integrate well?'

All sorts, he insists. Anyone can integrate. Local people are friendly here – a truth to which I can fully attest. 'We're accommodating.' The trick is to find your niche. He doesn't quite know how to explain it, but some people 'just fit'. He was out with an incomer just this morning, for example. The two were clearing up some rubbish that a farmer had dumped.

It's true that quite a few of the incomers are a 'bit weird', he observes. But he doesn't have a problem with that. Many of the locals are weird too. So the two groups mesh well. He interlocks his hands to demonstrate this mutual affinity. And it cuts both ways. On the one hand, incomers are 'dilut-ing' the local pool of people. That much is undeniable, he asserts. But on the other, they positively enhance the town, bringing money, energy, ideas, vitality. Take the book festi-val, he says. It's economically vital for Hay. All in all, it's a 'double-edged sort of thing', he thinks.

'And when it doesn't work, why's that?' I ask.

He grins. Well, it's more of a smirk than a grin, really.

There is little doubt in his mind. The biggest mistake incomers make is coming in and trying to boss everyone around. 'They say, "We're going to take over this, we're going to deal with that."' The local population don't like that. Being told what to do by 'someone who's been here five seconds'. How can he put it? It doesn't go down well. 'In fact, they resent it.'

I'd heard the same from our local MP a few months beforehand. I'd gone to speak to him about another matter, but had asked as I was leaving what his advice would be for people moving into the area. Throw yourself into lots of interest groups, he said. The choir, the gardening club, a sports team, whatever. 'But don't, under any circumstances, become chair of a committee for at least two years.'

To be fair to Rodney, he has more than served his term. He first came to Hay in the 1970s, and has been living here permanently for six years. He helps run the local chapter of the University of the Third Age, an education movement for retirees. He volunteers as a steward at the festival. He was active for a while in a local theatre group. As with Andrew and Louise at Eighteen Rabbit, he could rightly be described as an active citizen. The core membership of Plan B, some thirty or forty people, are all cut from a similar cloth.

'So the whole anti-supermarket affair . . .' I pause, looking for the right way of phrasing the question. Mr Golesworthy raises an enquiring eyebrow. I become suddenly nervous. 'Urm, how do you read that, then? I mean, was it incomers trying to push their weight around?'

Behind my question is a shared acknowledgement that the anti-supermarket lobby was largely financed and supported by those 'from off'. Personally, however, I don't see it as a power-play. I read it as a protective measure, an attempt by those who revel in Hay's particularities to prevent the town's homogenisation. Safeguarding, basically.

First things first, he says: he was one of those most in favour of the development. To his mind, the deal was almost all upside. Hay would land a £30-million investment, a state-of-the-art school and a new community centre. Some local businesses might be hit, he accepts, but the overall effect on trade would be positive. 'Instead, what have we got?' he continues, sloping the back of his hand into the palm of the other. 'The community centre is shut, closed, gone. The school hasn't been built. Powys keeps producing plans, but I've not seen a planning application yet.' Until he does, he refuses to believe anything.

His lower lip is trembling. He has grown visibly angry.

As for Plan B, yes, he thinks they represent a 'minority pressure group'. They went directly against the wishes of the local population, he contends. 'It's all right for people coming in from off who have plenty of money. What they don't realise is that jobs aren't well paid around here.' Local people don't have disposable cash. One in six children qualify for free school meals. At the moment, there's only the Co-op and Spar to choose from, both of which are overpriced in his view.

The Plan B lobby are hypocrites to boot. He names two prominent anti-supermarket campaigners, who, according to his sources, both receive regular deliveries from Tesco's, the devil incarnate if Plan B's own rhetoric is to be believed. 'Where were they shopping locally? They weren't.' There's one rule for them, and one rule for the *Untermenschen*. I look confused. 'German,' he clarifies. 'The subhumans.'

We are not going to see eye-to-eye, I realise. At the same time, I can understand his frustration. He wants what he thinks is best for the town. To his mind, that means a little more choice. Many locals agree. And both he and they believe that an unelected group of wealthy incomers is preventing that from happening.

His mobile phone goes off, the ringtone the same monotone bleep-bleep of the alarm function.

'Hello Alan . . . I've done all that . . . I've got a meeting at eleven . . . Yup . . . Yup . . . I'll be an hour . . . yeah, so twelve o'clock should be okay . . .'

As he continues his phone conversation, it dawns on me that the leaders of the Town Council and Hay Together are really not so different after all. Both claim to have the town's interests at heart. Both recognise that a rural town such as Hay cannot stand still. Both accept the need for a clear path forward. It's only when they look to the future that the chasm between them reveals itself. Their views on what direction the town should take and who should get to decide are starkly opposed. Nor does it look like an accord will be found. Because of the bad blood over the supermarket, the two men are not on speaking terms.

'. . . Right, well, if they all need replacing, then replace the lot . . . Okay . . . okay matey, bye.'

He hangs up, then asks if I have any more questions. 'Or are we done?' The inference is that we are. In case I'm in doubt, he at last removes his feet from the table.

Thanking him for his time, I begin to gather up my things. As I'm putting my notebook in my bag, I sneak in one last question. About the Community Plan, could he tell me what timescale the Town Council has in mind? He doesn't know, he says. The National Park is pushing them to involve Hay Together and as a consequence he has removed himself from the whole process. 'Because of my personal prejudices.'

'But will it be a five-year plan, say? Or a ten-year plan?'

We've moving towards the door by this stage. 'I don't talk about that,' he says, his tone blunt. 'That's communism.'

*

Andrew from Eighteen Rabbit calls the Chamber of Commerce meeting to order.

It is now midsummer and the air in the back room of the tapas bar is stifling. Two tables are laid out at right angles. Rays of bright evening light shine through the open window behind the chairman's seat. Accompanying them is the feeblest of breezes, barely a whisper. Andrew enquires if everyone has a copy of the agenda. One of the eight attendees signals that he doesn't, and the owner of Hay's fair-trade store hands him a sheet from the pile in front of him.

All of the attendees are shopkeepers in the town. Most are relative newbies. The only one who's been in business any real length of time is Marina, who runs a furniture and antiques store at the top end of the high street. An old-school retailer, she refuses to set up a website and swears against ever using email. In all the years she has had the shop, a 'sale' sign has never once hung in the window. But everything is meticulously chosen and artfully displayed, and over the years she has built up a loyal clientele. The fact that she's outlasted almost every other antiques dealer in town indicates her business nous.

With curly, voluminous grey hair and a wardrobe full of loose-flowing, robe-like garments, Marina is recognised as one of the town's 'characters'. She is also something of a mystery. One of those rare incomers who somehow feel part of the fabric. No one can quite remember when she arrived or where she came from. And although everyone knows her and she seems to know everyone, she is not one for joining in. In fact, she actively stands apart, positively keeping herself to herself. A woman without ties.

She is not a member of the Chamber of Commerce and never has been. In fact, this is the first time she has ever attended one of its meetings. She has something to say.

Before that, the Chamber has its formal business to work through. Andrew states his ambition to be done in under an hour. He hurries the group on to the first bullet point on the list. A pending meeting with the organisers of the literary festival. Discussion centres on the shuttle bus service between the car park and the main site. Last year, it didn't stop in town. The traders would like to see that changed. Andrew is tasked with the negotiations.

Next comes an update on a voucher scheme that the Chamber proposes to introduce. The idea is that people will be able to gift a five- or ten-pound coupon to friends or guests, redeemable in shops around town. It fits neatly with the Totally Locally campaign that Andrew is pushing. Proofs of the voucher still haven't come back from the designer. Again, the chairman is charged with following up. Tabled next is a discussion about a recruitment drive, but the Membership Secretary hasn't turned up so it's pushed back until the next meeting.

Under Andrew's professional direction, the group see off the remaining topics relatively rapidly: the proposal to start a closed Facebook group (approved by majority), arrangements for the Christmas lights, provisions for a replacement Sunday bus service, a change of signatories to the Chamber's bank account.

That leaves ten minutes for any other business. It's looking good. Andrew kicks off, saying he thinks the Chamber should formally institute a revolving chairmanship, 'so no one gets dumped with the job indefinitely'. Everyone agrees. Mention is made of the Chamber's invitation to join a delegation from South Korea, which is visiting the king of Hay to learn more about the booktown model. Finally, the owner of the craft beer shop asks if the Chamber can write a formal letter expressing its concern about the possible closure of the high school. The request goes to a vote. Seven hands go up.

'Right, then, anyone for any more?' asks Andrew.

No one says anything. He turns to Marina, who has sat in virtual silence throughout wearing a look of detached interest at the evening's proceedings. 'Marina, is there anything you'd like to add at this juncture?'

Andrew is no psychic. It's fairly obvious that she is not there to discuss bus routes and coupon schemes. More to the point, he's had a tip-off. Word is that Marina has come along with the intention of 'kicking up a fuss'. Hay's shopkeeping community is like that. Secrets are impossible. Cash tills have ears.

'Yes, thank you, I would,' she says, and leans forward over the table.

Everyone's gaze turns in her direction. A few eyes roll.

She dives straight in, her mind set and her manner assured. The reason she is here, she explains, is because of serious concerns about the proposed renovation of the castle. 'The plans, the absence of consultation, the lack of forethought about what exactly will happen to the town.' She fears that the restoration project will lead to the creation of a 'National Trust tourist trap', replete with dishcloths and tearooms.

'Yeah, okay Marina, if I could just . . .'

The antiques dealer continues, acknowledging Andrew's attempt to interject but politely ignoring it. She hasn't finished.

Architecturally, Hay has one unique attribute at the moment, its own romantic ruin. Look at any postcard or publicity for the town, and the castle is always featured front and centre. The rooks' nests, the sprawling ivy, the spacious lawn. That's all going to go, she warns. The town's primary asset is about to be stripped. Instead, we'll have what everybody else has got. A blank tourist destination.

She'd like to share a quick anecdote, if she may. Andrew nods, a fixed smile on his face. His one-hour goal is now irretrievably lost. A few weekends ago, she was walking up through town. A tourist in front of her stopped and turned to his companion. 'And I heard him say, "This is like Bourton-on-the-Water in the crap Cotswolds."'

Now she knows the Cotswolds from old. She has seen how it's gradually turned into a twee tourist Mecca, every new holiday home and fresh coachload of visitors sucking that bit more life out of the place. 'I've been warning for a long time that the same thing will happen here.' She's just really concerned, she says. 'Really, really concerned.'

'Oo-kaaay,' says Andrew, who, in one simple word, manages to convey both doubt and disagreement.

Marina is not deaf to the chairman's scepticism, nor blind to the passive expressions on the faces around the table. She hasn't come to rant, she assures them. Her main purpose is to make a request. Would the Chamber of Commerce arrange some kind of public meeting? People are asking the castle committee questions, but they are being 'fobbed off'. She feels if the business community were to mobilise as one, then they could begin to get some straight answers.

It's the same fight as Rodney's repeated. A sense that the town is on a precipice. A feeling that change is afoot, that conformity is coming. And a bubbling anger. Anger that those affected aren't having a say, that the wishes of a minority are being pushed through without contest.

As with the Castle Trust, Andrew sees things differently. Decaying romance is all well and good, but it doesn't shift product. In his view, the more people the town can attract, the better. Unlike Marina, he doesn't own his shop. And, with the change of premises, his monthly rental bill has just skyrocketed. It won't pay itself. Most of the small business owners around the table are of a similar mind.

In his position as chairman, however, he adopts a more conciliatory tone. His role is to see that all the views of local businesses are given an equal airing, he explains. One thing he would say, however, is that the plans for the castle are only provisional at this point. That's what he understands, anyway.

Marina shakes her head. That might be what they're saying in public. She's convinced that the die is already cast. Before we know it, there will busloads of grannies and Japanese tourists flocking into town.

One of the shopkeepers cuts in. 'And what's wrong with that, exactly?' They will scare everyone else away, Marina responds. The owner of the stationery shop comes to her defence. 'It's well known that coach trips spend one pound on a cup of tea and that's it.' It's going to become a wedding venue, someone else has heard. A cookery school is the rumour another person picked up. Another suggests it's to be turned into a museum dedicated to Richard Booth.

Andrew cautions everyone about getting ahead of themselves. He has a 'good dialogue' going with the London-based architects appointed for the job. He suggests speaking with them. Marina raises her eyebrows. She knows someone who tried already. 'They got a nasty rebuttal.' Plus, has anyone seen the other projects they've done? she asks. They did the refit of the Ashmolean in Oxford, didn't they?

Andrew replies. They did, Marina confirms. And has anyone seen it? 'I went,' she says, and snorts indignantly. 'It's all
about increasing footfall. It's nothing to do with the museum itself.' No one responds.

Anxious to draw a line under the subject and bring the
meeting to a close, Andrew comes back to Marina's request.
Supposing that the Chamber can arrange a meeting with
the castle committee, what questions would she like to ask?

Before she answers, she feels a need to clarify her position. She's not about maintaining the castle in aspic.
Everyone accepts that. As a minimum, the building needs
stabilising. And the town needs to attract visitors. This
much she accepts; she is 'no fool'. But Hay is the Town of
Books, she emphasises. If you take that away, you're left
with a place that looks much like every other place. 'Because
if the booktown stops, what is it then? The Town of What?'

'So the question is . . . ?' Andrew asks, his pen in his hand,
ready to jot down her response.

She looks down at the back of her hands, which are
spread out on the table, fingers splayed. Her mouth fixes in
frustration, her bottom lip gripped between her teeth.

'Have the trustees got an overall, long-term vision?' she
says eventually. 'Not just for the next two years or ten years.
But a vision for long after they're gone.'

Andrew duly notes the petition on his pad. We can certainly try to put it to them, he promises. There's no guaran-
tee they'll listen, of course. But the important thing is to be
proactive. At least that way, the Chamber can 'stake a claim'.

The meeting disbands and everyone heads home. I cadge
a lift off Andrew in his hybrid Prius. We glide silently
through the streets, down past the clock tower and then out
over the Wye towards Clyro. He drops me at my door. I

wave him goodnight. 'Night, man,' he says, and pulls off.

I stand on the pavement for a few seconds, looking up at the cluster of trees opposite. The sky is cloudless. In a short while, the stars will blanket the night sky. For now, the late evening light still has breath. The leaves rustle softly, their tips turning a shimmery silver in the twilight.

It may well be that Marina's fears prove unfounded. This tiny, village-like town tucked away on the Welsh border has pedigree. Surprises are its forte. Becoming the first Town of Books; creating a literary festival miles from anywhere. A seam of creativity clearly cuts through its soil. For all we know, the castle's restoration committee may have donned their hard hats and be mining it this very minute. I hope so.

According to Robert Golesworthy, Hay's idiosyncratic spirit all comes down to ley lines. Perhaps he's right. A powerful sense of the magical certainly seems to cling to the place. With it comes an energy, an aura, an ambience. Call it what you will, but it is real, it is in the ether, it exists. Breathe and you can taste it on your tongue. Walk and you can feel its mass beneath your feet.

The future can follow one of two broad forks. Residents both old and new can seek to impose their will on the town. That way lies more shouting and scuffling, more power struggles and rancour. Or they can release their grip a little. Free up the town to indulge its own predilections, to decide its own course, to speak its own mind. If that sounds fanciful, then good. More flights of fancy are what the world needs.

Up on the old castle tump, somewhere amid the cluster of branches, an owl hoots. I take my house keys from my pocket, open the door and call to Emma that I'm home.

Epilogue

The day I came to Clyro I remember fixing my eyes on a particular bough of an apple tree in the orchard opposite the school and the Vicarage and saying to myself that on the day I left Clyro I would look at that same branch. I did look for it this morning but I could not recognise it.

Kilvert's Diary, 2 September 1872

'You got plans for the rugby, then?' Des asks, his accent pure Radnorshire, soft and lyrical.

The match is all everyone has been talking about for the last few days. England versus Wales, Saturday evening, group stage of the World Cup. I haven't decided yet, I reply. 'How about you?'

He hasn't made up his mind either. It's a friend's birthday on Saturday and they're planning to head out for a few drinks in Hay beforehand. He invites me along and I readily accept. Then I remember that I have to take Seth and Bo over to Llangorse for an indoor climbing lesson, so I might not be able to make it after all.

Let's meet for the match instead, he suggests, looking down from the top of a stepladder, paintbrush in hand, dabbing at the chipped stonework that Emma has asked him to repaint.

Sounds good, I tell him, and we talk through the various

viewing options. The Con Club has a big TV, he says, although it tends to get packed out quickly. Same with the British Legion. The Rose & Crown? I suggest. Des looks doubtful. More of a football pub in his view.

Eventually, we settle on Kilvert's Inn, which has a large saloon bar with a widescreen television. I like the choice, partly because the idea of sitting in a pub named after a man who never frequented pubs rather appeals, and partly because it's practically on the English border, which to me, as an Essex émigré, feels comforting.

The last time I followed English rugby with any close attention was in my teens. Among my friendship group, there was one boy, Ali Thomas, who considered himself Welsh and we would rib him mercilessly for it. That was back when England dominated among the home nations. Today, not only is the Welsh rugby team in the ascendency, but I am living on Welsh soil with children who hassle me to buy them the red, dragon crested kit of the national team.

The game is just kicking off when I turn up and Des is standing on a chair, fist pressed against his heart, singing the Welsh national anthem with uninhibited gusto. He looks well-oiled and happy. An enclave of other Welsh supporters surrounds him, several of whom are wearing the national strip and all of whom are singing in similar voice.

Among the group is Gareth, a quietly spoken man whom I met during the Hay festival, where he runs the bookshop. Originally from the Monmouthshire town of Pandy, he now lives in Clyro, in the house next door to Ty Melyn. Outside the festival period, he works as a landscape gardener. He is the possessor, as he's proving this very minute, of a mellifluous baritone.

Sitting across the table from Des, lips sealed shut, is

Danny. The two men are brothers-in-law, both married to sisters from the Golesworthy clan. Robert Golesworthy, of the Town Council, is their wives' uncle. A close enough bond for Des to call him 'Rob'. Both Des and Danny are strikingly good-looking, the one tall and fair, the other dark and stocky.

I first met Des at the school gates. He has two sets of twins, all four of whom go to Clyro Primary. For a while, I would take our boys along to an informal football class that he used to organise on Sunday mornings at the school. Our paths crossed again through Cherryshoes, the band that Rob from the Majestic Bus plays in. Since meeting Rob, I try to go along whenever they have a local gig. Des, who used to be a professional session musician in his younger years, is their lead guitarist.

Climbing down off his chair, Des pushes forward a seat that he has set aside for me. The saloon area is already rammed with people crowding in to watch the game and I had resigned myself to having to stand. Thanking him for his forethought, I place my jacket over the back of the chair by way of surety. Then I go in search of the bar, which is located on the other side of the room through a thicket of jostling bodies.

I plunge into the morass, eventually emerging out the other side to discover a lengthy queue for drinks. As I wait my turn, I spot Tim from my running club. Dressed in a floral, slim-fit shirt, he is standing a few feet away with his back to me. I tap him on the shoulder.

A one-time insurance executive, Tim has washed his hands of corporate life. He built himself a green-roofed studio in the garden of his house, which borders King Richard's palace up in Cusop Dingle, and he now dedicates his days to creative pursuits. Sculpture and figurative painting, mostly.

His wife, Emma, a freelance management consultant, is a fellow runner with Hay Hotfooters. She's on her way back from holiday, he tells me when I ask after her. In fact, he has to pick her up from the train station in the second half, a prospect he isn't terribly amused by. 'Drink?' I ask him. He's fine, he replies. 'Got to drive, haven't I?' A grimace crosses his face. I order a pint for myself, and one each for Des and Danny. Holding the three drinks in a tight triangle, I venture back towards my table. Tim wishes me luck, whether for the crowd ahead or the game I'm not sure.

In truth, I'm largely indifferent about who wins. My usual bias in sporting matches is towards the underdog, although today no one seems able to agree which of the two teams that is. From Des's nail biting, he appears to think the upper hand is with England. As the game progresses, the score reflects as much, with Wales's larger neighbour gradually stretching ahead.

Early into the second half, ten points separate the two sides England looks unassailable. Choruses of 'Swing Low, Sweet Chariot' start breaking out.

A takeaway pizza arrives for the group of women on the next table. Des, who appears to know them all, successfully solicits a slice.

Support in the pub is split broadly half and half. Wales cling on with occasional penalties, but their supporters are growing progressively quieter. Des begins to lose some of his animation, slouching further and further back in his chair, muttering about keeping ball in hand and silly errors. 'There's no pace, no pace,' he mutters repeatedly. Gareth, on the other hand, is cursing loudly at the referee.

I spot others I know among the audience. Several are

Welsh. Tom, a young and serious-minded novelist, who is part of a book group I recently joined, is shaking his head. Finn, a photographer with a huge following on Instagram who joins our weekend hikes, is looking equally glum. In better spirits is Val, the gallery owner from Surrey, who is perched on the edge of her seat in front of me. Aware of the mixed emotions in the room, she is keeping a diplomatic lid on her excitement at England's growing lead.

In front of her is Simon, who owns a pottery shop in town. He went to art college with Bernie from the market. They both moved to Hay years ago. Another incomer from across the border, Simon keeps his celebrations equally restrained, marking each new point with a clenched fist and a wry smile.

Far less sensitive is a heavy-set gobby Englishman on the sofa directly in front of the television screen. Legs splayed, lager in hand, he's been offering an ongoing obnoxious commentary since the beginning of the game. 'Way-yals,' he keeps saying in what he thinks is an amusing Welsh accent. No one laughs, not even the pub's English contingent.

I look over to Des, who is scowling. I nod towards the back of the man's head and raise my eyebrows. One of the women on the next door table catches my gesture and says someone should shut him up. Des tells her not to fret. Just ignore him, he says. 'He's not from round here.'

The words stick with me as the game plays out. Des, whose mum owns the newsagent's in Hay, knows almost everyone in town. This man's face isn't one that he recognises. He'll be a weekend tourist most likely. Maybe even staying at Kilvert's itself.

What hits me about Des's comment is the weight of implication that it carries. The man is from off, he's saying.

Not that he isn't welcome, in principle. Not that he doesn't have as much right to be here as anyone else. But he's an outsider, an alien, parachuted in, oblivious to the cultural dynamics of the room, indifferent to who he might be offending. His behaviour may well be accepted, even approved of, wherever it is he's from, but here it jars. Yet because he knows no one in the room and because he has nothing of himself invested here, he doesn't care.

Best to just let him be, is Des's verdict. It's no good reasoning with a man like this. Anyway, tomorrow morning he'll be gone, back to wherever he calls home.

On the screen, the game is beginning to show signs of turning. The Welsh convert a succession of penalties, pulling back to within four points of England. They are back in it, the momentum all theirs. The red shirts in the pub find their voices once more. The fat-necked Englishman is still sounding off, but his confidence is shakier than before.

Ambivalent until now, I feel myself silently willing Wales on, my allegiances won over by the red team's courageous fightback on the pitch as well as by Des's desperate muffled prayers on the seat beside me ('Just one try, please. Come on. Just one, just one'). A darker side of me would also like to see the big-mouthed Englishman get his comeuppance.

I realise this second sentiment is petty and spiteful, two traits that are never attractive whatever the motive. In this respect, Kilvert was a better man than I. Rarely in his diary does he express ill feeling towards his fellow man. Not that he's without cause. Behind the lush romanticism of his prose, life in Clyro was not all burnished sunsets and neighbourly conviviality.

On the few occasions a barbed remark does slip into the *Diary*, the effect is deafening. One such clangorous example appears during his final days in Clyro. It is his penultimate Sunday in the parish and he is describing his walk across the hills to the isolated chapel of Bettws. Mr Irvine, his replacement as curate, is strolling at his side. The new man is due to preach from the first chapter of Paul's letter to the Philippians in the morning service. Kilvert is down to read prayers.

Back in his lodgings that night, the diarist dips his pen in the inkstand on his desk. I picture him sitting there a moment, looking out towards the Swan for almost the last time, summoning up images of that final walk, savouring the summer smells in the fields and the sun on his back. 'Every tree and hill and hollow and glimpse of the mountains was precious to me.' He is there, retracing his steps, his sentimental spirit half a pace ahead.

Then, all of a sudden, lurching uninvited into the shot, spoiling this halcyon scene, comes an impostor. The 'stranger' Mr Irvine, for whom none of this makes any sense, from whose perspective the contours of the valley and the twists in the path are but 'nought', empty of significance, devoid of meaning.

Even if he appreciates the inherent beauty of the landscape, as a newcomer, he has 'no dear associations with the place', no memory bank on which to draw, no recollection of walking that same route in a snowstorm or on a sultry spring day with thunder clouds rolling around the sky and the 'green and pink of the trees thickening with bursting buds'.

Kilvert's caustic tone is perhaps not surprising. During these last days of August 1872, a whirlwind of emotions is coursing through him. His decision to take up the curacy at his father's parish represents the subject of much conjecture.

Was it a broken heart? A career move? A earlier promise to his family? We may never know the true reason, although part of him manifestly desires to stay. That morning in Bettws Chapel he would burst into floods of tears.

Leaving is made harder by the depth of affection lavished upon him by his parishioners. The old school house next to Pottery Cottage 'thronged with people gentle and simple' for his farewell party. Speeches were made and gifts presented. The diarist struggled to find the words to respond. 'My heart was full and I could not speak what I would.'

None of this fully explains his abject dismissal of Mr Irvine. Maybe he was a city man with disdain for country ways. Perhaps he was disdainful of Kilvert's precious Wordsworth. *The distant hills / Into the tumult sent an alien sound / Of melancholy.* Even so, to write so disparagingly of the man seems highly out of character. Irvine is not the problem, I'd wager. It's Kilvert. The prospect of these mountainous borderlands so soon being lost to him fills him with an intense despondency. Its vistas, its people, its 'sky a cloudless deep wonderful blue', all gone. There's envy there too. Envy that so much beauty awaits Irvine, a beauty the new man is too blind to see but which, over time, may come to beguile and overwhelm him as completely as it did Kilvert.

If Irvine is at fault, it is primarily by virtue of his newness. The giveaway is there in the phrase 'dear associations'. I feel I know what the diarist is getting at. Consider the Begwyns. The first time we walked with the boys to the peak of the moor above Clyro, where Kilvert would watch the lapwings 'wheeling about the hill in their scores' and where the gorse 'flamed fiery gold', we thought it a beautiful picnic spot. Nothing more.

Now when I picture it, I call to mind Seth dangling from the branch of a tree after he slipped when climbing. I remember Bo's fourth birthday, with all his friends playing hide-and-seek in the evergreens. I think of getting hopelessly lost in a snowstorm with my friend Chris when out for a night run. I recall the boys' excitement the first time they flew a kite. Places have layers, undercoats. The longer you're in a place, the deeper and thicker they run. The truth of this occurred to me recently. We had B&B guests staying and, being a Thursday, I urged them to go along to the weekly market. 'Oh,' the woman responded, 'we have a market where we live too.' I wanted to counter her. Tell her that she hadn't tried Bernie's sausage rolls yet or tasted Lucretia's fruit cake.

But I didn't. Commendable though they are, the market's gastronomic virtues aren't the reason I have become a weekly regular. Sharing a word with the stallholders I've come to know. Bumping into friends. Trading gossip. These are my chief motivations for going.

None of this our B&B guests would compute. *Where we live too.* I could visualise it through their eyes, as visitors, as people attached to their own place somewhere else. Hay's market may not quite be as 'nought' to them, but it's unlikely to be very much more.

Which is why I let it drop. After all, it wasn't so long ago that I viewed it the way. It was only yesterday that I was Irvine.

*

We had arrived in Kilvert's old stomping ground wondering if it was a place we could one day call home. I had assumed this would be a decision of my own making. Was it somewhere that I liked? Did it suit my needs? Would its residents be people we could relate to? Would we find friends? In all these respects, we struck lucky. The boys are happy in school and now have an army of little buddies in the village. Emma is almost impossible to keep up with, always finding new projects to develop and new people to meet.

I love it too. My runs in the hills. My shed. The changing colours of the mountains. Sharing smiles in the street. The bookshops. The festival on our doorstep. Having our own king, a permanent Lord of Misrule. I even love the weather; gnarly and rain-soaked one minute, dazzling and cloudless the next.

What I hadn't contemplated was the reverse. Would this place accept me? Would it allow me to call it home? As an adult, I have lived in plenty of places that have met my needs and desires. London, most obviously. Buenos Aires too. Yet none felt like home.

Cities can spurn you, turn on you, spit you out without a care. That wasn't my issue though. Passing through was. Working, studying, playing, that's what drew me. Not find-ing a home. My big-city experiences have all essentially been flings, one-night stands dragged out over years. Perhaps the cities guessed that. Accustomed to movers and takers, may-be they are wise to my type. I kept my true self hidden from them. What's to say they didn't do the same in return?

My objective in coming to the Marches was different. I came looking to put down roots. I expected to find Updike's plumbers and widows. And find them I did, both literally and figuratively. Many have become good friends. I have not yet persuaded Pat into Booths' café, but she had cake and tea with us at home on Christmas Day. A wider network I know to wave to in the street and chat to at the school gates. Farmers, teachers, retirees, office workers, shop assistants, cleaners, taxi drivers, electricians. People, in short, not in my game.

Scrolling through my phone, I must be close to Dunbar's magic 150. People I hadn't met until a short while ago, but who I'd now feel comfortable calling up any time. And it's reciprocal. People regularly pop in when they're passing. Ann for a cup of tea, Rob to use our washing machine when his isn't working, my neighbour David to give us surplus tomatoes from his greenhouse.

They're a mix, too, of locals and incomers. On first moving here, I couldn't have imagined it playing out like this. It felt like a 'them' and 'us' split. The Marches was their turf. We were the interlopers, building our bungalows and buying up their old barns. The consequent logic was simple: if I wanted to belong, I'd have to shed myself of my incomer skin and somehow take on becoming a 'local'.

I never could, of course. Not in the strict sense of being 'born and bred'. I could not rewind my infancy. The childhood memories of the drinkers at the Rhydspence could never be mine. I would never enjoy acquaintances of the same longevity as Geoff or Les.

This wouldn't have surprised Kilvert, familiar with the Gospels as he was. *Nicodemus saith unto him, How can a man be born when he is old? Can he enter the second time into his mother's womb, and be born?* Yet genealogy is only one route to belonging somewhere. Nor, I've come to learn, is it even the most important. There are born-and-breds who forsake the Marches and make their home elsewhere. There are others who stay but never really fit; they're either too snobby

or too solitary, too busy or too aloof. By the letter, both are
local, but nothing more. And then there are others who
arrive 'from off' and appear to assimilate fully. They become
mainstays of the community. Treated as though they have
belonged here forever. So how do they do it?

Time certainly helps. Some outsiders arrived aeons ago
and never left. Over the decades, folk begin to forget where
they came from or when. Marina is one of these, a local by
dint of endurance. It is as if the landscape begins to absorb
them, enveloping the person into its folds, binding them to
itself.

We talk of 'putting down roots' as though the work is
entirely of our own doing. Us cementing our place. Us
anchoring ourselves in. Yet if the ground is stony or the earth
is barren, such efforts will be in vain. If anyone is to stay and
grow and weather the years, the place itself must welcome
them, must nourish them, must allow them to flourish.

Kilvert hints at this, writing about how the hills 'grow
upon us'. It's a figurative phrase, but I wonder if his intent
isn't partially literal. The hills subsuming him somehow,
incorporating him into them. When circumstances eventually tear him away, the landscape stays with him. A physical
adjunct almost, as real as a foot or an ear.

Years later, late one spring night in Wiltshire, he turns his
mind back to the rolling hills of Radnorshire and the 'never
to be forgotten' day when he walked alone from Clyro to
Builth and first saw the Rocks of Aberedw.

The morning sun shining like silver upon Llanbychllyn
Pool, and [when I] descended from the great moor upon
the vale of Edw . . . Would God that I might dwell and die
by thee.

He is back there as he writes, stealing glimpses as on the path to Bettws. The writer and poet Margiad Evans conveys the same in *A Country Dance*, her sublime inter-war novel about a love affair in the Marches. English-born Olwen Davies, Evans's heroine, is being wooed by the Welsh-speaking Evan ap Evans. She insists he address her in her native tongue, to which he replies that having a Welsh mother makes her only half English. 'No, not that even,' he adds. 'For you have lived in the mountains.' Her surroundings have begun to wash off on her, her suitor is saying. They are getting under her skin, reshaping her identity.

By the same token, people can live for years in the Marches and remain permanent newcomers. Such folk usually keep to themselves. They buy a smallholding and throw their energies into breeding pedigree goats or growing champion marrows. If they socialise, they do so among a small self-enclosed circle of equally private individuals. Or, alternatively, they fill the house with people from elsewhere, importing friends from the city for a relaxing weekend in the country. From a community perspective, they are social hermits, ostracised at their own volition. If and when they leave, as the anthropologist Tamar Kohn observes about the blow-ins to an Inner Hebridean island, 'people forget their names'. I am sure they don't care a jot, but to my mind it sounds like a terrible indictment. Or a missed opportunity at the very least. There is another route to belonging, a simpler one by far. Now I see it, I spot it threading through Kilvert's *Diary* from first page to last. It is there in the Jesse Norman book that Rodney gave me as well. Norman uses a technical term for it, 'philic association', a complicated way of describing the knit that grows out of φιλία, ancient Greek for 'friendship', 'tie', 'affection', 'regard'.

Kilvert would have preferred Updike's approach to saying exactly the same, the habit of loving and knowing your neighbour 'in the old, old sense'. Kilvert genuinely cared for his flock, drawing alongside them in life's troubles and celebrating with them in its joys. 'A home to me for nearly eight years,' he reflects during his last week. Its residents, 'like brothers and sisters'.

Inevitably, not all saw it similarly. The young curate was of too low birth for some and too high birth for others. He himself didn't see it that way, though. For Kilvert, everyone was his neighbour. 'God bless and keep you all' was his prayer on departing; local and incomer, farmer and townsperson, adult and child.

So it was that he could wave his handkerchief from the carriage window of his departing train at 'all the old familiar friendly houses'; the Bridges at Pont Vaen, the Dykes at Cabalva, the Dews at Whitney Rectory. And so too, as he drove away from Clyro for the final time, 'all the dear people were standing in their cottage doors waving their hands'.

Belonging was never the end point for Kilvert. He came primarily to serve, not to settle. Integrating into the community was, and is, only ever an outcome, the overspill of a caring ear, a kind word, a latch left off the hook.

*

Back in the pub, the match has finished. Against everyone's expectations, a late try saw Wales eventually pip England to the post. No one can quite believe it. England are out; Wales march on. Walking over to the television, I stand with my back to the wall and take a photograph looking out into the room.

Des and Gareth are dancing on their chairs, ecstatic at the unexpected victory. The table of women is a blur of motion, all of them hugging and jumping at once. Tom and Finn are both holding their pints of beer high in the air. The English supporters, in contrast, are leaning forward, heads sunk into hands. Wan, defeated smiles paint the faces of Simon and Val. The rowdy Englishman is nowhere to be seen.

Danny slips off home after the final whistle, leaving Des to enjoy the moment. It is late by now and, after the initial euphoria has subsided, the pub soon begins to empty.

In a voice hoarse from shouting, Des tells me about his friend Mally. He used to say that the England versus Wales games were class war. Public-school types against valley boys. Des doesn't see it that way. 'For me, it's just war.' Laughing at himself, he slaps me on the back and asks what he can get me to drink. 'Same again?' I nod and thank him, grateful for the offer and for becoming part of the knit.

Acknowledgements

John Updike's assertion that 'it's good to live between a widow and a plumber' was foremost in my mind as I set out to write this book. It did not occur to me what it would be like for the widow or plumber to live beside me, a writer. So, to my fellow residents, a huge and heartfelt thanks for overlooking this oversight and so generously allowing me to share in your lives. Your contributions and kindnesses inform every page of this book, and beyond.

I am enormously indebted to those who took the time to read the manuscript at various stages and offer honest feedback: Maria Carreras, Nancy Durham, Jules North, Barry Pilton, Rebecca Spooner. Particular thanks to the ever-sympathetic Iain Finlayson.

This book would not have happened were it not for the support, patience and timely interventions of two very special people: my agent Georgina Capel and editor Walter Donohue. An enormous debt of gratitude to you both.

For their expertise at tightening text, illustrating covers and making maps, hats off to Trevor Horwood, Joe McLaren and Kevin Freeborn, respectively. At Faber & Faber, thanks to Eleanor Crow, John Grindod, Samantha Matthews and everyone else who worked behind the scenes.

This book has benefited from the practical and professional support of countless individuals, including: Fiona Balch, Emma Beynon, Roger and Dot Carswell, Patricia Daly, Jasper Fforde, Peter Florence, Andy Fryers, Steve

Acknowledgements

Greenow, Sally Gregg, Phil and Kath Keene, Sian Lazar, Ali McCowliff, Chris North, Laura Paddison, Alasdair Paine, Clare Purcell, Ben Rawlence, Owen Sheers, Richard Skinner, and my parents Douglas and Vanessa.

My understanding of Kilvert's life and times was greatly enhanced by A. L. Le Quesne's *After Kilvert*, Frederick Grice's *Francis Kilvert and His World*, and David Lockwood's *Francis Kilvert*. The online archive of the Kilvert Society's biannual *Journal* also proved a source of unexpected scholarship and enduring entertainment.

To Emma, Seth and Bo, thanks, gracias, diolch yn fawr. I owe you everything.